"Interesting and very entertaining—I read it with pleasure."

—**Tracy Kidder,** winner of the Pulitzer Prize and
New York Times bestselling author of *Strength in What Remains*

"Part Gen-X guide to genealogy, part rollicking road trip for roots—complete with somebody named Cousin Mooner—Buzzy Jackson's book is funny, illuminating and profound. If your idea of genealogy is grandpa hunched over that tattered ancestral chart he keeps in the back of his suspenders drawer, think again."

—**Ariel Sabar,** winner of the National Book Critics Circle Award and
author of *My Father's Paradise*

"Oh, no! Who let Buzzy Jackson in and showed her our secret handshake? It's as if Tony Horwitz or Sarah Vowell invaded the hallowed halls of gene-alogy and exposed our past-adoring, source-citing, ancestor-worshiping un-derworld. How will we ever live this down—or keep all the wannabes out?"

—**Megan Smolenyak Smolenyak,** author of
*Who Do You Think You Are?: The Essential Guide to
Tracing Your Family History*

"This is a delightful book—fun to read, but educational. Much recom-mended for anyone who has considered searching for their ancestors (or loves someone who does so). Jackson is so friendly, her outlook so generous—from a cruise ship in the Caribbean to a forgotten graveyard in Alabama to a crowded library in Salt Lake City—she is the perfect companion for this adventurous trip into the world of genealogy."

—**Karen Joy Fowler,** *New York Times* bestselling author of
The Jane Austen Book Club

"There are many books that will tell you how to trace your ancestors, but almost none that tell you what it actually feels like to do it. Buzzy Jackson captures perfectly the mixture of frustration, astonishment and delight all genealogists feel, and does it with humor, good grace and great narrative skill. Her book is indispensable for anyone thinking of researching their own family, and for anyone wondering what makes family historians tick."

—**John Grenham,** Ireland's foremost genealogist

"Buzzy Jackson launches herself with verve and enthusiasm into the arcane but friendly and increasingly democratic world of genealogy and genealo-gists, about which she knew next- to- nothing at the outset. The fastest of fast learners, she soon finds herself comfortably at home, and has produced a book which is cheerful, cheering, and challenging. Shaking the family tree will be a tonic for those who already know at least something about their ancestry, and an inspiration to those who don't."

—**John Titford,** English genealogist and author, Trustee and
Chairman of Examiners, the Institute of Heraldic and Genealogical
Studies, Fellow of the Society of Genealogists of London

ALSO BY BUZZY JACKSON

A Bad Woman Feeling Good: Blues and the Women Who Sing Them

SHAKING THE FAMILY TREE

Blue Bloods, Black Sheep, and Other Obsessions
of an Accidental Genealogist

BUZZY JACKSON

A Touchstone Book
Published by Simon & Schuster
New York   London   Toronto   Sydney

Touchstone
A Division of Simon & Schuster, Inc.
1230 Avenue of the Americas
New York, NY 10020

First Touchstone trade paperback edition July 2010

TOUCHSTONE and colophon are registered trademarks of Simon & Schuster, Inc.

For information about special discounts for bulk purchases, please contact Simon &
Schuster Special Sales at 1-866-506-1949 or business@simonandschuster.com.

The Simon & Schuster Speakers Bureau can bring authors to your live event.
For more information or to book an event contact the Simon & Schuster Speakers
Bureau at 1-866-248-3049 or visit our website at www.simonspeakers.com.

Designed by Akasha Archer

Manufactured in the United States of America

10   9   8   7   6   5   4   3   2   1

Library of Congress Cataloging-in-Publication Data

Jackson, Buzzy.
    Shaking the family tree : blue bloods, black sheep, and other obsessions of an
accidental genealogist / by Buzzy Jackson.
        p. cm.
    "A Touchstone book." Includes bibliographical references and index.
    1. United States—Genealogy. 2. Genealogy—Social aspects—United States.
3. Genealogy—United States—Psychological aspects. 4. Jackson, Buzzy.
5. Jackson, Buzzy—Family. 6. Jackson, Buzzy—Travel—United States. I. Title.
CS49.J25 2010
929'.1072073—dc22

                                                                        2010009670

ISBN 978-1-4391-1299-1
ISBN 978-1-4391-4926-3 (ebook)

This book is dedicated with love to my family—
past, present, and future

Thirteen Generations of American Jacksons

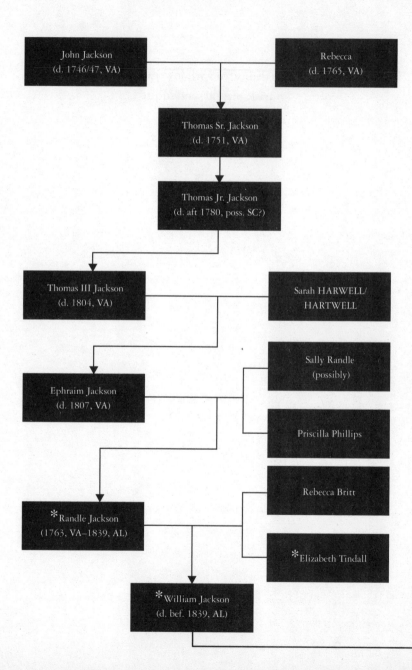

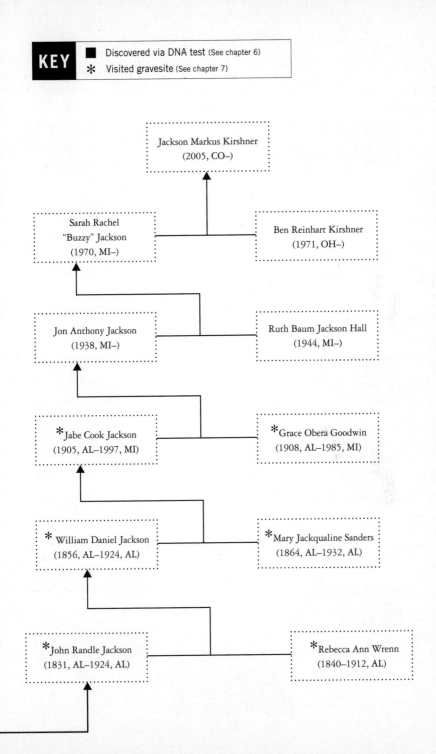

KEY

■ Discovered via DNA test (See chapter 6)
✳ Visited gravesite (See chapter 7)

Jackson Markus Kirshner
(2005, CO–)

Sarah Rachel
"Buzzy" Jackson
(1970, MI–)

Ben Reinhart Kirshner
(1971, OH–)

Jon Anthony Jackson
(1938, MI–)

Ruth Baum Jackson Hall
(1944, MI–)

✳Jabe Cook Jackson
(1905, AL–1997, MI)

✳Grace Obera Goodwin
(1908, AL–1985, MI)

✳ William Daniel Jackson
(1856, AL–1924, AL)

✳Mary Jackqualine Sanders
(1864, AL–1932, AL)

✳John Randle Jackson
(1831, AL–1924, AL)

✳Rebecca Ann Wrenn
(1840–1912, AL)

CONTENTS

8

The Mountain and the Cloud; or, A Pilgrimage to Salt Lake City's Family History Library

All genealogical roads eventually lead to the Family History Library in Salt Lake City, a mind-blowing archive run by the Church of Latter-Day Saints (aka, the Mormons). I speak with the chief genealogist at the FHL, the man responsible for its hundreds of billions of records, as well as with the collections director who oversees the archives in Ukraine where one half of my family's archives probably still sit. Mostly I marvel at the several thousand genealogical pilgrims (most non-Mormon) who visit the FHL every day.

9

Ask Yourself Why You're Doing This . . . and Keep Asking

A reflection on the unending nature of genealogical research, which is both a good and a bad thing. I assess my own progress, and wonder if any other Jackson descendant will ever visit that overgrown cemetery in Sumter County, Alabama, where a dozen of my antebellum ancestors lie.

1

Ask Yourself Why You're Doing This; or, Genealogy for Beginners

Ask yourself why you're doing this."

Pat Roberts, a woman with a stylish haircut, some serious jewelry, and the no-nonsense voice of a high school guidance counselor, stared out at the group of strangers who'd shown up for the introduction-to-genealogy seminar that morning at the Boulder Public Library. I suddenly realized what was coming: just like that guidance counselor, this enigmatic gatekeeper was about to tell us whether our expectations were realistic or just plain ridiculous.

"Ask yourself why you're doing this," she repeated, this time with a rhetorical spin. "If I put that question to each of you, I'd get twenty different answers. So ask yourself: What do you hope to find?"

Other people's history

In my case, it was a circus tent and a dentist. And a cattle farm in Mississippi and, of course, Windswept. I'd come to the Boulder

Public Library looking for the truth, if it existed, behind both the tall tales told by my family as well as the silences. I didn't suspect scandal, but I wouldn't be surprised to find some. This seemed realistic; at least, it didn't seem totally absurd. I was also looking for one other thing: a strategy.

I was looking for Jacksons—my Jacksons, among an ocean of people who shared my name but not my DNA. Jackson is the twentieth most popular surname in the United States; in the year 2000, 666,125 Americans were named Jackson. We are legion—but whom did I mean by "we"?[1]

My father, Jon Anthony Jackson, is one of eight children spread out over seven states. They like each other, yet they rarely see each other. As a family, we neither send nor receive regular Christmas letters. Frankly, most of us probably feel virtuous if we can remember all the cousins' names. Now that my grandfather Jabe and grandmother Grace Jackson are dead, there is no central "home" to return to—not that many of their children visited much, anyway. Whether that is normal, I don't know, but it sure didn't make for a strong sense of heritage. I'd spent seven years getting a Ph.D. in history . . . *other* people's history. It had never occurred to me to look into my own.

Recently, this lack of family narrative began to bother me. The furthest back I could trace my ancestors was three generations: my great-grandparents. That barely got me into the nineteenth century, and I started to feel a little, well, irresponsible about it. I'd spent a lot of time in graduate school tracing the history of African-Americans, people who lamented their history of enslavement not only for its obvious privations, but also because of the way slavery erased their family connections, as parents, children, siblings were separated and sold, names changed, and records lost. Something similar had happened on my mother's side of the family, Russian Jews who fled persecution to come to the United States in the brief window of time when such a migration was possible.

So what of the Jacksons? I knew they'd arrived in this country before my maternal ancestors, but how much earlier? I had no idea, and no one was discussing it at the Jackson family reunion, because there was no reunion. Ever. Oscar Wilde wrote that "to lose one parent . . . may be regarded as a misfortune; to lose both looks like carelessness." So what if you've misplaced your entire family tree?[2]

Life offers some reliable milestones guaranteed to thrust family in our faces. Weddings, for example. My husband, Ben, has two uncles, one aunt, and four cousins. Me, I have six (surviving) aunts and uncles just on the Jackson side alone, with who knows how many cousins (and, sadly, I didn't). For a couple trying to plan a small wedding, you'd think the Bride's Side of the aisle would be the problem here, but no. No, because it barely occurred to me to invite any of my Jackson relatives: I hardly knew most of them. The wedding planner in me was relieved, but the Jackson in me felt, for the first time, a little sad about the etiolated state of the Jackson family horticulture.

Another major milestone was the birth of my son—or rather, the forty weeks leading up to it. It was a magical time filled with excitement . . . and paranoia, nausea, and more questions about my family health history than I'd ever imagined possible. Causes of death, incidents of stroke, commitments to sanitariums? I needed the information fast. The eventual birth of my healthy son did, of course, provoke all the expected but nevertheless poignant emotions related to the Circle of Life and the perpetuation of the family line, but honestly? It was the endless medical interrogations that really got me thinking about where this baby came from.

Weddings and births are happy reminders of the ways we are all connected to the billions of human beings who walked the planet before we got here (over 100 billion at last count). Funerals, of course, prompt similar thoughts, and also force us to think about our own mortality. None of my grandparents were at my wedding; they had all passed away by then—but I had only attended one of their funerals. I was never very close with any of them, but with the birth of my son, I found myself missing my grandparents and trying to remember how they looked, how they sounded, and the stories they'd told.

Jabe Cook Jackson was the most riveting storyteller among them. Born in Alabama, he was one of those southerners who turned every utterance into a memorable bon mot. Some family stories are told more often than others; among Jabe's eight children, each one might have a different version of a canonical yarn, and each version would be equally funny and vivid. Sheer numbers contributed to a Jackson family narrative pieced together according to the rules of the old game of Telephone; stories are repeated and commented upon, then subtly changed and passed not only from father to son, but also from sister to brother.

Growing up—and even now that I am, *ahem,* grown up—every once in a while a relative would drop a Family Bomb. A Family Bomb was one of those Jackson family stories so bizarre and unexpected that it threw everything into a new light. They usually appear in a conversation apropos of nothing in particular. One involved a mysterious black "brother" of my grandfather—a Family Bomb first dropped when I was about twenty-two. My dad just happened to mention it during an otherwise unremarkable conversation: *Oh, and another thing: your white, southern grandfather grew up in Jim Crow Alabama with a black orphan boy around his own age whom he considered a brother. Never knew what happened to him.* Right. Or: *Actually, when we first moved to Kingsley, the whole family lived in a circus tent.* Sure. And: *You've never met those cousins? They're the ones who own a cattle ranch, and when they got tired of asking the bank for money, they started their own.* Their own what? *Their own bank.* Oh.

So there was the black brother question, the circus tent issue, and the First Bank of Jackson mystery. There were others, too. Why, at Grandpa Jackson's funeral, did my righteous, devout Christian aunt Mary insist to the undertaker that my Baptist-minister grandfather—her father—was Jewish? Why did my grandparents name their home in Kingsley, Michigan, Windswept? It sounded like a southern plantation—was it an homage to a lost antebellum homestead? I didn't know. With all these questions in mind, I began to seek answers.

I hoped my background in American history would help. I had a lot of experience with old records and dusty documents, but I had never applied it to my own family. I'd gone to the introduction-to-genealogy course that morning in an attempt to bring all my Jackson relatives, dead and alive, together—if only on paper. I wanted to gather them up and make sense of them if I could.

The name gatherers

Within one second of walking into the meeting room, I'd made my first major discovery: *I am not alone.* It's not that I found my long-lost Jackson cousin sitting there. It was that I found so many other people, strangers to me, each on their own identical quest.

I am not alone is a sentiment that resonates on many levels when beginning a journey of family history. In this case the numbers signified something surprising: forty-seven people had taken time off work or arranged a babysitter in order to come to the Boulder Public Library on a Tuesday morning, all to get help with their family trees. I was definitely not alone.

It didn't surprise Pat Roberts, of course. As the secretary of the Boulder Genealogical Society and its director of education, Pat had witnessed what the rise of the Internet had wrought: a whole new generation of genealogy enthusiasts eager to Google their family trees. Once the province of orphans and aspiring Daughters of the American Revolution, the world of genealogical hobbyists is now exploding in popularity, thanks in part to the immense new repositories of data on the World Wide Web. That's why Pat was here: to guide all of us in this journey—a journey that more and more people were making every day.

How many people are actually doing genealogy? According to the official Directory of Genealogical and Historical Societies, Libraries, and Publications in the United States and Canada, there are twenty-two thousand genealogical and historical societies; twelve thousand genealogical and historical periodicals; and ten thousand public and private genealogical and historical libraries, archives, and collections. Looking through the directory, I found an average of thirty to fifty genealogical societies per state, divided by county, city, and sometimes by special interests such as ethnic affiliation. That's a lot of genealogical societies—heck, that's a lot of societies, period. So much for bowling alone.

Not everyone interested in genealogy joins a society, though. Most genealogy hobbyists do their stuff on the Web, and I found even more numbers there. As with most genealogical quests, you can't go wrong by starting with the Church of Latter-Day Saints (aka the Mormons). The LDS Church began compiling family history data for religious reasons a century ago and these days their archives contain information on over one billion people. The church's Family History Library has always been open to the public, but until recently that required traveling to Salt Lake City. In 1999—hallelujah!—the church launched www.FamilySearch.org, the Web version of the Family History Library archive. Since then, over 150 million people have visited the FamilySearch Web site, with one million registered users and more than fifty thousand people accessing the site every day. And that's just *one* archive. In the past few years dozens of new free and fee-based Web sites have popped up to offer different types of searches, whether for census information, birth and death certificates, or—my personal favorite—tours of "virtual cemeteries," where one can peer at all those faded headstones without scuffing a slipper. It's pretty clear: one reason more people are interested in genealogy is that it's gotten so much easier to do.

The people gathered in the Boulder library that morning probably started their searches online. If their explorations were anything like mine, they'd experienced an initial thrill (Hey! Someone named Desmond Jackson is also looking for *his* ancestors!) followed by a slow dissipation of excitement (Okay, there are, um, a *lot* of people named Jackson looking for their ancestors . . . and somehow we're all looking for different people). I now knew what a helium birthday balloon felt like as it shriveled and drifted to the floor a few days after the party. It felt like it was time to get help.

Sometimes I think nothing in this world would ever get done without the no-nonsense grit and guidance of women over forty. Pat Roberts knew what we needed and she was willing to help. She smelled our desperation as we filed into the conference room, lunging for her information packets. We needed guidelines. We needed parameters. We needed to focus, people. Pat would provide a Plan of Action.

We'd already asked ourselves why we were doing this. But Pat was not going to make us state our motivations aloud. "Some people want to find a celebrity ancestor," she said. "In my case, my husband challenged me to find out if his family tradition was true—were they descended from a signer of the Declaration of Independence?" Pat had a friend named Jane who was already experienced in genealogical searches, and she also encouraged Pat to dig in. "I was intrigued," Pat said. "I came down here to the Boulder library and ordered microfilm from the National Archives. I turned my children loose in the children's section, and they played while I looked at the microfilm."

I groaned. Seven years of graduate school had left me a battle-scarred veteran of the University of California's army of ancient microfilm readers, massed in a herd in the half-height stacks of a dusty, windowless no-man's-land somewhere beyond the periodical room. I thought my labor in the archival mine shafts had ended when I submitted my dissertation: Did my interest in genealogy mean I'd have to descend again?

"This was 1973," Pat continued. "The copies came out on thermo paper—you can't even read it anymore. Microfilm . . ." She shook her head. I did, too. "You cranked it . . . it's ugly . . ." Yes it is. I could almost see my as-yet-unpopulated family tree begin to wither, leafless.

"But what we did back then was a totally different type of genealogy," Pat said.

I perked up and I'm pretty sure several others in the room, perhaps with their own hellish microfilm memories, did, too. Pat explained that while it was still necessary to use microfilm from time to time, the Internet had revolutionized the practice of genealogical research. Not only were many archival resources online, but "now, with the Internet, we're communicating with people we never would have found before . . . ever, ever, ever." It was now possible to find distant relatives online—relatives who might already have done a lot of your family research for you. Now we were getting somewhere.

"We're getting our hands on stuff we never would get before," Pat said. "Back then, genealogists were just name gatherers. We collected as many names, births, marriages, and deaths as we could. If it looked reasonable, we jumped on it. But we were not doing good genealogy." What she meant—and this was something I would hear a lot as I learned more about the changes in genealogy—was that very few people made much of an effort to actually verify the information they found in family Bibles and in the stories of Aunt Ida. If it was a name or date: it was good to go. Over the past few decades, even before the Internet arrived on the scene, genealogists have gotten more professional in their research. Proper citation is a big deal these days, as is good record keeping. There is more information to be had, which means there is a lot more information to organize. "I can do in two weeks what it would take me two years to do back then," Pat said, referring to her early days of research in the 1970s. My friend Matthew calls these TGFI moments: Thank God For the Internet. I hoped to have a lot of them.

Six degrees of Juan Baca

I'd begun my genealogical research on the Internet, first by looking for information about my family, but since I didn't know much
about them or where to look, I started looking at other people's family trees and then at the genealogists themselves.

And I started to think about death.

You might say death is what genealogy is all about. One of the
less publicized benefits of genealogical research is its role in providing a gentle acquaintance with the idea of death . . . specifically,
one's own. As I read through the family stories of online genealogists, I was struck by their casual, even cheerful way of noting the
deaths of family members in the course of relating some larger story
about their research. They're not morbid, nor are they flippant;
they're simply more at ease with discussions of death because it's
something they consider every day. It's even more profound than
that, though, because I think their deep understanding of their roots
is a tangible source of comfort in the face of death; to them, death is
both unavoidable and familiar. And, of course, their own work offers
the promise that someday one of their own ancestors will, in turn,
remember them. When it comes to postlife expectations—divine
resurrection aside—what more can one hope for?

Genealogy hobbyists are not just a bunch of well-adjusted
funeral attendees, though; they're also nerds. I love nerds. My definition of a nerd is someone who is extremely interested in . . . something. Anything. Whether experts on sports scores, *Star Wars,* or
Michael Kors, they're all nerds to me. These are people of passion,
and the object of their fascination is less important than their zeal
to know everything about it. With genealogy, there is a lot of "it"
to know, from understanding the limits of mitochondrial DNA to
locating the long-lost manifest of an ancient schooner, these people
demonstrate that *learn* is the most active verb. My name is Buzzy
Jackson and I, too, am a nerd.

Skeptics often distrust the motivations of genealogists. Isn't this obsession with ancestry just . . . self-obsession? Isn't it just another narcissistic pastime, sort of a "six degrees of separation" game in which one's own name takes the hallowed central spot usually reserved for Kevin Bacon? (Genealogy Nerd Fact #37: In New Mexico, people use the name "Juan Baca" instead of Kevin Bacon. No one really knows why.) Common sense and the math of genealogy say no. Once one reaches back past, say, one's grandparents' generation, there are just too many ancestors for anyone to feel a seriously intimate connection. Consider the generation before your grandfather— there are sixteen people involved there. And the rules of exponents reveal that this number just keeps getting bigger and bigger—yes, exponentially—with each generation, eventually resulting in thousands, then millions of ancestors. When you go way back, say, five thousand to fifteen thousand years ago, you hit what genetic researchers call the "identical ancestors point," which basically means this: if you look back far enough, we're all cousins. If nothing else, this provides some long-sought scientific backup for the conceptual framework of *The Patty Duke Show.*

If this is narcissism, then it's a form of self-love that extends to the whole human race. Genealogy math is full of strange facts. A recent *New York Times* article provoked hundreds of angry reader responses when the author asserted that less than 50 percent of any one person's ancestors are men. Reader, he proved it. (His calculations looked pretty convincing to me; but I should confess that I was an English major.) Then there's evolutionary biologist Richard Dawkins's explanation of how our "250-greats grandparent" is not only a grandparent shared by you and me, but also the grandparent of all living chimpanzees. Even for hard-core Darwinians, this can be a little hard to digest.[3] Personally, I was thrilled. Nerd alert.

Being nerds, genealogists love freaky details. Want to excite a genealogist? Just mention the 1890 Census . . . then hang on. The 1890 Census is the *Rosebud* of American genealogy. As the first machine-tabulated census, it reported the United States' total population (exactly 62,622,250) in six short weeks, unlike the 1880 Census, which wasn't completed until two years before the next census took place. Administered at a crucial time in America's immigration history, the 1890 Census provided a quantifiable measure of a new, multiethnic population. The data gathered included information on country of origin, race, ability to read and write English, and much more (including whether anyone in the house was officially "idiotic." Now that's information you can *use*).

Stored in the basement of the U.S. Department of Commerce Building in Washington, D.C., this trove of (future) genealogical information caught fire one night in 1921 and a quarter of the 1890 Census data was incinerated, with another 50 percent damaged by smoke and water. The accident became a key factor in the formation of the National Archives, a presumably safer home for America's in-box. But even that couldn't save the apparently doomed 1890 Census. Sometime in 1934 or 1935, all those punch cards disappeared—forever—when the librarian of Congress (who shall remain unnamed here) tacitly authorized their destruction along with a lot of other "scrap" paper.

Many, probably most nations have their own sad story of archival loss. Ireland lost nearly its entire collection of public archives, including all its census information, when the public records building in the Four Courts blew up during the Battle of Dublin in 1922. Only the few materials that had been left in the reading room were saved. Stories like these make genealogists (and historians, I must add) physically ill. So much information, lost forever; it's the Library of Alexandria all over again.

Genealogists are a dogged and frankly obsessive bunch. Human beings are record keepers. The first human records were stories, oral histories of tribal origins told to one another around the African cooking fire. Then came art and writing. Many of the oldest cave paintings depict what may be family groupings, perhaps the earliest expressions of the family tree. And virtually every ancient religion begins and ends with a story of lineage: So-and-So begat So-and-So, and so on. Historians argue that one of the hallmarks of the modern age was the emergence of bureaucracy.

Wherever you find bureaucracy, you will also find genealogists, because genealogists live for records. They may (and constantly do) scorn the carelessness and poor handwriting of the scribes and clerks who noted names and addresses in decades and centuries past, but they also deeply appreciate the fact that such documents exist. Genealogists will go to nearly any length to find a key record. And genealogists are all around us.

I had no idea.

They walk among us unnoticed; they look just like everyone else. But secretly, internally, they are plotting and planning their next research step: a trip to that remote county courthouse in Iowa; a friendly visit with the widow of the man who used to take roll at the Odd Fellows Lodge; a mental list of microfilm to be requested from the Family History Library. They're always up to something. One unproven statistic you hear a lot in the genealogy world is the "fact" that genealogy is the second most popular use for the Internet. Guess what the first one is.

Genealogists are everywhere. With their history of immigration, I assumed that Americans' interest in genealogy was probably unique, but no. It seems that anywhere people have parents you'll find an interest in genealogy. Take the United Kingdom, for example, where six million viewers tune in every week to watch the celebrity genealogy show, *Who Do You Think You Are?*

In the United States, the record-shattering TV premiere of Alex Haley's *Roots* in 1977 is credited by most genealogists for the huge upsurge in genealogical interest among all Americans, especially among those with African heritage. The African-American theme has been a strong one in American genealogy ever since, with the DNA-aided discovery in the late 1990s of the African-American descendants of Thomas Jefferson and his slave Sally Hemings. *Roots* got an update in the 2006 PBS series *African-American Lives,* in which historian Henry Louis Gates guided Oprah Winfrey, Chris Rock, and several other prominent African-Americans back to their African ancestors with the help of genealogists and geneticists.

Now I was hooked. African-Americans like Henry Louis Gates found white ancestry where they didn't expect it. With a name like Jackson, it seemed possible that I might have African-American relatives I'd never met; the offspring of a relationship between one of my southern, slave-owning (or so I assumed) Jackson ancestors and, perhaps, a slave, just as the white descendants of Thomas Jefferson discovered African-American cousins they'd never known existed. I wasn't harboring conspiracy theories; everything I'd learned about American history supported this possibility. It was certainly worth looking into.

Pat's plan

It was all this that brought me to the library that morning. As I looked around at my fellow Beginning Genealogists I did feel a certain kinship, despite the reservations I shared with my fellow skeptics. The biggest turnoff for me was the notion of racial or lineal purity: a tacky sort of bloodline-based quest for status that kept registries like *Burke's Peerage,* the ultimate Who's Who of the royal set, in business. As I'd explored it, though, I recognized a different, simpler impulse: the desire to understand oneself, through a better understanding of one's own family.

"Decide where you're going," Pat instructed us, "and then you can figure out how you'll get there."

I was looking for Jacksons. Check.

"You may find a family line that speaks to you," Pat said, "and other ancestors who don't want to be found. That's all right; all genealogists hit a brick wall at some point." We all nodded, confident it would never happen to a single one of us. "For instance, you might end up looking for Johnsons." She rolled her eyes. "Johnsons are almost as bad as Smiths!" Nineteen people in the room laughed. I did not laugh. If Johnsons were almost as bad as Smiths, Jacksons must be worse. Even a beginner genealogist knows that Smiths are the laughingstocks of Anglo-European genealogy, the dynastic equivalent of a common housefly. Smiths are everywhere and there are too many of them. Apparently Jacksons were nearly as bad—the moths of genealogy, perhaps. Maybe we could be the cute ubiquitous surname family, like ladybugs. It was a stretch, I knew.

"Don't get discouraged," Pat said, oblivious to the black cloud of demoralization hovering over my head. "There are ways of getting through those brick walls . . . though it might take years to do it." She then began to list the research strategies available to us, we lucky genealogists of the Internet age. She handed out a sheet listing over one hundred Web sites related to genealogy, from state-sponsored archives to Ellis Island passenger lists. TGFI, baby.

While the Internet is a genealogist's best friend, it cannot do the research for you. As Pat explained, although the Internet had revolutionized access to genealogical information, the basic steps of genealogical research had not changed very much since the era of the rotary phone. She outlined them for us over the next couple of hours, but I provide them here, in their distilled form:

- **Start with yourself.** Write down everything you already know and can verify about your family history. Interview yourself and your siblings (who may know different family stories—or different versions of them—than you do) then work back.
- **Interview as many living relatives as possible.** Whether by phone or in person, talk to your relatives, especially the oldest ones, about the family history. Ask to see family

mementos such as family Bibles, old photographs, and journals, even quilts that might contain data on your ancestors.

- **Collect as many relevant records as possible.** Vital records are key; these are records of birth, death, and marriage. Other useful records include those concerning military service, employment, census information, city directory information, etc. Depending on the record, you'll find these online, in local courthouses or libraries, and in archives such as the Family History Library and the National Archives.

- **Ask for help.** You don't have to hire a professional genealogist, though it's an option. You can also get great advice from librarians and members of the historical organizations where your family lived. But if you ask any genealogist, they will tell you the single best resource you have is other genealogists. By simply joining a local genealogical society (believe me, there's one near you), you'll end up meeting a lot of other people with similar interests and helpful strategies. One of the hallmarks of genealogy is the sense of mutual support. Genealogists live to share information, and that's true whether you're dealing with someone in your own genealogical society or simply the name and e-mail address of a genealogist across the world that you met in a virtual genealogy chat room.

- **Go deeper.** Once you really get rolling, you can consider other research methods, including DNA testing and visiting the actual locations where your ancestors lived. Many hard-core genealogists plan all their vacations around family history research. Depending on how far back you get, this might mean a trip overseas.

- **And, the most important step of all: stay organized.** Be methodical in your research; write everything down to avoid doing the same searches twice. Keep notes about what you've looked at and what's left to do. Find an organizational system that works for you and stick to it. These days, most genealogists use computer programs to help them keep track of their family tree and their research trail. Invest in one.

We've all read the enigmatic phrase on the shampoo bottle: *Lather, rinse, repeat.* It's the same with genealogy. The basic steps—interviews, archival research, expert consultation, travel—will repeat themselves, over and over, for as long as you stay involved. That's both the beauty and the curse of genealogy: it never ends. On the plus side, your research skills improve every time you go at it, making future work a little more smooth. And for addicted genealogists, there really is no downside.

The daylong course at the library continued, and my disappointment at having a common surname dissipated. We looked at Web sites. We discussed common mistakes. We learned.

In the year that followed, I learned much, much more. That day at the library was the beginning of a journey that would lead me to an abandoned Alabama cemetery and a beach in the Caribbean. I would be politely spurned by one relative and rib-crushingly embraced by another. It was a path that would lead me through four time zones and at least three regional dialects and ultimately reward me with the genealogical equivalent of a million-dollar lottery ticket. It would also force me to think more deeply about the cycles of birth, life, and death than I ever had before. My research would make me mourn the loss of my grandparents and appreciate the health of the family still with me.

What I learned on this journey changed my perspective on some of the biggest life issues any of us contemplate: my relationship to my family and my sense of my own life path. It also changed my life in smaller, concrete ways. I learned things about American history I'd never heard about in graduate school; I tried new foods; I forced myself to study the basic tenets of genetics in order to understand my DNA results; I changed the medications I take on a daily basis as a result of learning new information about my family's medical history, and much, much more (let us not dwell on the number of extra pounds I gained while "researching" the gastronomic heritage of my southern forebears).

Just as I began this journey I happened to hear an interview with the actress Tilda Swinton, who belongs to one of only three families able to trace its lineage back to the ninth century (they are known as Clan Swinton, in *Burke's Peerage* terminology). When asked about what it must be like to belong to such an old family, the beautifully spoken Tilda Swinton sighed, betraying just the tiniest speck of irritation. *"Everyone's* from an old family," she said. "Mine just wrote everything down."[4]

There you have it. Every single one of us alive today is by definition a member of an "old family." We don't hear about "young families" because . . . they died out. In genealogy, you're either old or you're dead. Whether last year or eight hundred years ago, when you're gone, you're gone. It's the chronicling of a family that links it to history. I wanted to know mine.

So, nerd that I am, I started at the beginning, just as Pat Roberts advised: start with yourself, then work backward. Lather, rinse, repeat.

2

They See Dead People But I Stick to the Living; or, Join Your Local Genealogy Society

Genealogy is perfect for boomers," Gary said. "For most of our lives, we didn't care about our past, about our parents' lives. It was all just . . . us." I understand completely. As the child of boomers, I've lived in their us-centered shadow my entire life. When they're gone, I'll be living in the shadow of the Echo Boom, to which both of my younger brothers belong. There's a reason they called my generation slackers—what else does one do, hanging out in the shadows all the time? But this is the stuff of contemporary demographics. Genealogists are interested in the past.

They see dead people

I was at my first Boulder Genealogical Society Meeting, where I'd gone not only to seek expert help, but also to learn about the people who spend all their free time in pursuit of history. Genealogists, I was beginning to discover, tend to have thought pretty deeply about why they're doing it.

"Now we're older," Gary said. "We have the time and the money and we want to know [about our roots]." He told me about a recent vacation he and his wife took in Illinois and Missouri, where they hit thirteen cemeteries and several county courthouses. "We didn't go to one quote-unquote tourist attraction," he boasted. I decided not to ask the obvious question: *Are* there any tourist attractions in Illinois or Missouri? It didn't matter. The Rouths see dead people. It's their hobby.

Up until now, I'd been feeling pretty organized. I felt prepped. I started planning a trip to Michigan to put my interviews to the test. I felt more than ready. And then I attended my first meeting of the Boulder Genealogical Society, and all my fantasies of expertise evaporated into the summer night.

I thought of you on the way to the Dumpster

It's a balmy seventy-five degrees at 7:35 P.M. as I walk up to the July meeting of the Boulder Genealogical Society (BGS). Held monthly in the basement of the Mountain View Methodist Church, the whole event emanates a nostalgic ambience made up of cool, waxed linoleum floors and faux-wood paneling that instantly evoked the postwar elementary school buildings of my youth.

The BGS members are not grade-schoolers, however. The crowd of forty-five or so attendees (of the 130 total members) are mostly gray-haired; I say mostly, because the few exceptions are the nine bald men and a scattering of brunettes in their forties. I arrive a little late (bad form, I know), entering in the middle of the monthly business announcements: an upcoming garage sale; an announcement for a contest starring "My Most Inspirational Ancestor." I find a seat on a folding chair in the back and try to give off polite, well-mannered vibes. Several people smile in my direction.

As it turns out, tonight's speaker is none other than Pat Roberts herself, lecturing on the topic of "Dating and Identifying Heritage

Photos." BGS members nod: they all have boxes of old pictures lacking names, dates, or any other identifying feature. To a detective such as Pat, every photograph contains identifying features.

"Don't even try to take notes," she says at the outset. "You'll never catch up. Mona will hand out CDs—it's a Word doc." The CDs start to circulate, each one sleeved in a transparent plastic case through which a decorative label can be seen. Pat made fifty of these lovely CDs for our benefit. Suddenly I do feel as if I'm back in elementary school after all, and Pat Roberts is the little girl in the front row with perfect ponytails who always wins the handwriting contest. You know that girl. Personally, I had a hard time learning cursive letters, but perhaps there's still hope for me, genealogically speaking.

What follows is an hour-long tour through the history of photographic technology, American fashion, and cultural norms that is worthy of a *CSI* plot, if not a Ph.D. degree. Before any of us in the audience get too overwhelmed with details about celluloid processing innovations or the relative weights of paper stock in historical *cartes de visite,* Pat reassures us that we can find all this information on our CDs. Good, because—surprise!—I can no longer read my own frantic handwriting.

I do take away one significant piece of advice: write the name and date and any other identifying details on the back of your important photos. Always. If you don't, your photos may end up like those poignant stacks of sepia-toned curiosities in the antiques shop: signifiers with no significance. She then shares with us the chilling title of one of her friend's genealogy lectures: "I Thought of You on the Way to the Dumpster." The Dumpster is where unlabeled photographs go to die.

Pat then cites the story of the Little Red Hen to describe the thankless job of being her family's designated record keeper. I guess being the Most Organized Woman in the World has its downside, after all. Everyone wants to see the genealogical results, Pat says, but no one wants to do the research. None of the kids, anyway. Almost every head in the audience nods in sympathy. Heads then shake sorrowfully as various BGS members lament their children's apathy.

Suddenly a balding dissenter pipes up in defense of youth (*Hey—teacher! Leave them kids alone!*). "You know, I didn't get interested in this stuff until I was sixty," he says. Others seem to agree. As a somewhat conspicuous member of Generation X, I sit up a little straighter (slackers be damned) and hold my head high. Looking around, I notice a few other (relative) youngsters, all female. And— holy generational gaps—one of them is sporting a rather large tattoo on her upper arm! I'm not inked myself, but I'm tattoo-friendly. I *will* meet this BGS member.

When the meeting ends, I grab a brownie from the refreshment table and do my best to mingle with anyone who will talk to me. It's easy mingling. First, Gary tells me about the boomers. Then I meet Shirley Huntbach, the BGS officer whose job it is to keep all the name tags in their wooden box. "We'll have to get you your own name tag!" she says, motioning toward my handwritten sticker. "Yes!" another woman exclaims, extending her hand and a million-dollar smile. This is Mary Ann Looney, the BGS membership director. They got lucky when they found these two. Warm, friendly, self-deprecating ("You might forget Mary Ann," she says, "but you're not going to forget Looney"—*wink!*), Mary Ann even looks a little bit like a slightly older version of Mary Ann from *Gilligan's Island*. I always thought Mary Ann was cuter than Ginger or Mrs. Howell. Mary Ann Looney is adorable. "We like to be known as the friendliest genealogical society," Mary Ann tells me. Mission accomplished.

Her arm linked in mine, Mary Ann begins escorting me around the room to introduce me. This feels a little like going to my mom's office holiday party, in a good way. Everyone is seemingly charmed to meet me; I'm not sure if this is because they have excellent manners, or because I'm with Mary Ann, or simply because I'm under forty. I don't really care, either. I'm not typically a joiner; I don't belong to any other clubs in town, but I'm starting to understand why one might.

Mary Ann introduces me to Dina Carson, another BGS board member. Like me, she's on the younger side. Unlike me, she is a committed, experienced genealogy fanatic who is currently overseeing the Boulder Pioneers Project, a listing of every individual living in Boulder County before Colorado achieved statehood in 1876. She's got long brown hair and a great smile; she's warm, bubbly, and full of friendliness like all her BGS compatriots. She's also really into graveyards.

"I photograph cemeteries," Dina explains. "I go to old, overgrown cemeteries, like ones near the old mining towns. If you don't get these photographs now . . . they'll be gone. Some of the stones are in really bad shape." Dina's interested in the history, but she also photographs these crumbling headstones as a service to other genealogists. She posts the photographs of the graves on the Web so that others can search for their gold- or silver-mining ancestors without having to travel all the way to the Rocky Mountains. It's not just the travel that's an obstacle. Visiting old cemeteries can be dangerous, too.

"I went to an old mining town cemetery in the mountains west of here," Dina told me. "It took me three full days to photograph it. It was a lot bigger than I thought.

"The first day up there, I just kept getting this weird feeling that somebody—something was watching me. It gave me the creeps. Not only was I far from my car, but I was out of anybody's sight. But I never saw anyone."

"Was the cemetery part of a ghost town?" I asked.

"There are some houses that weren't too far away," she said, "but the most recent grave was from the 1920s.

"The next day I went back up there and I start walking down the road that goes through the cemetery. Suddenly I got that hair-standing-up-on-the-back-of-my-neck feeling—I'm thinking it's a big cat," she said—a mountain lion. "I thought—you know what? I have a gun in the car; I'm going to take it with me. I go back to my glove compartment and put the gun in my fanny pack."

"What kind of gun is it?" I hear myself asking, despite the fact that I know nothing about guns and won't be able to appreciate her answer, whatever it might be. It seems like a logical question, though. And I'm mingling!

"It's a forty-five-caliber Colt. It's a fairly big gun—it would stop somebody."

"It would stop me," I say. The sight of any gun—a Super Soaker, say—would stop me. I keep this information to myself.

Dina shrugs. "Just the sight of it would stop most people. I get a little ways back down the road and sure enough I hear something. Then I see him: a guy's standing there, not ten feet away. You know how you get that feeling that someone is just up to no good? I get that feeling. I worked as a paramedic for twenty years. I know when they're bad actors. So I take the gun out and I say, 'You *really* have to go someplace else.'

"He's just staring; he's got this look on his face like he's not real sure what to do next. And I keep pointing it at him and I say, '*Seriously:* you should run.'"

"So what did he do?" I ask.

"He ran."

Dina seems unfazed by this experience. I'm still trying to process the idea of keeping a gun in the glove compartment—though I know lots of people must do this. I'm glad she mentioned the paramedic thing, though. It helps explain her coolness in the face of danger. Dina goes on to assure me that this type of thing—creepy guys lurking behind headstones—is not typical of her experiences photographing cemeteries. Frankly, the idea of the mountain lion is scary enough for me. The stalker and the gun merely add another level of paranoia to the scene.

So far Dina's collected over 7,500 names for the Boulder Pioneers Project. She also owns her own graphic design business. When I ask her about where she finds the time to do all this (volunteer) genealogical work, she tells me she just makes the time. She devotes every Wednesday to photographing the contents of various local archives. As far as her personal family history research goes, she laments that she's "plagued by Smiths"—with that surname appearing on both sides of her family tree. I get the feeling she's exhausted her own research and decided to dedicate her skills to the service of genealogists everywhere.

It's not uncommon. "Genealogists are so helpful," Shirley tells me in a separate conversation. "Even before the Internet, you might write a letter to someone who seemed to know something about your family line, and you'd get a whole packet of documents back in the mail—all from someone you've never met! It's one of the best parts of doing genealogy," she says, and the others standing with us nod in agreement. "It's just such a friendly, helpful group of people." It sure is.

Just as the meeting is breaking up, I spot Pat Roberts. She seems to recognize me from the intro course. "Why, hello!" she says, a little surprised to find me here. Although part of the goal for the library class is to publicize BGS, the promotion is not overt. None of the other people from the library appear to be here tonight.

"Hi, Pat," I say. "Thanks so much for your course; it really helped me get started."

"Well, you made it here, so that's a good sign. It's a nice group," she says, looking around at her fellow BGS members. "You'll get a lot of help here."

I found Mary Ann Looney and gave her my twenty-five-dollar membership fee. Joining a genealogical society wouldn't transform me into a genealogist overnight, but the help of its members might push me in the right direction.

Pleased to meet me: the self-interview

I felt ready to dig for my roots, but sticking to Pat's directions meant that I should interview myself first. Then I'd move on to living relatives, and only then start researching the dead.

I knew of only one family member living in any of the seven states adjacent to me: my aunt Joanne in New Mexico. I had never met her. The only blood relative in my own state was my three-year-old son, and interviewing one's children is the opposite of genealogy. I didn't spend much time interviewing my two younger brothers, Devin and Keith, because as the arrogant oldest sibling, I was sure I knew more than they did. I threw some questions their way via e-mail and in response I received support for my quest and wishes of good luck. Genealogy really does favor the old.

My self-interview, on the other hand, was more revealing than expected. As it turns out, I'm fascinating! No, that wasn't it.

The self-interview revealed not only how little I knew about my family history, but how poorly documented my own personal story was. It took several hours of scouring my files to find a copy of my own birth certificate. I never found anything that proved I was married, a sad fact demonstrating that it doesn't necessarily take decades or centuries for records to become lost; in my case, it only took six years. I resolved to do better. And I hoped that my own ancestors were a bit more type A.

I knew from past interviewing experience that there were two kinds of questions, each important in its own way. The first was the question requiring a specific, factual answer: *What year was your paternal grandfather born?* Or, *What was your mother's maiden name?* The answers to these questions will further your research later, when you start plugging names and dates into search forms for census and vital record information.

The second kind of question was a little trickier. These questions were designed to provoke a thoughtful response: *What kind of neighborhood did you grow up in? What's your earliest memory? What did your grandmother's voice sound like?* These questions try to root out impressionistic details. They are manipulative, in that each question has multiple agendas. Perhaps a discussion of an old neighborhood will lead to reminiscence about childhood friends. Maybe the memory of grandmother's voice will induce a reverie about what grandmother was like. Above all, you're trying to avoid a yes or a no.

No matter how well you formulate your questions, it may still be difficult to get the material you seek. I once interviewed the musician Lucinda Williams. When I asked her if classic blues singers such as Bessie Smith had influenced her own work, she flatly said: "No." I ran through the names of several other musical greats, each time getting the same response, until I finally mentioned Bob Dylan. Bingo: she talked for a quarter of an hour about how much his music meant to her. I think she was testing me. Relatives will test you, too.

Shocking Fact #1: Mom and Dad had lives before I was born

I knew that interviewing my parents was going to be a different experience from interviewing my aunts and uncles, so I devised two strategies. I usually talk by phone or e-mail my parents every few days or weeks (they're divorced, so I communicate with them individually). This regular, friendly contact meant that I could conduct a more casual, ongoing form of interview with them, asking questions as they came up in my research. A professional genealogist would no doubt advise me to sit down with each of them formally for a lengthy interview, given life's unpredictability, and it is a very good idea. But I didn't do it that way, at least not initially.

What I did do was ask each of my parents for a basic time line of their lives, beginning with the year they were born, and following them through each residence (including addresses, if they remembered them) and major life event (names of schools, years of graduation, notable achievements, military service, marriage, divorce, etc.). I let them decide how specific they wanted to get, figuring once I got the basic outline, I could go back for more details. I also asked them to send me copies of any important documents they had: birth and marriage certificates, immigration paperwork, and the like.

I called my mom first, and I got a lot of great information, using her time line as a guide. But it was e-mail that saved me. There were just so many little questions that arose after our phone conversation ended, I started to compile a list: What year did you graduate from high school? How long did you live in New York? When I reached five questions, I'd e-mail it off to her. Then I'd start a new list. I always felt I knew my mother really well, and I do. Yet when I started to read my parents' time lines, I realized how vague my understanding of their lives really was. This first stage of family research provided a much clearer view of my parents. At times I felt as if I were watching a silent Super-8 movie unspool in my imagination. If I learned nothing else from my genealogical quest, this would have been precious enough.

My dad took the time line seriously. Attention, budding genealogists: try to have a writer for a parent; it worked beautifully for me. My dad, who is a novelist, wrote me long, beautiful e-mails about his family memories. He wrote of how his interest in bird-watching led to his work as a writer. He wrote of how his father's religious convictions had begun with a seemingly miraculous experience of being visited by God. The details my father provided from the kind of texture that is usually impossible to re-create once you start going back into history beyond your parents' generation. Sometimes it's even lost there. As soon as I began my research, I realized how lucky I was to have a parent who could recall these facts of history—names, places, and the reasons they moved on or stayed put.

When it came to my Jackson aunts and uncles, however, I knew

27

I had to be more deliberate. After all, I barely knew any of them. I decided to compile a list of what I knew—or suspected—about the family history, and then see if they could fill in details. I used my dad's time line to start out. Then I contacted his sister Nancy, one of the aunts I knew best. I'd heard a rumor that she'd done some genealogical research herself.

Big score. Nancy mailed me many sheets full of family trees, with names and dates I'd never seen before. Equally important, she provided me with the names and contact information for our southern Jackson cousins, many of whom she had met personally. Nancy was one of the only surviving seven Jackson siblings who had made any effort to stay in touch with her cousins. They didn't know it yet, but I was gearing up to call on them, too.

Oral history is a huge part of genealogical research, so I knew I didn't have to reinvent the wheel here. I went online and found several good resources for doing family interviews, including the Oral History Association (www.oralhistory.org), About.com's genealogy section (www.genealogy.about.com), and Cyndislist.com's Oral History page (www.cyndislist.com/oral.htm). After reading through their do's and don'ts, I was able to create a list of basic questions to use as a starting point in my research. It looked like this:

Family-History Questions

1. Please tell me when and where were you born. Are there any stories about your birth, or about your mother's pregnancy with you?
2. Can you tell me your earliest memory?
3. When and where were your parents born/married? Do you know any stories about their courtship or life together before you were born?
4. Tell me about your name: Do you know how was it chosen? Do you have a nickname? How did you decide to give your children their names?

5. Did your family have any close friends or neighbors when you were growing up, and if so, what can you tell me about them?

6. Was your family religious? What holidays/rituals did they observe?

7. How was your family perceived by others in the community?

8. Tell me about your a favorite pet or toy as a child.

9. When did you start to feel like a grown-up and why?

10. How did you meet your husband/wife/partner?

11. Tell me about an experience that taught you something about yourself.

12. What are some of your strongest memories of your parents/siblings/children and spouse?

13. Can you tell me any stories you've heard about our ancestors?

14. Are they any special family traditions or stories you can share with me?

15. Do you have any old photographs you can show me?

16. Do you have any strong memories of significant events—wars, elections, sporting events, etc.—and how your family reacted to them?

17. Did you ever meet your grandparents or great-aunts/uncles or great-grandparents?

18. What did you/your parents do for work?

19. Has the world changed since you were a child and if so how?

20. Is there any message or idea that you would like to pass on to future generations of your family?

Clearly, this list of questions was already too long. There was no way I was going to get through all of them. But they did provide a starting point. And they could be adapted, given the situation and the direction in which the interview was going. I kept the list long to give myself options; if I got all the way to Vermont to interview my aunt Claudia, I didn't want to run out of things to talk about.

To this list, I added another set of topics specific to what I already knew about the Jackson family history. Most of these fell into the categories of rumor and myth, so I wanted to find out if there was any truth behind them.

Jacksoniana

- Have you ever heard a story about my grandfather Jabe Cook Jackson performing a miracle to save his father's life? If so, what can you tell me about it?
- Have you ever heard of an ancestor named Bullwhip Jackson?
- Jabe Cook Jackson once told a story about a "little black boy" who was adopted by his family in Emelle, Alabama, and grew up with them there. Do you know anything about this?
- Is it true that our family is related to William Faulkner?
- Why did Jabe Cook Jackson and his wife, Grace, name their home in Michigan Windswept?
- Is it true that before Windswept was built, Jabe, Grace, and their eight children lived in a circus tent?
- Is it true that Grace Jackson saw ghosts?

I figured these questions would get them talking.

My parents are from Detroit—different Detroits. As with most of the folks who grew up in Detroit in the postwar era, they each now live elsewhere, part of the epic Detroit diaspora that saw a million people leave the city over the past four decades. My parents moved west. Mom sends a check every year to the Detroit Art Institute; Dad follows the Red Wings.

Interviewing Mom

Being Jewish, my mom's family lived in Detroit's Jewish neighborhoods. In a certain sense, however, all of these neighborhoods were only temporarily Jewish. My mother was the middle of three children, and by the time she was born, the family had already moved twice, always moving northwest from downtown. Just the usual white flight: the WASPs moved first, then the Jews, then the blacks, and the recent immigrants.

My mother's mother, Mary (née Mindl) Yaffe, was born in 1906 in Rovno (now known as Rivne), a city in the Russian territory of Volhynia Gubernia, now located in Ukraine. This region of Russia was where the pogroms first began. Hoping to escape the rising tide of anti-Semitism, Mary's father, Herschel, emigrated to the United States in 1911. Her mother, Rochel, brought the children over ten years later, arriving at Ellis Island as so many millions of immigrants had before them.

My grandmother's future husband, Ephraim Hersh "Herman" Baum, was born in Sambor, Galicia, a few hundred miles southwest of Rovno. He came to New York, too, staying in the Bronx at first and then moving to Detroit. But he didn't go directly to the United States. An early Zionist, he first went to Palestine in the late 1910s, where he spent at least some of his time laboring on a collective farm. In 1929, he came to the United States. Herman and Mary were married in 1938 in Detroit and had three children: Martin, Barry, and my mother, Ruth. In 1948, Herman died of a heart attack at the dinner table. He was forty-six years old.

My mother was the source of all this information. She had shared bits of it with me over the years, but until now I'd never paid attention long enough to piece it all together. It really was a mystery; the Baums and Yaffes were not big on family history. Both the trauma of the past—the pogroms, the harassment, the fear of the czarist army—and the horror of what might have happened had they not left Russia—virtually the entire Jewish population was murdered by the end of World War II—prevented them from dwelling on it. Like so many other immigrant families, the Yaffes left literally everything they knew behind and forged new lives, new communities, in a new land. Yet making a radical break like this was not easy. One consequence was a virtual erasure of the history they'd left behind.

As a result, very few records of my grandparents' lives made the trip to North America. What my mother did have was a file folder stuffed with poor photocopies and old letters, a random collection of family documents.

Just to give an idea of the kinds of documents you may come across in your family research, I'll list them here. The folder included:

- A photocopy of an undated, unidentified (please don't tell Pat Roberts) photograph of my mother's father, wearing what appears to be either a dentist's smock or an ancient football uniform.
- Two photocopied pages, in Polish translated into English on additional pages, from the *Birth-Book of the Jewish Registration District of Sambor, Galicia* (1902), detailing the date of my maternal grandfather's circumcision as well as the names and addresses of his parents, his grandparents, and the midwife.
- A handwritten (by my mother) family tree going back three generations, including only one surname, no dates, and a list of questions at the bottom (e.g., For some reason I'm thinking I heard that G. G. Baum married his first wife's sister . . . ?).
- A 1920 certificate from a kibbutz in Israel that seemed to relate to my grandfather's membership in a Zionist Pioneer organization.
- A 1929 visa from the government of Palestine stamped "Emergency Certificate—not renewable" allowing my grandfather to travel from Palestine to "Syria, France, Italy, Argentine [sic] and the United States of America."
- My grandparents' 1938 marriage certificate.
- Certificates of citizenship and naturalization for my grandmother and grandfather (1936 and 1941, respectively).

- A 1961 letter written in Hebrew from a relative in Israel I'd never heard of and a 1998 letter from a relative in Ohio I'd never heard of.
- A photocopy of some notes scribbled on a check register by my mother during a phone conversation with her cousin, Nessa Baum—content mostly indecipherable.
- My mother's birth certificate.

And that, friends, was the Baum/Yaffe equivalent of the family Bible. While it may not seem like much information, it's actually more than many Jewish families can claim. The Jewish birth-book, in particular, contained incredible details about not only my grandparents, but also their addresses, employment, and even the names of my great-grandparents, the godfather of the baby, and the midwife.

Some Jewish families lost their genealogical data when they fled Eastern Europe and others simply wanted to forget about the past. "Starting life over was the point," my mother told me. "The idea was to wipe out our history and leave it behind. My family had no interest in remembering or revisiting their past. They were deeply traumatized by that experience—fear kept the history buried; perhaps fear of being deported again." In contrast to the Jacksons, the Yaffes and Baums told no stories about the old days or the old country.

My mom learned not to ask many questions. On the phone one day during one of our casual genealogical conversations, she told me about calling her mother on her wedding day. When she and my father applied for a marriage license in 1969 in Missoula, Montana, she realized she didn't know where her father was born. "I called my mother and she was rendered speechless—terrified." These simple facts—name; date of birth; place of birth—the foundational data of genealogy itself, provoked horror in my grandmother. Questions like these seemed benign but could, in her experience, lead to destruction.

For my Jewish ancestors, family reunions and trips to visit the old country were beyond consideration—they were perverse.

The family of Israeli novelist Amos Oz was also Russian, and were émigrés from Galicia—his father from Odessa, his mother from Rovno—like my grandmother's family. In Oz's family memoir, *A Tale of Love and Darkness,* he describes the feeling these exiles had, looking back at the home they'd left behind. "I have no desire to go back for a visit: what for? . . . To grieve? . . . Not for what once was and is no more, but for what never was . . . Russia doesn't exist anymore. Russia is dead."[1] Everything of value in their lives was in the future, not the past.

Interviewing Dad

In November 2000, just before the presidential election, the radio program *This American Life* broadcast a segment entitled, "Nepotism: A Beginner's Guide." In it, reporter Adam Davidson marvels at the differences between his family and George W. Bush's—differences of class, status, and financial achievement that amaze him, since he and George W. Bush are ninth cousins whose ancestors lived in Plymouth, Massachusetts, in the eighteenth century. "Why did he get the presidential nomination handed to him," Davidson asks, "and I have to borrow money from my girlfriend to pay the rent?"

The genealogist Gary Boyd Roberts explains what happened to their distinct branches of the family tree. Although both Adam Davidson and George W. Bush shared the distinction of having colonial-era American ancestors, that in itself did not guarantee a future of wealth and power for the extended family. Bush's ancestors left Plymouth in the late eighteenth century, branching out to Vermont, Ohio, and, as we know, Texas, and ultimately Washington, D.C. Along the way, the Bushes became a dynasty. Davidson's ancestors, on the other hand, stayed in Massachusetts for the next 250 years, in which time they became, in genealogist Boyd's (joking) terminology, "swamp Yankees."

My husband and I heard the story and we both found it fascinating. "Your dad's side of the family has probably been here for a while," Ben said. "I wonder why they didn't . . ." I knew where he was going with this. Why hadn't they done better? Why had our family gone the swamp Yankee route (so to speak) rather than the presidential one?

I'm aware of the prestige granted to people whose ancestors arrived on the *Mayflower*, but it never occurred to me that there was any real advantage to having immigrated to North America in the seventeenth century. Sure, it's harder to be a recent immigrant; recent immigrants tend to suffer more from bigotry and have a harder time finding their place here. But unless we're talking about the advantages of having had an ancestor, say, buy the first shares of Xerox stock, or claim the deeds to the real estate that eventually became Beverly Hills, what other advantages could there be?[2]

I didn't know much about the Jackson side of my family, but I did know this: they came to the United States before the Baums and Yaffes. How much earlier, I had no idea. I knew my grandpa and grandma Jackson (Jabe and Grace) had moved to Michigan from Alabama in the 1920s or '30s, but how long had they been in Alabama before that? Not a clue.

In learning about my grandparents, e-mail saved the day. My father lives in Montana. He and I don't see each other as much as I'd like, but we do communicate by e-mail several times a week. His are probably the best e-mails I receive, always full of brilliant details, steely opinions, and good humor. Another benefit to interviewing your relatives by e-mail is a purely logistical one: the beauty of cutting and pasting.

In the spirit of jumping straight into the deep end of the gene pool (sorry), I'd plunked down the cash for a genealogical software program, in my case Reunion—the only one designed for Macs. There are a number of these programs available for PCs; the main purpose they all serve is to provide a platform in which to record, save, and display all of one's genealogical research. Along with the Internet, these software programs have revolutionized genealogy, allowing even the most amateur genealogist an elegant way to access one's data.

Whenever my mom or dad wrote me an e-mail containing details about an ancestor, I could simply copy that information directly into my genealogical software program. Good-bye, onerous audiotape transcriptions; hello, keyboard shortcuts.

I got a lot of great details from my dad through these e-mails. He provided details about his childhood and early adulthood; about meeting my mom in college; about how he decided to become a writer. He told me wonderful stories about his father, his mother, and even his uncle, John R. Jackson, who had stayed down south when Jabe and Grace moved north. He told me one tale about his grandfather, Willie Jackson, but the family stories seemed to end there. It seemed he didn't know anything about his great-grandfather or anyone before that.

I think part of the reason my dad knew so little about his southern roots was that Michigan is so far from Alabama. It's 850 miles from Emelle, Alabama, to Detroit, Michigan. That's a good, long way even in 2010; in the 1930s it was even farther. Grace and Jabe occasionally went back home to visit and their oldest children were sometimes sent to Alabama for summer vacations with their grandparents, but by the time they had eight children, none of them were taking any interstate car or train trips. They couldn't afford it. Nor did minivans exist. Managing a family of eight is a feat of economics. My dad, who now hosts his own radio food program, told me that he didn't eat in a proper restaurant until he was fifteen years old—and he paid for it himself with money earned on a paper route.

Hearing my dad talk about growing up in that huge brood, I started to get the feeling that one of the unexpected consequences of having such a large family is isolation. A family of ten becomes a social unit unto itself, a tiny kingdom with Mom and Dad at the top, looming above the crowd as the ultimate providers and arbiters of punishment. The oldest kids take on many of the child-rearing responsibilities, looking after their little brothers and sisters while Mom cooks and Dad works. In the Jackson family, the kids formed two semidistinct groups; an older set, composed of Don (1929), the oldest, and the next two kids: Joanne (1931), and Mary (1932). After them came my dad, Jon (1938), then Nancy (1939), Larry (1940), Jabe Cook Jr. (1942), and Claudia (1945). Don, Joanne, and Mary were so much older than their younger siblings that they were almost a second set—often a primary set—of parents to the youngsters. When I tried to imagine the logistics of transporting all these kids—even, say, six of them—from Michigan to Alabama in the 1940s, I understood how they lost their connection to the South so quickly.

The basic facts were these: Jabe Cook Jackson met and married Grace Obera Goodwin in the 1920s in Alabama. They moved to Detroit, where Jabe found work as a machine repairman in the auto industry, working for Dodge, then Plymouth, then Pontiac. He moonlighted as a baker to make extra money to feed his growing family. Jabe Cook Jackson spent most of his working life in the factory but he did not leave Alabama to escape rural life; he simply needed a job. The life he left behind—subsistence farming in a tiny community isolated from most expressions of modern progress— was, in fact, the one to which he always longed to return.

As my dad told me, Jabe Cook Jackson "cultivated himself as a latter-day patriarch, styling himself on those pastoral Hebrews of yore." It may be most accurate to say that he aspired to the *lifestyle* of a biblical patriarch: agrarian, huge family, long life, personal relationship with God. This explains why he and my grandma Grace retired to Windswept, a romantic name for a funny little code-violating dwelling in Kingsley, about fifteen miles south of the Grand Traverse Bay of Lake Michigan.

At Windswept, Jabe grew vegetables, raised goats, dug a well, planted trees, canned fruit, grew grapes for his homemade wine, and baked his famous coconut cakes a few times a year. I needed to go to Windswept if I wanted to learn more about him, Grandma Grace, and the rest of the Jackson family. Although Jabe and Grace were now dead, my aunt Mary lived there, maintaining both the house and the legacies of her beloved parents. Traveling to Michigan wasn't going to take me back to the beginning of the Jackson history, but because Jabe and Grace were buried there, it was something close to going back to the very end.

The plan was already forming, and thanks to my new friends at BGS, I had a pretty good idea of what it would entail: "not one quote-unquote tourist attraction," for starters. I wasn't going to hit thirteen graveyards; just one, where my grandparents were buried. Everyone else had died somewhere else—probably Alabama. As for the county courthouses, I would try. But I also knew I could get the few vital records pertaining to my grandparents in Michigan online, through the state Web site. I was going to see two dead people and the family they left behind.

3

Interview Your Relatives and Go to Your High School Reunion; or, Rust Never Sleeps

One of the appeals of genealogy is its emphasis on Life's Big Issues. Birth. Death. And time. Time is everything to a genealogist. Time is the medium in which a genealogist's work exists. Time is also the enemy. With every day that passes, another memory fades. With every year, a lost connection. Have you ever seen a box of old letters in an attic or in an antiques store? Time made them mysterious. What used to be a snapshot of someone's uncle Harold is now, after years of forgetfulness and a few moves from state to state, just a sepia-toned portrait of an anonymous man standing in front of an anonymous house. Once upon a time, that photograph was a token of love and remembrance. Now it's just an unidentified relic.

I once heard a truism about buying a house or planting a tree: last year was always the best time to do it. The same goes for interviewing one's aging relatives. Time is the enemy and rust, as Neil Young observed, never sleeps. My conversations with the Boulder Genealogical Society members hammered home the importance of oral history as a keystone for genealogical research, so my path was clear: I needed to interview my relatives and I needed to do it as soon as possible. That's how my three-year-old son and I ended up flying across the country in the midst of one of the worst hurricane seasons on record.

I wasn't flying anywhere near a hurricane, but you know how these things go: flights in the Gulf Coast were canceled and then rerouted northward, so while my son, Jackson, and I avoided Hurricanes Gustav and Ike, we were hit by Hurricane FAA and its hundred-mile-an-hour gate changes and flight cancellations. All we could do was wait.

A good sign

It was a gorgeous day for flight—in Denver. Unfortunately, we left Colorado airspace around 8:35 A.M. and that was the last we saw of blue skies. We arrived for a change of planes in Chicago and the full force of the travel cyclone hit us at full velocity. Jackson and I ran—well, I ran, pushing him in a stroller—from one alphabetically ordered concourse to another. Peripheral rainstorms drifting from the edges of Hurricane Ike were lapping up against Chicago, and every other terminal was out of power due to the weather, leaving long hallways lighted only by flashes of lightning. After half an hour we finally made it to a blessedly bright Concourse G, where we were planning to meet my mom. I finally relaxed. My son, Jackson, was always relaxed.

Fifteen minutes later we found mom, who walked off the Jetway and into a major flashback—almost total recall of her trip through O'Hare Airport thirty-seven years earlier—traveling with eleven-day-old Buzzy (me) en route from Traverse City, Michigan, to Missoula, Montana.

"The airport must have been a lot smaller then," I said.

She shrugged. "It seemed huge."

My mom looked at Jackson and me. That trip through O'Hare in October of 1970 had been a big deal. It wasn't just that she had an eleven-day-old baby, but that she had to make the trip from Michigan to Montana at all. The doctors had told my mother that her baby was due in August. That worked out well, since my dad's first year of graduate school at the University of Montana started around Labor Day. The baby would come in August, then the three of us would drive out to Montana together. That was the plan.

August came and my mom and dad got ready to move. The end of August approached and there was still no baby. My dad waited as long as he could without jeopardizing his teaching fellowship, but eventually he had to go. Advised by her doctor not to fly so "late" in her pregnancy, my mom stayed put in the old farmhouse they rented just outside Traverse City.

The house, which is still standing, looks like the model for an Edward Hopper painting. It's a tall white plain clapboard house with a stingy front porch, sitting on a hill on Solon Road looking over the rolling farmland. No other buildings can be seen, just this towering, severe yet beautiful house. It's a lovely setting, but like a Hopper painting it evokes loneliness, and I imagine my mom was pretty lonely after my dad left her there alone to give birth. It wasn't quite as tragic as it sounds. His brother Jabe and Jabe's wife, Maggie, lived nearby and they watched over my mom and waited with her. The story goes that Jabe drove her around through the rugged country roads in his Volkswagen Beetle, hoping the bumps would induce labor. Like most labor-inducing remedies, this one didn't work.

I was not born in August. I was not born in September. I was born in October. How did the doctor get the due date so wrong? My mother doesn't remember. I suppose he thought the pregnancy was much further along than it actually was. This story came up thirty-four years later when I was pregnant and my mom came out to be with me for the birth. She arrived a few days before the due date, just to be sure, and then we waited. And waited. We waited until Jackson was finally born nearly two weeks past his due date. At the time, it seemed like an unendurable wait, until I was reminded of what my mom went through.

As we sat together at O'Hare, I looked forward to seeing the house on Solon Road again. Now that I was familiar with the intensity of emotion leading up to childbirth, everything from joy to fear to hope to fear and then, more fear (I'm just talking about my own experience here), I considered that house my real birthplace, rather than the hospital at Munson Medical Center where I was actually delivered. I suppose I wanted to claim a more poetic birthplace—but why? The question gets to the heart of how we tell our own origin stories. No detail is accidental. If I claim the Hopper house as my birthplace, I am claiming a romantic beginning for myself. It's a human impulse and one connected to our sense of narrative logic. Just as in a Charles Dickens novel, we like to believe that tiny clues to our destiny reveal themselves from the moment we're born. But in life, just as in *Great Expectations,* they only emerge in retrospect.

My mother, my son, and I waited in O'Hare for eight hours, then finally boarded the plane to Traverse City. Waiting was now officially a key theme for this trip.

Windswept and the house next door

We were fortunate to stay in the house next door to Windswept, where my aunt Mary now lives alone, during our visit. The house next door is owned by Harry and Jeanette Veeder, old friends of my dad's who bought the land on impulse after visiting Windswept with him during college. The story of how the Veeder family came to own a house next door to my grandparents is a good example of the kind of textured detail that disappears from most family histories within a generation. That's because it involves nonfamilial relationships, in this case the most common and valuable of all: friendship. As most of us know from our own experience, friends are often closer to us than family; sometimes they become our family. But genealogy depends on a paper trail and the echo of DNA, neither of which documents friendship.

Professional genealogists know that there is much to be learned about our ancestors by paying attention to the names of their neighbors (typically listed on the lines above and below our kin on the census form as from house to house census takers went, in sequence, we hope). You might find another relative—someone with the same surname—living next door. It's also possible that the people who lived next door were close friends of your family; they may have moved to this new street as a group, possibly from another town or another state. Comparing their records—the birthplaces of both family's children, for example—might provide a clue as to where your family lived before. If nothing else, checking the names of the neighbors might spark your memory, reminding you of stories you heard about old family friends. That's worth something, too.

My mother, my son, and I stayed at the Veeders' house on this visit, but I doubted whether my son would ever return. The Veeders talked of selling the house, and Mary had already put Windswept on the market. This was probably his one and only trip to a place that had once meant so much to his ancestors.

On our first morning in Michigan, we went over to Windswept to see my aunt Mary. Before leaving for the trip, I'd had a series of absurd conversations with her by telephone as I tried to arrange the details of our interview. Each time I'd attempt to schedule a time and day for it, she'd put me off, saying, "Oh, honey, I'll be here. You just get to Michigan and we'll figure it out then." With so many people and places to see, I was worried about having enough time for everything. Mary refused to play along. This was a good lesson about interviews: as much as I wanted to pat myself on the back for getting organized enough to go out and see my relatives, I still couldn't force them to talk to me. I knew Mary would eventually consent to a conversation, but on her terms. I accepted that.

Jabe and Grace Jackson bought the property in Kingsley when they lived in Detroit and for a while there was nothing on it. With eight children, there was no way they could all fit in a tent . . . not a regular tent, anyway. So Jabe bought a circus tent.

The fabled circus tent! I'd heard rumors of this. Shortly before going to Michigan, I talked to my aunt Claudia in Vermont, and it was she who told the story.

"People in Kingsley thought the circus had come to town," my aunt Claudia told me with glee. "We partitioned it inside with canvas panels and it was our first home up there while they built the house. Dad bought old wood to save money," she said, "and he even pounded the nails out to use them in other places. He used a Coke bottle partially filled with water for a level." Mary corroborated the story, which is as close to the hard truth as I was going to get in the *Rashomon*-like retelling of the family history narrated by half a dozen siblings. I felt vindicated. And thrilled by the whimsy of it; it seemed like something out of a John Irving novel. Funny how fiction always creeps back in, isn't it?

Fifty years later, the circus tent is long gone. Windswept is fully equipped with running water and even cable TV, thanks to my aunt Mary. Mary is seventy-seven years old. She is almost totally blind, due to glaucoma. If Mary were a cookie, she'd be a gingersnap: tough but sweet. She lacks self-pity and spends her time productively, refusing to dwell on the negative.

Mary has lived at Windswept since the late 1960s, when she and her daughter Candiss moved there from Detroit after her divorce. She became her parents' caretaker and it is a role she seems happy to have taken on, but I can never help wondering if she didn't sometimes feel . . . cloistered. Burdened. But perhaps that's just me. If you ask Mary, she will tell you that her parents were wonderful and that living with them was a privilege. I wasn't going to challenge her on this, but I did keep it in mind as I interviewed her, knowing it would color her memories. We all do it.

A footpath stretches between the Veeders' house and Mary's, winding through the pines planted by my grandpa Jackson to anchor the sandy soil that gave the house its name. Large sand dunes still rest farther behind the house; my father and his siblings used to play there. I love watching my own son run along this path, unaware of the history all around him.

Mary was warm and friendly and down-to-earth. Jackson was pretty shy with her. She enticed him with a local specialty: cherry-flavored doughnut holes. He liked that, but when she tried to kiss him, he wiggled away. "It's good that you've taught him not to be too friendly with people," she said. "You don't want him overly friendly with strangers." My mom and I laughed, sensing there was a backhanded compliment in there somewhere.

Mary was glad that I was interested in the Jackson family history, but she was worried about giving away too much information . . . about the house, about the family . . . she is protective, even suspicious. As she's aged, she's become aware of the ways in which unscrupulous people target the elderly. She is very careful about giving away information, which is a good thing. I sympathized with her, even as I wanted her to spill all the family beans.

Another lesson I learned that day with Mary is that you can ask your relatives to talk to you, and they might talk, but not necessarily about the things you had in mind. Mary likes to talk about religion—her own faith, and the faith of her parents. I tried to guide her back to family stories and she kept talking and we got somewhere. My philosophy of interviewing is to guide but not insist, because you may miss a wonderful story that they want to share and which you never knew existed.

I did bring my list of questions, of course, as well as a digital voice recorder that I connected to my iPod. Like most people unaccustomed to being recorded (i.e., all of us noncelebrities), she found the device irritating at first. It made her feel self-conscious, and she fussed about whether it was actually working. She soon forgot about it, though, which is the case with most interviewees. The only advice I can offer here is to find the smallest recording device you can; the smaller it is, the sooner they ignore it.

Mary and I talked for about two hours, spread out over two consecutive days. This was as much or more than I'd hoped to get from her, so I was thrilled. Overall, I collected some good stories from Mary as well as some nice old photographs. She wouldn't let me borrow the photos, but she did let me photograph them with my digital camera and they reproduced surprisingly well. Another benefit of this strange photographing-photos technique was that I instantly created digital versions of these old family treasures, and I could add them to my genealogical software program as more data.

Pat Roberts, my BGS guru, had advised me to look for a family Bible. These often contain handwritten family trees in the endpapers and sometimes one can find important family documents tucked inside. When I told Mary that I'd like to see the family Bible, she got very excited. I was sure I'd hit the genealogical jackpot. She brought out her father's Bible to show me. She held it up. I reached for it and she subtly pulled back. I was not to hold the Bible.

"Can I look inside it?" I asked.

"Of course," Mary said. She set it down on a table and began flipping through the pages. "You see, Daddy took lots of notes in his Bible," she said. I did see that. The entire thing was highlighted and annotated in the margins. This was a well-used Bible.

"Is there anything written in the front or back," I asked, "like a family tree?"

"Nope," Mary said, without checking to see. She slammed the book shut. "This is a very precious book," she said, and carefully placed it back in its special spot on the shelf.

And that was that. No Bible scouring for me. Not this time, anyway. I suppose a more cutthroat genealogist would have . . . what?

Snuck back into Aunt Mary's house while she was on her morning walk? Furtively snapped a photo of the Bible's front and back pages while Mary fetched the kettle? I just couldn't do it. A huge part of doing genealogy is about getting to know your family—the living and the dead. My visits with Mary had accomplished that, and if there was more to be discovered in that family Bible, well, it would just have to wait.

Letting go on Jabe Mountain

The next day we headed out to Jabe Mountain. *Jabe Mountain* is the term my cousin Mooner (not her real name; nicknames run in the family. We also have a cousin Flipper) uses for her rural childhood home on the Leelanau Peninsula, now that her father lives there alone.

A commercial-welder-turned-metal-artist whose pieces looked something like a hybrid of Alexander Calder and Ralph Steadman, Jabe was still working a lot, with pieces ranging from the four-foot-tall horned satyr guarding his driveway to the dainty sugar bowl and spoon on his kitchen table, all made of stainless steel. They've only gotten weirder since his big motorcycle accident several years ago, which seemed to bring him into even closer contact with the freakiest reaches of his creativity. He'd recently customized the front license plate of his truck. First he'd replaced it with a handcrafted steel grille that read, simply NO. Later he explained that NO replaced his original plate creation: RECLUSE. He said too many old ladies kept asking him to explain what recluse meant. "With 'No,' no one asks you to explain," he said.

Mooner and I agreed: Jabe is doing well, all things considered.

I attempted to interview Jabe about the family history, but didn't get very far. He was so excited to see all of us that the idea of sitting down with me for an isolated conversation was out of the question. He wanted to play with Jackson and show him all of Mooner and her brother Nick's old toys. Jackson was, of course, totally into this plan. I could feel myself getting stressed out—I'd traveled a thousand miles to interview him, and now he wouldn't sit still?—but then I decided to take a deep breath and go with the flow.

It was a good decision, because as it turned out, while I was upstairs gently and unsuccessfully cajoling Jabe into talking, my mom and Mooner were sitting downstairs at the kitchen table, where they'd taken it upon themselves to interview each other about their Jackson family memories. Those twenty minutes of conversation were filled with more details about my grandparents than I ever would have expected.

Lesson #3: Don't be afraid to let your relatives interview each other.

At the BGS meeting I'd attended just before leaving on the trip, a member advised me to visit the county records offices in Traverse City and Detroit to obtain vital records on myself and death records on my grandparents. It gave me a mild panic attack when I realized what a short time I'd planned for the Traverse City portion of our trip. But I did a little Internet research and discovered that these records were available by mail, once you knew what to ask for. With so little time available in the Traverse City area, I decided to prioritize my meetings with actual living relatives rather than spending the time in government waiting rooms.

I did one other thing before I left: I asked Mary for directions to the cemetery where my grandparents were buried. I hadn't attended either of their funerals and I'd never seen their graves. A friend from the BGS had advised me to ask for specific information about where in the cemetery my ancestors were buried. This was the kind of invaluable advice that probably saved me an hour of walking through the cemetery, and something that would never have occurred to me on my own.

I found them just where Mary indicated. There they were, buried together outside Kingsley, Michigan, just a few miles from Windswept. GOD FEARING COUPLE, the headstone read. As I stood there in the slanting light of autumn, I felt . . . something. I wasn't sad, but I did feel a pang of regret. I wished I'd known them better. I wished I'd gone to their funerals. At least I'd made it here, to their graves. I took a few photographs and then I said good-bye.

With that, we were off, headed south to Detroit: not to see more Jacksons, for the Jacksons had left Detroit long ago. No, we were going to see the Baums, the Kratchmans, and the rest of the relatives on my mom's side of the family. It was time to leave the oceanic vistas of Lake Michigan; the cherry-flavored doughnut holes; Jabe Mountain; and Windswept itself behind. It was Jewish deli time.

Traveling with a celebrity in Detroit

Let's say you meet someone at a party in Los Angeles. You ask where he lives and he responds, "Detroit." Sounds pretty straightforward. But he's probably fudging. He doesn't live in Detroit proper—the 148 square miles of formerly grand, now heavily gutted architecture and boulevards—he lives in Metro Detroit, a six-county aureole of green lawns, sprawling houses, and enigmatic high-tech office parks surrounding what used to be an economic colossus. Like a black hole, Detroit's core has collapsed, and now everything surrounding that economically ravaged interior is pulling in the opposite direction in an attempt to resist a similar fate.

My extended family lives in Metro Detroit, cousins, aunts, and uncles scattered around its rolling hills and broad traffic arteries. We stayed with my mother's cousin Michael and his wife, Bunny, in their beautiful old home. Coming straight from the charming funkiness of Traverse City, it was a shock to walk into this light-filled lakeside house with its Fairfield Porter and Alex Katz paintings and a kitchen straight out of *Architectural Digest*. When I say it was a shock, I mean it was a very, very nice shock, like being gently hit in the face with a goose-down-filled, lavender-scented, eight-hundred-thread-count pillow.

Our priority on this trip was to visit Aunt Selma, Michael's mother and my great-aunt. At ninety-seven, she was our oldest living ancestor and sister to my maternal grandmother, Mary. Selma had a strong narcissistic streak driving her forward in life. I mean that in a good way; her high self-regard was impressive and even charming in a woman over eighty. I have strong memories of visiting her at her gorgeous Birmingham home, a paradigm of midcentury modern architecture and furnishings that would make the set designers of *Mad Men* drool. Her beloved husband, George, died in 1983, and Selma maintained their house as a tribute to all George had provided. When my mom and I visited, Selma would lead us down to the basement, where her vast cedar-lined closet was located, and would gift me with a few choice items, knowing I had an appreciation for vintage clothes.

My mother and I looked forward to these closet tours with a mix of anticipation and dread, but always with humor. For my mom, they were a flashback to her own encounters with Selma as a younger woman. Selma could be a bit of a frenemy when it came to trying on clothes, and by that I mean she was a master of passive-aggressive commentary. "You have a good eye," she'd say as I picked out a bracelet-sleeved patterned silk blouse. "That's original Pucci. But I'm sure it's much too . . . petite for you." My mom would discreetly roll her eyes and urge me to try it on anyway. When it fit, Selma would suddenly remember that the blouse had actually been a little big for her, back in the day. This went on for as long as we were down there, but it didn't bother me. The tsk-tsking was a small thing to endure when I considered her generosity and some part of her truly did want her old clothes to go to someone who cared. I still have them, and I cherish them: handmade party dresses with matching bolero jackets; floor-length velvet evening gowns with rhinestone zipper pulls, and a collection of incredible vintage purses.

My mom and I were pretty sure that Selma's vanity would keep her strong. And, in fact, when we tried to schedule a time to visit her at the senior center where she now lived, she informed us that she had a hair appointment that day and it would be impossible to cancel it. The fact that we'd traveled 1,400 miles to see her on this short trip didn't enter into it. *Beauty is your duty,* I could almost hear her say. In the end, she did manage to postpone her parlor date by a half hour in order to accommodate our visit.

By ninety-seven-year-old standards, Selma was doing incredibly well. She seemed physically strong, independent, her mind sharp. By Selma standards, however, she seemed a little down. Cousin Bunny said that depression is undertreated in the elderly; perhaps we expect the aged to be depressed? It seemed as if it might be true in Selma's case. Still, she was thrilled to meet Jackson, her great-great-nephew, and he was thrilled to accept her never-ending stream of cookies.

I talked to Selma a bit about her childhood. She repeated some of the stories I'd already heard, about how much fun she had on the ship that brought her family to America; about how wonderful her husband had been; about how wonderful her grandchildren were. I couldn't draw her out about anything else, she just wasn't in the mood. I tried to remember the lesson I'd learned on Jabe Mountain: Be flexible. Acknowledge that you can't force your relatives to talk, and then accept it. You can always try again. I told Selma I'd give her a call. She nodded.

A few weeks later I received an e-mail from my second cousin Lou, one of Selma's beloved grandsons. It was a PDF file, a digital version of a personal narrative Selma had dictated to a genealogist a decade earlier. In it was the story of her family's terror in Russia as they waited to emigrate, as well as photographs and documents pertaining to her life and the lives of my grandmother and great-uncle Victor. I'd had no idea the booklet existed. This was a happy, unexpected by-product of making the effort to get to know my family, and wonderful genealogical data.

If you want to know what it's like to travel with a shirtless Brad Pitt, just take a toddler to a senior center. Children are more than popular at old folks' homes: they are celebrities. They leave a wake of goggle-eyed, smiling people in their oblivious wake as the je ne sais quoi of their youth shines forth in every direction. We stopped briefly in the lobby gift shop at Selma's and within thirty seconds one of the residents was offering to buy Jackson a candy bar. Offering him—not asking me. I wasn't the Angelina to his Brad Pitt; I was merely one of their children's six anonymous nannies.

The celebrity madness continued that night when we met the rest of the family at the Stage Deli for dinner. As we walked through the dining room to a booth, older folks leaned out of their chairs trying to catch his eye and make him laugh. My mom recognized it right away: it's what she calls The Dream. My mom spoke about this at my wedding: the realization of the immigrant's hopes for the future embodied in their children. I've never seen the power of youth expressed more vividly than on that day. Each time Jackson's chubby fist lunged for another bite of bagel, the room swooned. The Dream in action: not only was there a future for the Jewish race, but it would continue to produce bagels. Praise G-d.

The next day we flew home. In the swirl of visits, doughnut holes, and bagels, I learned one important lesson: it's not easy to do genealogy while lugging along a three-year-old (even a wonderfully patient and good-natured three-year-old with a very helpful grandmother to help out). There are so many little things that come up—places you want to see; people to talk to; depositories of vital records that suddenly occur to you—and it's difficult to change plans when you're responsible for others with their own agenda, especially if that agenda involves an hour of intense LEGO construction followed by two more of throwing sticks into a stream. It's not really fair to expect a three-year-old to sit through all the interviews, tours, driving, etc., and eventually he will get cranky and whiny, no matter how good-natured he is. Let's face it: it's hard to do anything productive when accompanied by a three-year-old. Genealogy included.

The special space-time continuum of high school reunions

A few weeks after I returned from Michigan, I took a quick weekend trip, sans three-year-old, to Northern California to attend my twentieth high school reunion. Weddings and high school reunions go together: they're events that remind us of the connections we share with others. At a wedding, one looks around at one's new in-laws and thinks: *Okay, all these people with their plastic cups and soggy hors d'oeuvres plates—they are now my family. Somehow we've all been brought together, stuffed mushroom caps and all.*

It really hits home once you have children, because suddenly your own kid is sharing DNA with your mother-in-law. I say this as someone blessed with a wonderful set of in-laws, but it's still a little baffling. It's the most obvious thing in the world, and yet it can really blow your mind: my child has as much of *those* people's genetic material as he does of mine! In my experience, every single aspect of conception, pregnancy, and childbirth is a source of just such obvious yet awesome mysteries.

Here's another awesome mystery: the language of teenagers. On the airport shuttle I—no, the entire shuttle car—was exposed to the insanely raw, vulnerable dumbness of teenagers in love.

Boy: I love the way you sign your name.
Girl: Shut up!
Boy: I'm serious. It's so cool that you only use capital letters.
Girl: Shut up!
Boy: I love you.

I will spare you the rest of this "conversation," though those of us on the airport shuttle are still suffering from post-traumatic stress disorder. Nevertheless, as I made my way toward a reunion with everyone who had known the sixteen-year-old Buzzy, I wondered: Is this what I sounded like in high school? I'm afraid so. I started thinking about my first boyfriend, R. I met him after one of the most significant events in my adolescent life, when, after eight years of wearing dorky glasses, I finally got contact lenses. Within two weeks I'd cut my hair into a stylish (I swear it was, at the time) Princess Diana bi-level, learned to apply mascara, began my freshman year of high school, and snagged a boyfriend. Contact lenses, apparently, will do that.

My conversations and love letters with R were just as inane as the dialogue reported above, though even as I write that I feel obliged to defend my first love. Our fluctuating emotional states may have been hormonally inflated, but it was also my first experience with the transcendence of romantic love—and lust. There is no lust like the lust of a teenage virgin.

Our relationship, if you can call an unending cycle of ecstasy, pain, breakup, and reunion a relationship, accomplished the same thing the shuttle-bus conversation did: it was a form of simultaneous action and rehearsal. The shuttle-bus kids talked for the sake of talking, which is another way of saying they were practicing conversation; in this case, the fine art of bullshit chitchat (bullshitchat?). For our part, R and I were practicing every aspect of the boy-girl relationship, from kissing to fighting to clever note writing. The novelty of love, along with the mind-blowing hormone overdose from which we were both suffering, compelled us to rehearse our parts over and over. And over and over again.

I thought of my mother—with pity for her suffering and gratitude for her patience. It can't be easy to watch your formerly levelheaded fourteen-year-old daughter suddenly devolve into a swooning, mooning gossip machine who's decided to subsist on only three grapes and a Diet Coke for her daily caloric intake. (This is true. It wasn't an anorexia phase or even a conscious desire to be skinny; I simply could not bring myself to eat whilst in the throes of love. This pattern repeated itself in the early infatuation stages of all my later love affairs; I found that, unfortunately, it always wears off.)

All these memories were crowding back into my consciousness as I flew westward over the Rockies and toward California. Our incredibly dedicated senior-class president had exceeded her campaign promise to oversee our future reunions. The fact that this, our twentieth reunion, was the third reunion we'd had (tenth and fifteenth preceded it) was evidence of that. No elected official had ever been so true to her word. The organizational superiority of the class of 1988 began to attract interested members of our proximal classmates from years 1987 and '89. It was, therefore, entirely possible that R, who was two years ahead of me in school (it seemed like a huge deal at the time) could make an appearance. I considered this possibility for ten seconds: not good. Today's experience on the airport shuttle was as close as I need to get to my teenage self. Seeing my classmates, none of whom I ever dated (I seemed to have a thing for the classes of '86 and '87), would be much less fraught.

High school reunions are fun, which is why I keep going. My experience at the ten-year one was positively life affirming. I walked into the banquet room and was confronted by a sight I'd never dared to imagine: X, one of the quietest, nerdiest girls in our class chatting comfortably with Z, a scrumptious stud who probably lost his virginity (happily) at age nine to some high school girl and continued getting effortlessly laid for the rest of his life. Yet there they were, the ugly duckling and Prince Charming, catching up on old times as if they were social equals. Which they now were.

People tell you lots of things when you're in high school: these are the best days of your life (False); and someday all this social warfare will be revealed as the petty bullshit you deep-down know it to be—a statement I'd always wanted to believe and one which, standing there in the foyer of a rented ski lodge, I suddenly knew to be true. That's why I keep coming back. Reunions are the big do-over we always hoped for.

I didn't feel that I had much to do over or live down (maybe that's why I have such a positive attitude toward these things), but that wasn't the case with my friend P, who had finally consented to attend after a mere twenty years of cajoling by yours truly. P had been a quiet but well-liked guy—an athlete and star academic—but in his own mind high school had been just one miserable moment after another and he could barely wait to leave it behind. I'd always felt that a trip back to one of our reunions would finally exorcise those teenage demons—especially because he'd be returning as a handsome, successful grown-up man married to a gorgeous woman. Right? It seemed obvious to me. I guess I'd worn him down enough, and finally something snapped, and here he was—here we were! We took a quick disco nap, slugged a gin and tonic for courage, and off we went.

There is a special quadrant of the time-space continuum reserved for weddings and high school reunions. I don't think Einstein went into detail about it and I can't provide a mathematical equation to explain it, but in layman's terms what happens is this: One enters the wedding/reunion space and suddenly hundreds of recognizable faces, each one sparking a different memory stream, begin to whir through one's consciousness. The nearly mechanical consumption of a sequence of alcoholic beverages serves to speed up this swirling reality, until somehow eight hours have passed by in what seems to be twelve minutes. Now, if one were to be sucked into a black hole, one's entire self would be compressed, flattened, and stretched into a filament so infinitesimally incomprehensible that existence as we know it would be nullified. That's my understanding, anyway. The difference here is that when one enters—and eventually emerges from—a high school reunion, the only organ to suffer such a fate is the liver and possibly the higher-functioning lobes of the brain. That was my experience, at least, and I once again stress that you'll have to ask a physicist if you want a full scientific explanation.

I did survive with a few memories intact. I remember standing at the door of the restaurant, waiting to claim my name tag. I remember ordering a margarita. I remember embracing Mehmet, a Turkish exchange student who'd made the trip back. He'd been my senior-prom date and I'm proud to report that he is now quite possibly the handsomest man on the Anatolian Peninsula.

Most importantly, I remember several of our class's cutest girls walking up to P and exclaiming: "You're hot!" Victory was mine. I replayed the moment in slow-mo over and over again in the days that followed. Needless to say, P had fun, too.

The twentieth reunion went down just like the tenth and fifteenth: hot, boozy, and loud. Former geeks mingled with former studs. Hair was a theme. For some reason, 95 percent of the guys had goatees and receding hairlines. Almost every girl's hair had gotten blonder. Boobs were much in evidence and they were still just as popular as they'd been in high school. Some of the heavier kids were now skinny and vice versa. A few of our teachers showed up, looking exactly the same (this was a little unnerving). We were still a little embarrassed to be seen drinking around them, but our level of inebriation was such that we managed to get over our mortification. Fast. Many photos of adorable children were passed around. Many business cards were exchanged. I was harangued by at least a dozen people about the fact that I had not yet joined Facebook. When I told people I was working on a genealogy project, most of my classmates said something along the lines of: "My mom/aunt/uncle is totally obsessed with that stuff!" If my eighty-five classmates were any indication, Generation X had not yet reached its genealogical maturity. I'd expected that.

We danced sweatily to the tunes of our adolescence. For the class of '88, this meant a lot of New Order, Guns N' Roses, and Prince. I realized that I'd spent my music-geek teenage years convinced that the music I loved (the Smiths, Duran Duran, the English Beat) would not stand the test of time, as the music of an older generation (Led Zeppelin, the Rolling Stones, Carole King) had. I was wrong. For a New Wave music dork like myself, this was a gratifying revelation.

As predicted, many interlopers from other classes showed up at our reunion. I danced for about twenty minutes with a guy who *really* loved AC/DC before it occurred to me that the reason I didn't recognize him was that he was a graduate of the class of 1978. With his shaved head and goatee, he looked just like every other guy I'd graduated with. Rock on. All interlopers were welcomed.

In some weird way, it felt as if all those mindless high school pep rallies had a purpose after all. Every class had chanted its superiority, trying to outshout the others. "We are rad! [It was the eighties, people.] We are great! We're the class of eighty-eight!" Why did we do this? I didn't know at the time and I don't know now. But it turned out that possibly we were better than the classes of '87 and '89, after all, because we were the only ones able to pull off a slammin' reunion every five years. The fact that our former upper and lower classmates were attending was the proof.

Seeing my old classmates was like reuniting with long-lost brothers and sisters. There were only eighty-five kids in my graduating class, so we really were a kind of family. We shared the same teachers at the same schools. We lost the same friends in car accidents over the years. We grew up together in the same small town and we watched that town get bigger and less affordable over time. We watched each other metamorphose from grubby little kids to preening teens to slightly wiser adults. And when we get together every ten years, we are thrilled to remember those former selves.

Looking around at my classmates in various states of embrace and exhaustion, I remembered one of the genealogical factoids I'd picked up recently: if we were able to play out every individual's family tree with enough detail, we'd find that each one of us has approximately four trillion twentieth cousins. These are crazy numbers: not only are they too big to comprehend, they also describe a population greater than the number of people who ever lived on earth (that's math for you). Nevertheless, the lesson I drew from it was the one I kept drawing on this journey: We're all family. Every one of those drunken sots at the reunion was a cousin—literally. During gatherings like weddings and family reunions, we enter a collective subconscious agreement to emphasize and cultivate those subtle relationships, which makes us feel even closer.[1]

The next day I tried to recount the happenings to my mom, who'd suffered through it all the first time with me in high school. She's attended her reunions at Cass Technical High School in Detroit, so she could relate to the strange mixture of delirium and emotion that overtakes these events. "I can't believe it's been twenty years . . ." I said. My mom shrugged. She believed it. At age thirty-eight I was finally starting to understand another important aspect of time: the way it moves faster, the older you get.

So much changes in one's first twenty or thirty years of life. And sometimes, it seems, relatively little changes after that. These new conceptions of time and aging were surely a part of why I'd gotten interested in genealogy in the first place. I was starting to experience the slightly desperate feeling of watching time slip away. I thought of the thousands of images and emotions I'd felt at the reunion the previous night. Very little of it could be captured in a photograph or even by writing about it. Genealogy, I thought, was the attempt to capture as many impossible details as we can. We focus on the big, boring details: birth certificates, marriage licenses, then allow our imaginations to fill in the rest.

The importance of backups: Not just for IT professionals

I came away from the reunion and the trip to Michigan with a new metaphor. Our family and our old friends are like external hard drives: they're independent memory banks reminding us of who we used to be. Sweet, caring, warm little hard drives. As we all know, however, no hard drive is foolproof. We need backups. And the backups exist in the old family Bibles, the stories of our great-aunts, and the moldering archives of millions of county courthouses, church records, and federal assessments around the world. Backing up is a life's work.

Almost exactly a month after we visited her, my great-aunt Selma died.

On a metalevel, I could barely believe it. This is *exactly* what genealogists are always saying will happen: there are so many stories of oral histories recorded just days before the subject dies. It almost seems as if interviews themselves might be some kind of a curse. But they're not. As a genealogist, you just have to be grateful you took the opportunity when it came.

That visit to Detroit turned out to be the only visit my son will ever have with that generation of his ancestors—the generation born in Europe. Shalameth "Selma" Yaffe Kratchman (1911–2008) was the only one left and now they're all gone. I took out one of her beautiful dresses and put it on, remembering her. And, I'll admit: the dress *was* a little tight. That made me laugh. I took a photo of Selma with my son, Jackson, on that day when we visited her in October. It's now part of the cosmic backup. But I should have taken more.

4

CSI: Lido Deck:
The Genealogy Cruise, Part I

I tried to do the right thing, genealogically speaking. I tried to start at the beginning, filling in all the boxes of the pedigree chart (that's the official genealogical name for a family tree) and collecting the relevant documentation—birth certificates, marriage certificates, census forms—as I went. But I was impatient—I wanted more, faster! So I took two slightly rash actions: I sent in for DNA testing kits for myself and my father (to get samples of the male and female chromosomes in my family); and I signed up for a genealogy conference—on a cruise ship. Two words I'd never heard side by side: *genealogy cruise.*

When I told my friends about the DNA tests, they were fascinated, if a little confused. "Does that tell you whether you'll get Alzheimer's?" some asked. (Answer: No, this is a genetic genealogy test, not a medical genetic test.) When I told them about the genealogy cruise, they simply went silent. My genealogist pals at BGS, however, got it right away. "A genealogy cruise—I've always wanted to go on one of those!" they'd exclaim. "You're really throwing yourself into this, aren't you?" another said. It was true. I'd only just started to look into my family history and I was already spending the big bucks on genetic testing and exotic conference going. But if genealogy teaches you one thing, it's that life is short. I wanted to wolf down as much genealogical data as possible. Whether I would be able to digest it was another.

The logic of the genealogy cruise

As I began looking into the culture of genealogists, I found that, in typical American fashion, no marketing opportunity was left untested when it came to harnessing the dollars, if not the sense, of the genealogy community. Where there were genealogists, there were people asking questions. And where people asked questions, there were experts. And all these questioners and experts could, theoretically, be brought together in one place . . . not just in a hotel ballroom for an annual conference, but on a giant ship where they would be bound together by the simple fact that, on a boat surrounded by the Atlantic Ocean, there is nowhere else to go. This is the logic of the genealogy cruise.

I'm making it sound as if these genealogists were forced at gunpoint to attend, but of course they—we—boarded willingly. The marketers, in this case the software company Wholly Genes (maker of the genealogy software the Master Genealogist) brought together a gaggle of the world's greatest professional genealogists and offered access to their wisdom as we sailed from New York City down the east coast of the United States and on through the western Caribbean (St. Kitts, Antigua, St. Thomas, and Puerto Rico). Admit it: it's a lot more inviting than a long weekend at the Indianapolis Sheraton. So I signed up.

I did so just in time. The cruise was almost full by the time I started looking into it, and though I asked around to see if any friends wanted to come along with me, I couldn't find any takers.

The idea of spending a week in a tiny cabin with my toddler son was a nonstarter (not to mention that my mother had convinced me of the probability that he'd fall overboard if we ever left our room). I would be going it alone. Has anyone in world history ever taken a Caribbean cruise alone? I wondered. I thought I remembered a scenario like this on one of *The Love Boat*'s more melancholy episodes. I steeled myself and hoped my cruise director would be as friendly as Julie McCoy (though perhaps a little less cheerful).

In all honesty, I was more than a little bit thrilled by the idea of seven days and nights in my very own room. As the mother of a three-year-old, I'd given up—grudgingly—on the idea of privacy and "alone time" for the past, oh, three years, four months, and twenty-one days. I knew I would miss Jackson. I might even miss him so much it would ruin my trip. But by God I would have my very own room for a week with my very own TV (two, as it turned out), my very own bed, and no one to tell me when to go to bed or, crucially, when to wake up. As far as this aspect of the trip went, I didn't care if we remained docked in Red Hook for the week: privacy would at last be mine.

I spent the week before I left running cruise scenarios in my head instead of sleeping: Who would I meet, what would we talk about, and, above all, what the hell should I pack? Appropriate attire became my number one worry. This was all my mind's way of distracting me from my real fear: to be discovered as a fraud whose genealogical knowledge was so flimsy that I didn't deserve a place on board. The eternal shorts vs. skirts question was so much more concrete—and easier to solve.

The day before the cruise I met with the fabulous Birdie Holsclaw of BGS for a quickie Starbucks date in which we reviewed the topic: With Whom Should I Talk and What Should I Say? (on the cruise, that is). Birdie knew or had at least met all the big genealogy muckety-mucks and they would all be on this trip—Elizabeth Shown Mills, Tony Burroughs, even Megan Smolenyak Smolenyak (yes, her real married name—and hereafter referred to as simply Smolenyak). Birdie gave me lots of good tips.

Birdie is surprising. She's sweet and cute, with dark curly hair and square glasses and a bashful smile. She is so NICE that it's easy to overlook how brilliant she is (because she doesn't shove it down your throat). She drives a Subaru. She knows almost everything there is to know about genealogy, and more than that, she knows a lot about the structure and organization of genealogists in the USA. She's a member of every professional organization. While talking to her I realized how lucky I was to have been embraced by the BGS. Its members are exceptionally talented and so supportive; they were constantly helping me avoid the pitfalls that face every beginner.

Birdie is also crazily tech-savvy, always whipping out her paperback-size netbook or her matchbook-size cell phone to Jott down a memo (it's a transcription service). Perhaps you're familiar with the digital native/digital immigrant theory. This is the idea that people born after, say, 1982 are digital natives—they are folks who use e-mail, iPods, and video-game controllers as if they were extensions of their own bodies. The rest of us pre-1980s babies are, in contrast, digital immigrants. We've learned how to use all this stuff, but we'll always be the older generation from the old country who e-mails in a funny accent. My point is this: I'm pre-1980 and Birdie Holsclaw is even more pre-1980 than I am, but the lady throws down like a digital native.

We all know the old joke about the elderly and their inability to program a VCR (forget about TiVo), but I'm starting to believe that if you want to find an older person who can rock a binary code, try a meeting of genealogists. Birdie explained Delicious.com to me. She explained RSS feeds to me. She receives David Pogue's *New York Times* technology column as an RSS feed. Aside from her family genealogy, Birdie's biggest project is assembling the genealogical records (and an overall history) of the Colorado School for the Deaf. What this entails is doing the basic genealogy for hundreds of past students, and she organizes her massive amounts of research data by creating a separate blog for each person: 153 blogs in all. Yes. Birdie is the author of 153 genealogy blogs, and counting.

Birdie is a digital badass.

Birdie hipped me to the technology and then she gave me a CliffsNotes overview of all the pro genealogists: who was friendly; who was intimidating; who was especially quirky. I'm not naming names, though. With all her knowledge and genealogical experience— Birdie had been doing genealogy for at least two decades and is personally acknowledged in the acknowledgments section of Elizabeth Shown Mills's landmark genealogy reference book, *Evidence Explained: Citing History Sources from Artifacts to Cyberspace*—it seemed absurd that I was going on this cruise and not her. On the other hand, she didn't have as much to learn as I did. That's what I told myself, anyway.

The day arrived. The shorts vs. skirt question was resolved, or so I hoped (skirts won). I flew into New York and stayed with two old friends in Brooklyn, not far from the cruise dock. We spent Sunday morning walking around Park Slope. Somehow even at that moment I knew that good coffee would be something I'd miss once at sea. With this in mind, I waited at Gorilla Coffee for fifteen minutes just to get a cup of the good stuff. Aside from getting some quality time with my friends, it was the single best thing I did in New York; the memory of that dark roast would both torment and soothe me during the next seven days of pale beige—I can't bring myself to call it coffee—hot water.

My friends delivered me, fully caffeinated, to Red Hook, Brooklyn, to meet my ship. I lived in New York City for a couple years in the 1990s and never once imagined the city as a debarkation point for cruise ships. Yet here they were, giant, building-size, Moby-Dick-white ships parked at the edge of Brooklyn. What would Walt Whitman think?

I threaded slowly through the security check-in and was

rewarded with a health advisory—dated that day—warning that the *Caribbean Princess* was vectoring a higher-than-usual rate of Norovirus, symptoms of which are: nausea, vomiting, diarrhea, etc., aka the flu. I wondered if the flu shot I'd gotten the previous week provided any protection against it. Aren't cruise ships known for their mass outbreaks of virus-borne illnesses? Where did the Legionnaires have their ill-fated conference—on a cruise? I looked around and discovered huge vats of Purell stationed nearly everywhere: not a good sign.

I'd only just begun to assimilate the idea of cruise ships in Brooklyn when I arrived at my cabin, looked out the window, and saw, not a half mile across the channel, two of the most important symbols in American genealogy: the Statue of Liberty and Ellis Island. I stood on my two-by-four-foot balcony and beheld the closer icon: Ellis Island, the venerated starting gate for most European immigrants in the USA.

Just beyond Ellis Island loomed the Statue of Liberty, the embodiment of . . . what, exactly? I want to say immigration, but that's not really it—not officially. The French designed her in honor of the centennial of the American Declaration of Independence in 1876. She's linked with immigration because of her proximity to Ellis Island and because Emma Lazarus, the writer whose poem "The New Colossus" is inscribed at the statue's base, referred to her as "Mother of Exiles." I think she's meant to be America's First Impression—the image others see when they come here for the first time. Her full name, after all, is the Statue of Liberty Enlightening the World. It's difficult to imagine such a monument being built today; in fact, the only massive construction project concerning immigration I've heard about is a giant wall along the Arizona border. The "tired . . . poor . . . huddled masses yearning to breathe free" are still drawn to the USA, but now instead of a three-hundred-foot benevolent warrior goddess they will face a twenty-first-century Checkpoint Charlie. Somehow I doubt this wall, if it's ever built, will become tomorrow's symbol of American hope. In the meantime,

Lady Liberty and Ellis Island top the list of American genealogical symbols, with Plymouth Rock pulling up a distant third.

Americans in general may love these symbols but it turns out that genealogists have a troubled relationship with Ellis Island. Back when genealogy was just a quaint hobby and not the obsessive, data-crunching pastime it's lately become, folks would show up on Ellis Island in a relatively passive mode. They were happy to pop on a pair of headphones and let the sonorous voice of Tom Brokaw guide them through the museum. All of which proves that with the passage of time and the voice of a trusted celebrity, even the groaning wheels of bureaucracy—Ellis Island was nothing more than a processing center, after all—can become tourist attractions.

Like most symbols, Ellis Island does not in itself accurately represent a complete story of the issue in question. In the case of American immigration, Ellis Island served as key processing point for only thirty-two years, between 1892 and 1924 (after 1924 the only persons processed there were war refugees and those with special problems with their paperwork). These, of course, were a busy thirty-two years: approximately 12 million immigrants passed through Ellis Island during that time, most from Russia, Italy, and the Austro-Hungarian empire. The big waves of Germans, Scandinavians, English, and Irish crashed onto American shores earlier in the nineteenth century, when immigration issues were handled by individual states.

Perhaps you've wondered why there were no similar waves of Asians, Latin Americans, or Africans during this period? That's explained by the anti-immigration furor that arose in the late nineteenth century and came to a head in the 1920s, resulting in laws such as the 1882 Chinese Exclusion Act, which did just what it said: excluded the Chinese. This is in contrast to 1907's "Gentleman's Agreement" between the governments of the United States and Japan, which sounded, well, gentlemanly on the surface but in reality was just another form of racial and national profiling, barring Japanese laborers from entering the United States. More race-based immigration legislation followed, with a flurry of quota bills passed in the 1920s, the quotas themselves based on the existing American ethnic makeup as represented by the 1890 and 1910 U.S. Censuses. Immigrants from other countries were finally allowed through the "golden gate" (as Emma Lazarus's poem puts it) in significant numbers only in the 1960s and '70s. Clearly there exists a whole epic of immigration that has nothing to do with Ellis Island. Still. Lots of people came through the place: Bela Lugosi, Isaac Asimov, Albert Einstein, and Irving Berlin among them.

If you're having trouble finding your ancestor on the Ellis Island rolls (data now free and searchable online thanks to the Statue of Liberty–Ellis Island Foundation) don't jump to the conclusion that a frustrated clerk changed Skorczewski to Smith. Genealogists and historians who have researched this say that not a single incidence of "Americanization" of names has ever been proved.[1] Although many foreign surnames were changed over time, this usually happened after immigration processing, encouraged either by fellow immigrants or sometimes by teachers in the public schools. Blame them.

If you still can't find that forefather, perhaps it's because he traveled first or second class. These well-rested passengers not only avoided the unpleasantness of steerage class, they also escaped the tedium of mandatory literacy tests, mental health inspections, and stinky waiting rooms, simply by paying more for their fare. American authorities assumed that those who could afford more expensive tickets were unlikely to become problematic citizens. I believe this is where we find the origin of the phrase "membership has its privileges."

Ellis Island stands in for all the thousands of other points of entry, official and un-, that exist wherever the United States bumps up against non-American land or sea. Its name is now a catchphrase for an idea about this country that most Americans like to celebrate: the up-from-nothing story of a newcomer who takes a risk, makes a move, and strikes it big. For a few immigrants, this is a recognizable story. For most, it was a dream.

On the second day of the genealogy cruise, Megan Smolenyak gave a talk about her experience tracking down the "real" Annie Moore, the very first immigrant to pass through Ellis Island. For decades, the story of Annie Moore was the tale of a young Irish woman who walked off the ship on January 1, 1892, at age fifteen and went on to move to Texas. Her descendants there know the story well, as do millions of visitors to Ellis Island who read the tribute to her that resides there under a statue in her likeness.

"It was the wrong Annie," Smolenyak explained. Smolenyak first got involved in the story when, in the course of researching a documentary on immigration, she found that Annie Moore's vital records showed her born in Illinois, to a family of Moores who had lived in the United States since at least the 1880s. When she got serious about solving the mystery, Smolenyak—like Birdie, a self-described "techie" who very much believes in the power of new gadgets and media to revolutionize genealogy—simply posted a $1,000 reward on her blog, asking for help in tracking down the "real" Annie Moore.

"With the power of the Internet and a handful of history geeks we cracked this baby in six weeks," she said. "We had the smoking gun."[2] This is the world of genealogy, remember, a realm in which smoking guns usually appear a little less, well, shiny and dangerous than those in a film noir. In *The Case of the Real Annie Moore,* the smoking gun was in fact the naturalization certificate belonging to Annie's brother, Phillip. Through this one document (supplied by the New York City commissioner of records Brian G. Andersson), Smolenyak tracked down Annie's great-nephew and then the rest of her extended family of descendants, many of whom now have names reflecting the ethnic diversity of their American-made marriages, from Scandinavian to Jewish, Hispanic to Italian.

The real Annie Moore never moved to Texas; in fact, said Smolenyak, "she never got further west than Broadway."[3] Annie Moore was the first immigrant to pass through Ellis Island and, fittingly, the story of her life was typical of most immigrants of her era. She married young and had perhaps eleven children, five of whom died before the age of three. The common thread in their deaths, according to Smolenyak, was "poverty." She never left the Lower East Side of Manhattan and died there of heart failure at the age of fifty. As sad as her life may have been, Smolenyak believes it was also a success story, for Moore "sacrificed herself for the good of her descendants," and those descendants are alive and well all over America today. Another example of The Dream, my mother might say.

In 2008, Smolenyak joined Moore's family at Calvary Cemetery in Queens, New York, to dedicate a new headstone for her formerly unmarked grave. She is buried there with six of her own children along with the child of a friend—not an uncommon practice among those who could not afford to buy individual grave sites. The event drew a crowd of over a hundred, with the consul general of Ireland in attendance as well as the Irish tenor Ronan Tynan, who sang the song "Isle of Hope, Isle of Tears" written in Moore's honor. Another notable Irish-American offered a tribute to Moore: then–presidential candidate Barack Obama sent a letter read by Smolenyak in which he honored Moore's sacrifices on behalf of her family.

Most in the large crowd at the cemetery were not relatives of Moore; they were simply people touched by her story and wishing to honor her life. They were the same kinds of people who do genealogy—people interested in the past and eager to somehow get closer to it. Smolenyak believes this impulse, combined with the accessibility of documents made possible by computer technology, is contributing to the biggest trend in genealogy today: the democratization of history. As more people discover history's inaccuracies and unearth formerly missing documents, history will be rewritten—just as it was in the case of Annie Moore.

The powers that be at Ellis Island were convinced. They changed the plaque at the base of the existing Annie Moore statue there to reflect the real story, though the statue itself appears to be modeled on a photograph of the mistaken Annie Moore. As no photograph of the real Annie Moore is known to exist, what more can be done? Like Ellis Island itself, the real Annie Moore is a symbol. She represents not only the challenges of life as an immigrant, but also the speed with which the details of a life can disappear. In less than a hundred years, the story of Ellis Island's first immigrant had vanished—until genealogists dug in.

To me, *The Case of Annie Moore* represented something else, too: the power of new technology. "I thank my lucky stars that I was here for the Internet," Smolenyak told me on the cruise. "And computers, too." I assumed all contemporary genealogists felt this way, but apparently not—not at first, anyway.

"I went to my first professional genealogical seminar in 1991," Smolenyak said. "Everyone rattled off the tools and techniques they were using. I was the first kid on the block to have a scanner, and I got crucified. They accused me of cheating, of not taking it seriously because I used, say, a fax machine. And then the same thing happened with genetic genealogy."

Smolenyak is the author of the widely consulted book *Trace Your Roots with DNA: Using Genetic Tests to Explore Your Family Tree.* "I took bullets for that book," she said. "For the first two years after it was published, no one would publish anything I wrote on DNA. I think they thought I was saying, 'Hey, you don't have to do that futzy old boring research anymore.' They didn't realize I was saying, 'No, it can help solve other mysteries. It can tell you to look here— and don't waste your time over there.'" Smolenyak is the perfect ambassador for twenty-first-century genealogy, not only because she's smart and has the energy and enthusiasm of a fourth grader hopped up on Halloween candy, but because she is so eager to embrace the fruits of technology offered to today's genealogists.

I, of course, began my research in the midst of this tech revolution, and for that I can only say, "Thank the Lord." I spent hundreds of hours in the carrels and stacks of libraries as a graduate student. But I'm not one of those who would wish the experience on the students who follow me. I've met quite a few older genealogists, though, who scoff at the Web, even though they know they're missing out. Some merely shrug their shoulders—they're okay with the fact that they'll never send an e-mail. Others are bitter. These are the folks who turned on Smolenyak when she started using a personal fax machine. They look back on the years spent trolling stuffy library basements for the least terrible microfilm machine, and they think: *If I had to suffer, so should everyone else.* I suppose those riding in horse-drawn carriages in the 1900s had a hard time enjoying being left in the dust by the newfangled automobiles driving by, too. Missing out on a mind-blowingly amazing new invention sucks. But it doesn't mean you shouldn't try it.

The very first thing many people do when using the Internet for genealogical research is to enter their surname and see what pops up. If you try this with a common name such as Jackson, you'll find many, many mentions of people named Jackson (most of them Michael) and no clues as to whether any of them are related to you. If, however, you search for the terms *Jackson genealogy,* you will be on your way to real research.

A surname search such as this one directs you to sites that are actually useful. They may be personal family surname sites, built by genealogists for the purposes of organizing family reunions, or they may be message board sites such as those on RootsWeb.com containing thousands of queries about Jacksons all over the world. Eventually, most of these searches lead you to one genealogical giant: Ancestry.com.

Ancestry is the big dog in the field, a subscription Web site offering four billion searchable records and serving nearly a million paying members. They have staffed offices on five continents, busily digitizing genealogical information on a global scale. According to one report, Ancestry employs over a thousand people in West Africa alone—searching, scanning, translating, and digitizing data from all over the continent. That's a pretty serious commitment to global data.

It is possible to research your family history without subscribing to Ancestry (subscriptions cost upward of $100 per year) through sites such as the LDS Church's FamilySearch, for example, but if you can possibly afford it, why wouldn't you? So much is there, waiting to be found, downloaded, and added to your family tree. Visiting Ancestry for the first time—or anytime, for that matter—can be dangerous, because it's so easy to fall down the genealogical rabbit hole. *I'll just do one search,* I thought that first time, typing in my great-grandfather's name, date of death, and last known residence. An hour and a half later I was on my twelfth census record, far from Great-Grandpa Willie and now lost in the data pertaining to a distant Aunt Rebecca.

This is where genealogical addiction enters. One genealogist I encountered confessed, "Once you start you can't stop! [It's] really bad when I start doing some research at night, I don't get to bed until the wee hours of the morning." Another dedicated "genie" concurred: "I work two full-time jobs and am allowed to be on the computer; so I can put in fourteen hours just doing genealogy!" (Names have been withheld to protect the employed.) The relocation of research from distant archives to desktop computers has allowed already obsessed genies to follow their passion into dangerous territory, sacrificing sleep, personal relationships, and apparently billable hours to the seemingly infinite records to be found online.

I wasn't addicted to genealogy—not yet, anyway—but I was fascinated by those who were. I'd spent seven years in graduate school listening to my colleagues complain about their never-ending research and now I was confronted with a group of people who coveted any spare moment into which they could squeeze three surname searches on the Library of Congress Web site. They were like grad students gone rogue. And the sophistication of their research skills often put doctoral candidates to shame. I certainly felt humbled in their presence.

Ellis Island will always be hallowed ground for American genealogists, but in terms of its significance for actual genealogical research, it's long out-of-date. When it comes to the bottom line: names, dates, documents, Ancestry.com is an equally sacred (Web) site. I'd joined Ancestry before taking the cruise, and I'd spent hours there amassing information on the birth, death, and marriage dates of various relatives. I hadn't exactly hit the dreaded brick wall in my research, but I hadn't exploded any family mysteries, either. I'd discovered that not only was I cursed with a common surname but my paternal ancestors were keen on repeating common Christian names as well, leaving their descendants to work out who was who among the three Johns and two Williams in five short generations. Awash in Willies and Johnnys, I tried to remember that I was just a beginner. I might not have much to contribute to the discussions on a genealogy cruise, but I had a lot to learn.

I stood on my tiny balcony and focused on the view. It was stirring to see Ellis Island, the Statue of Liberty, and Manhattan from the deck of a huge ship, just as my maternal ancestors might have— though I'm pretty sure none of them were treated to the smooth sounds of the "Jamaican Me Crazy Sailaway Party" on the Fiesta Deck as they sailed by.

Nor were they surrounded by the cast of *The Sopranos*, as I seemed to be. I don't know who I expected my shipmates to be. Few of my friends had ever been on a cruise. Most of my expectations were shaped by two towering landmarks of American popular culture:

1. *The Love Boat:* the aforementioned ABC television show (1977– 1986), which was not only the first hour-long series to feature a laugh track (a dubious achievement) but also represented the acknowledged apotheosis of the "all-star cast anthology format" along with its sister show in ABC's Saturday night "one-two punch": *Fantasy Island* (1978–1984). *The Love Boat* was actually based on the memoirs of a real cruise director and the cruise line featured in the show was indeed the very same Princess line on

which I was traveling. I wasn't quite expecting to order drinks from Isaac, the chatty bartender, or—God help me—fend off the lecherous advances of "Doc," the ship's chief medical officer but then again maybe I was.

2. The legendary essay "A Supposedly Fun Thing I'll Never Do Again" (1996) by David Foster Wallace, in which the irreplaceable DFW describes, in nail-curling detail, his experience aboard a Celebrity Cruise through the Caribbean. I was intimidated by the idea of writing in the shadow of this essay until I read Chuck Klosterman's essay "That '70s Cruise" (2005), in which he describes the surrealism of a classic-rock theme cruise and in doing so acknowledges the burden all writers on cruise ships face with respect to DFW. At first I thought: *Super, now I have to slither out from under two big cruise-ship-writing shadows.* Then I thought: *The fact that cruise travel still exists even in the post-DFW world means that more needs to be said about cruises, even if it will never again be said as brilliantly as DFW.*

As a matter of fact, the passengers described by DFW were not much different from my shipmates. He boarded his cruise in Fort Lauderdale, Florida, and the locals there were formerly locals of the Northeast, where I was now awaiting departure. Northeasterners are used to dealing with the urban annoyances common to life abutting Interstate 95: traffic, noise, long lines, chaos. They are yelling to each other down the hallways and across the exterior balconies of the *Caribbean Princess* because yelling is what they do. I already felt far from home, though the ship was still tied to the dock.

Sunday evening

I did not attend the Jamaican Me Crazy Sailaway Party, despite the temptation of free rum punch. I didn't realize this would be the last free alcohol of the cruise. Instead I unpacked and got acquainted with my stateroom: three hundred square feet containing one queen bed, one couch, one balcony, and two televisions. God Bless America.

It was time for the Wholly Genes sign-in at Club Fusion (Promenade Deck 7, Aft). Based on the decor, I got the impression that Club Fusion would be the karaoke HQ for the *Caribbean Princess*. Would I, in fact, be performing karaoke at some point in the next week? Anything seemed possible. I grabbed a schedule and a name badge and was invited to sit down with two women perusing their swag. Their names were Millie and Patsy and they'd left their antigenealogy husbands behind. I liked them at once: two well-dressed, no-nonsense New Englanders who embodied what I imagined to be the typical New England Historical Genealogy Society membership. Smart, educated, and a little edgy. Millie and Patsy were old friends from college who had lost touch with each other until running into each other at a New England Historical Genealogical Society (NEHGS or, as its fans call it, "HistGen") lecture in Boston a decade ago.

They both seemed skeptical of the whole cruising thing. "Have you ever been on a cruise before?" I asked. "Oh, no," they both said quickly, as if wishing to set the record straight. They were not, as it were, traditional cruisers. "We thought the speakers would be interesting," Patsy told me. Millie nodded. They raised a collective eyebrow as they looked around the room with its disco ball, tightly packed cocktail tables, and casino-style patterned carpet as if to say, *We're not interested in any of . . . this*. They were interested, however, in the very first genealogy event of the cruise, a lecture that very night by David Lambert of HistGen. "David is wonderful," they assured me. I planned on it.

The most important war in American history

I found my way to Café Caribe (Lido Deck 15, Aft) and settled in for the first lecture of the cruise. We were sailing somewhere off the coast of Maryland by now. David Lambert was younger than I expected, in his thirties or so, I'd guess. He spoke quickly, with a Boston accent, and instantly reminded me of some of my husband's high school friends from Brookline, just beyond the Boston limits but within range of the T. These are guys who not only remember every published professional sports statistic, but also the winning times for the fifty- and hundred-yard dash as ran by their peers in eighth grade. It's a *Rain Man*–esque facility for data crunching, and Lambert had it, too, although in his case he applied it to military records going back four hundred years. I was intimidated, but my shipmates were clearly energized.

To get us all in the mood, Lambert started with a test, asking people to raise hands if they had a military veteran ancestor and he begins naming wars: from Iraq I and II all the way back to the Pequot and King Philip's war. I hadn't thought about the Pequot War (1636–1637; Massachusetts Bay Colonists + Narragansett + Mohegan vs. the Pequot) since graduate school. It appeared that others didn't have this problem, judging by the nodding and note taking and hand raising going on around me.

Lambert then asserted that King Philip's War (1675–1676; New England Colonists vs. King Philip [aka, Metacom, grand sachem of the Wampanoag] and his Wampanoag Confederacy) was the most important war on this continent because the destruction wrought by the Native Americans was so intense that it provoked the colonists to require that every able-bodied male own a flintlock rifle and know how to use it. By the time of the Revolutionary War, every family had at least one of these rifles and the British were surprised by the Americans' shooting skills and the quality of their weapons. "They were also surprised," Lambert said, "by the fact that Americans shot officers"—that is, they did not follow the typical rules of engagement. We all followed along, wondering why history wasn't this interesting or violent when we learned it in high school.

Lambert was still looking for veteran ancestors and asking for hands in the air. This was the first time I witnessed the game of genealogical one-upsmanship: How far back do *you* know your genealogy? Most of us stopped raising our hands around the Civil War, but some of our grinning companions were still grabbing air, waiting for the Revolutionary War veterans to be called. This was very HistGen, and clearly many of those sitting here in Café Caribe tonight were already well acquainted with our host.

Lambert is the official online genealogist at NEHGS and the author of many genealogical books and articles. According to the HistGen Web site, he is also "the tribal genealogist for the Massachuset-Punkapoag Indians of Massachusetts [and] serves on the Board of Directors for the Stoughton Historical Society, of which he has been a member since the age of 10." Later in the cruise Lambert would admit to me that his genealogy obsession flowered at age seven, when he began saving money to order vital records by mail. That, friends, is how you become the Encyclopedia Brown of genealogy. And his fans here clearly loved him for it.

Lambert acknowledged the attrition rate among the hand-raisers and offered this nugget of genealogical counterintuition. "I'm seeing fewer hands go up as we get further back," he says, "but remember: we actually have more ancestors the further back we go . . . so keep looking." He's right, of course. The spreading branches of our family trees get broader as we travel back in time, so it is quite likely that many of us have colonial ancestors—we just haven't tracked them down yet.

From this point on, the talk gets technical, down to the real nuts and bolts of how to track these missing veterans. Another professional genealogist, the venerable Craig Roberts Scott, chimed in. Scott's many genealogical credentials as a researcher, author, and teacher are too long to list here, but he is notably the president and CEO of Heritage Books, a genealogical book publisher and an expert on the records held by the National Archives as well as on military history. Scott represents the hard-core genealogist fringe, and I'm not saying that just because he sports a beard known to the tonsorial cognoscenti as the "chin curtain" (picture C. Everett Koop/Abraham Lincoln/an Amish farmer).

Scott began by pooh-poohing our frustrations with colonial record keeping. "If genealogy were easy," he said, "it wouldn't be as much fun." Everyone laughed at this except me.

He dove back in. "Subscription services," he says, meaning Web sites like Ancestry.com and Footnote.com—the engines of online genealogy, "are cheating." Now it was nervous laughter. Could Scott be one of the digital naysayers? Hard to believe, considering his line of work. Yet whether or not anyone agreed with his skepticism, Scott had just given voice to everyone's private neurosis, the possibility that we might be doing *bad genealogy*.

What is bad genealogy? As I would learn many times over on this cruise, bad genealogy is the kind of family-tree keeping that everyone used to do and many still practice. It's the making of pedigrees without substantiating Grandpa's stories. It's accepting that what is written in the family Bible is The Truth. It's genealogy without footnotes. And, as the Queen of Footnotes herself, Elizabeth Shown Mills, would soon tell us: even the most detailed footnotes are worthless if they cite bad sources. As the author of the Birdie-acknowledged *Evidence Explained: Citing History Sources from Artifacts to Cyberspace,* she ought to know. But I'm getting ahead of myself.

Craig Scott was just getting started. He moved on to maligning our research, in a friendly way. It is not enough, for example, to check the muster rolls of the Revolutionary War for information on our ancestors. "Shame on you for not checking the neighbors of the relative on your muster roll!" he admonished us. The neighbors? Yes.

So, herewith:

Genealogy Cruise Tip #1 (and it's a comment I'll hear again and again this week): Look at the people around your ancestor when you're reading his/her name in the census record/muster roll/city directory. I'd heard this, but Scott reinforced it.

Why should you care about the person who answered the

questions in the house next door to your great-great-grandma on the day in 1830 when the U.S. Census taker knocked on the door? Well, knowing the names of neighbors, friends, and relatives of your ancestors can provide clues about ethnicity, income brackets, and more.

A few months postcruise this tip resurfaced when Mona, a friend from BGS, told me about the research she'd been doing on "Rocky Mountain Joe" Sturtevant (1851–1910), a colorful character in the mold of Buffalo Bill whose autobiography was equally creative. Mona had noted the names of Joe Sturtevant's neighbors in the 1900 Colorado Census, one of whom was Jemima S. Peck. When she dug further back into Joe's past, she discovered an old advertisement from Wisconsin listing Jemima Sturtevant Peck as a milliner for hire: this, Mona realized, was Joe's mother. A quick check of earlier censuses in that state showed that her name changed between censuses: she'd remarried, and by 1900 was living next door to her son, Joe. This discovery opened up a new batch of names for Mona to track down— many of the folks in Jemima's house were probably related to Joe, too.

Now, there's shame, and there's shame. I knew Craig Scott was joking (sort of) when he wagged his finger at this audience of eager beavers. But seriously: if you've traced your ancestry back to the Pequot War, there's no shame in your game. That's what I wanted to say to my shipmates, but as I looked around at their faces, one thing became brutally obvious: these folks were here to play ball. Professional ball. I, on the other hand, signed up for Fantasy Baseball Camp, only to arrive at Red Sox Spring Training. Perhaps I could serve as ball boy . . . for the ball boy.

Dave Lambert and Craig Scott gauged the determination level of this crowd long before I did and they now launched into phase two of their lecture, which I hereby dub "Clues for the Hard Core." They include the following nuggets of delightfully arcane information:

1. If you're looking for an ancestor who served in the Civil War army, try the records of the Civil War *navy*. Because they may

have signed up for the army but were then detailed to the navy—apparently this happened a lot.

2. A good source for military records is state adjutant offices. Finally, a way to combo-pack your errands when you're making your weekly trip to the state adjutant's office.

3. In 1963, Confederate widows (that is, women who were once married to veterans of the Confederate army) were granted pensions by the U.S. federal government. Before then, Confederate widows were reliant upon the pensions (if any) offered by their respective states. The last living Confederate widow, Maudie Hawkins (1914–2008), married an eighty-six-year-old Confederate veteran in 1933, when she was nineteen. When she died, that was the end of the U.S. Federal Government Confederate Widows Pension Fund.

4. If you're trying to track down your veteran ancestor's DD214 (Defense Department Form 214) form (a history of military service handed to a soldier/sailor/marine detailing his or her military service), try that ancestor's local county courthouse, because they were deposited in county courthouses after each war from World War I on. And yes, Lambert and Scott rattle off Defense Department forms and National Archive record numbers as if everyone knew these details. Don't they? I don't.

Now, if you're looking for military records, these tips might help. If not . . . Lambert and Scott offered some more general genealogical suggestions that I found toothsome. Here come Genealogy Cruise Tips #2 and #3:

Genealogy Cruise Tip #2, courtesy of Craig Scott: Remember the Archives Rule of Three: if the first archival employee can't find what I want, I ask two others. (Although maybe not on the same day or in front of each other, he cautions.) Don't take no for an answer.

Genealogy Cruise Tip #3, courtesy of Dave Lambert: Always consider the next generation of genealogists. If you have a box of family documents and you don't think anyone in your family is interested in them, give it to a local historical society or genealogical society . . . or give it to NEHGS, a place Lambert describes as "everyone's attic . . . because we're interested in everyone."

And with that bit of advice, I took leave of my fellow genies and of the Café Caribe, which was, of course, still serving food at this late hour; in fact, it served food twenty-four hours a day. Just before the military records talk, I had dinner alone at the buffet. I had the misfortune to stand in line behind a gentleman (sure, let's call him that) who, when asked by the lovely Bulgarian buffet attendant whether he would like more crab legs, replied, "What do you think I came on this thing for? Yeah, I want more crab legs!" then rolled his eyes and shrugged, looking at me as if we were in this together, we high-rolling, cruise-loving, crab-leg-scarfing Americans. I avoided his gaze, pretending to search for more hand sanitizer (the stuff was indeed everywhere on this germy ship). The Bulgarian attendant ignored him, politely, but I did hear her sigh.

It wasn't just the hand sanitizer that was everywhere; so were the ship employees who were working double duty while this Norovirus cloud hovered over us. Part of the Code Red policy requires that ship guests not handle the food-serving implements. This means employees had to stand around the buffets ladling salad dressing and scooping pats of butter in addition to their normal jobs. The exhaustion was evident in their faces, and this was only the first night of the cruise. I asked a Polish employee in the gift shop about it (every employee wears a name tag identifying her name and home country), and she said, "Yes, it's tiring working sixteen-hour days. But it's a lot better now than it was on the last cruise. Everyone was, uh . . ." She searched for the word, then mimed the action of something spewing from one's mouth.

"Throwing up?" I suggested. "Yes," she said, then she delicately pointed to her backsides: "and from here." Better never looked so good.

Monday, 9:20 A.M. Stateroom 301, Dolphin Deck

Good morning, shoppers.

I was greeted by Freddie, "Your Port and Shopping Guide," on the TV. I couldn't read her name tag through the screen but based on her appearance and accent, I'm guessing she hailed from the Netherlands or maybe South Africa. She's the blond, blue-eyed face of Princess's QVC culture, and the Princess Shopping Channel is the first thing that appears each time the TV is turned on. I was not expecting this, but I'm not surprised, either. If people come on these cruises for crab legs, they probably come on the cruises to buy diamond tennis bracelets, too.

Freddie was urging us all to buy lots of jewelry. Her goal is to "make you happy and put smiles on everyone's face." And to make us buy stuff. She wanted us all to meet her at the Princess Theater this morning at ten A.M. for the Princess Port and Shopping Show. There, she would explain where to go, what to buy, and . . . what else? Oh, free gifts. I've already been offered the chance to win a "crystal ship" each time I made a purchase at one of the ship's boutiques. Q: Am I the only passenger whose primary reference for the term *crystal ship* is the song about heroin by the Doors? A: Apparently, yes.

Here on board the *Caribbean Princess* there is a store that sells glass figurines. Let me emphasize: this store sells *only* glass figurines. Okay, *crystal* figurines (Freddie corrected me). Clearly, I'm not someone who digs glass (crystal, whatever) figurines. But even for those who do, how many do they need? I know it's a dumb question. And yet . . . bafflements like this are the kind of thing that really do make me feel apart from the rest of my shipmates—not the genies, per se, but the other 2,700 folks on board. They covet glass (crystal) figurines: I am perplexed by them.

Freddie was still yammering on. At the end of the cruise, she promised, each one of us will come find her somewhere on board and say, "Freddie, I did it all, I saw it all, and I bought it all." So far, I was only succeeding at complaining about it all. But I vowed to try to improve my attitude. I felt this could be achieved even without the purchase of a glass (crystal) figurine. It was worth a shot.

And here's a happy thought: room service on the *Caribbean Princess* was free! I ordered two cups of coffee, which were terrible, and read a few pages of *Roots*. I finally drew back the curtains and discovered the only thing on this cruise so far that had fulfilled ALL my expectations: the ocean. It may have been making me slightly ill, but it was awesome, beautiful. And it was vast. No land in sight.

I alternated between watching the amazing ocean from my balcony and, yes, watching one of my two TVs. But, incredibly, the ocean lost, because—I am not making this up—*The Love Boat* arrived. I had a Baudrillard moment, trying to fathom the simulacrum here. You could look it up, but basically the issue is one of hyper-reality. For years I grew up watching *The Love Boat* every Saturday night, a representation of life on a cruise ship based on a book written by a former cruise director. The exterior shots showed one of the Princess Cruise Line's ships—a boat that looks more or less exactly like the one I'm on right now. That's right, I was now on the "real" Love Boat. I thought I'd been prepared for this moment by the stream of sarcastic quips dispensed by friends before I set out to sea: "Tell Gopher I said hi," and "You can always drown your sorrows with Isaac on the Lido Deck." Ha. I was now snuggled up in my Dolphin Deck stateroom staring at . . . what—the fake Love Boat?—on-screen.

How could it be fake when it starred Jaclyn Smith, Sherman Hemsley (the eponymous Mr. Jefferson of the TV show), and holy-mother-of-sitcoms John Ritter? I knew it would be a classic episode when I saw that not only was John Ritter going to spend the cruise in drag, but pervy "Doc" would battle Captain Stubing for Ritter's affection. Jaclyn Smith would fall in love with the private detective (played by Dennis Cole, an actor who was in almost every TV show of the 1980s and whom I never saw again. He looks like a grown-up

Ricky Schroeder. I later learned he was Jaclyn Smith's husband) hired by her neglectful husband to spy on her.

No, this Love Boat—the one on-screen—was clearly the *real* Love Boat. Not only that, this was the very episode in which a female passenger (Jaclyn Smith) went on her cruise . . . alone! I was definitely on a *version* of the Love Boat. What I was on could in fact more accurately be called the Lunch Boat. Because somewhere on this ship food was being ladled out, that much I knew. I did notice, however, that the aesthetics of the shipboard experience appeared to be identical—from the wildly patterned textiles of the carpets and drapes to the leaping porpoise ice sculptures—on-screen and off.

I eventually managed to extract myself from the postmodern tractor beam of my television (I think its magnetic power intensified in such a small space) and ventured out to partake in some genealogical offerings. I snagged a seat in the Princess Theater for the day's first lecture, "Beyond Y-DNA: Your Genetic Genealogy Options," by Megan Smolenyak Smolenyak, of course.

Goddesses of genealogy

Mere moments after Smolenyak began her presentation, I realized that she was right: most of the people in this floating theater—and maybe the world beyond it, too—were suspicious of DNA testing. I could tell, because as charming and nonpatronizing as Smolenyak was, she was nevertheless treading lightly. She was gently advising us as to what DNA can and can't do.

Personally, when I heard about genetic genealogy (the use of DNA testing to assist in genealogical research), I was thrilled. I'll admit it: I believe in Better Living Through Chemistry and pretty much any other branch of modern science or Western medicine. When I was pregnant, I signed up for every test available. I figure if generations of medical students ruined their eyesight and social lives to improve health outcomes for their fellow Homo sapiens, who was I to turn my back on their efforts? I embrace the successes of Western medicine, from ibuprofen to albuterol. Given my self-identification as a cheerleader for the Enlightenment, I naturally took a shine to DNA testing. Thanks, Science! Looking around the banked seating here, however, I could see that my fellow genealogists were much, much more skeptical than I.

Perhaps DNA is tainted by its association with crime and infidelity. Just a few years ago, the only people who got DNA tests were suspected felons and serial adulterers. Not anymore. A proliferation of DNA-testing businesses has now emerged, and you can use DNA testing for various purposes, from forecasting the future of your health to peering backward into history to find your genetic ancestors. This is where Smolenyak comes in. She was tired of the prevailing opinion of geneticists that genealogists "don't understand" DNA. She not only understood it; she wrote the book on it.[4]

Smolenyak explained the difference between Y-DNA and mtDNA and HVRs and CRS and haplotypes and a bunch of other genetic acronyms that I will introduce you to later, Dear Reader. She disabused us of the fantasy that a DNA test could magically reveal a long list of actual names of actual people to whom we are related. No. That is to say, DNA may be able to tell you that you are related to Genghis Khan, or to one of the so-called Seven Daughters of Eve. But that doesn't really tell you . . . much. Sure, it's cosmically awesome to get scientific proof of your relation to some long-dead conqueror, but the fact that you're here, alive in the twenty-first century, already tells you you're from a long line of somebodies, doesn't it?

Judging by the crowd response, I think she may have convinced some of her audience that it's worth a few hundred bucks to do a test. I'd done one and so far I'd discovered that my paternal (Y-DNA) haplogroup is I1a, a marker associated with northwest Europe. My maternal (mtDNA) haplogroup is K, associated with Western Europe and is particularly prevalent among Ashkenazi

Jews. The bottom line: no surprises. I was a little disappointed that the results didn't turn up anything truly unexpected, but also comforted by the fact that the results seemed logical. I knew there was more to be done with my DNA results, but I'd have to do more traditional genealogical research—hitting the archives—to figure out what else they might mean.

At the moment, however, I had little time to ponder genetic mysteries. I felt a sizzle of energy pass through the room as the next speaker approached the lectern. It was her: Elizabeth Shown Mills herself, in the flesh. The genius had landed. Somewhere inside, I could picture Birdie Holsclaw, back in Boulder, her face aglow with admiration for this genealogical goddess.

I thought I'd spied Mills the previous night skulking around the fringes of the military records lecture but now I saw I was wrong. That attractive blond lady standing by the door in the Café Caribe was not half as glamorous as the woman at the lectern today. Mills could pass for Dolly Parton's younger, more normal-looking sister, with a similarly charming southern accent—and I say this as a fan of Ms. Parton's intelligence, wit, and beauty. She has that polished prettiness you see in women from the American South or in Los Angeles, just north of Beverly Boulevard. The hair: done. The nails: done. The smile: perfect. The demeanor: poised, confident, and a little bit feisty.

She'd drawn a big crowd. Bob Velke, our conference director and host, did something I'd never seen before: after describing Mills as "a woman who needs no introduction unless you just landed on this planet in a spaceship," he actually proceeded *not* to introduce her. Instead, he encouraged the curious among us to read her bio in the back of the conference handout. And she began.

In the world of genealogy there are stars, and then there are figures like Elizabeth Shown Mills, who constitutes her own galaxy. She earned this status not merely by demonstrating her prowess as a genealogical researcher—as a teacher, lecturer, and as the former editor of the *National Genealogical Society Quarterly* for fifteen-plus years,

87

she's proven that many times over—but by writing a series of books that revolutionized the field: *Evidence! Citation & Analysis for the Family Historian* (1997) and its mammoth, comprehensive successor, *Evidence Explained* (2007).

These guides to the citation and analysis of historical records are breathtaking in their ambition and achievement. Imagine for a moment that instead of the fourteen-member advisory board (plus, undoubtedly, hundreds of unnamed staff researchers and writers) credited with the creation of *The Chicago Manual of Style,* that august reference book had been written by one single author. Try to conceive of the mental fortitude, the attention to detail, and the incredible filing system that must exist in the world of Elizabeth Shown Mills, and you will stand back in awe with the rest of us as we shake our heads and mutter sotto voce about all the ways in which we are going to get organized this year . . . for sure.

ESM wrote the genealogical version of *The Chicago Manual of Style* by herself (she had some help from far-flung consultants, including a little from Birdie Holsclaw). In doing so, she raised the bar for family history research. By providing clear methods for citing even the most arcane records (Aunt Millie's Bible; a few sheets of loose-leaf paper containing the deathbed scribbling of a nearly-forgotten ancestor), she denied lazy researchers the comfortable refuge of ignorance, e.g., "I would write all the boring citation information down but I just don't know how to credit this source." Now you do. You can either thank her or curse her; some genealogists do both.

"Research is not a matter of looking up the answer," Mills said from the stage. "Research is tracking down the answer." She followed this with a quote from Lee Fleming, chief archivist of the Cherokee Nation: "Undocumented genealogy is garbage genealogy." Sighs emanated from the seats around me: were we all garbage genealogists in Mills's eyes? Perhaps.

She surged on, a one-woman crusade against sloppy scholarship. I started to wish I'd heard this lecture on my first day of graduate school because it would have clarified my methods and goals. This lecture was really a *lecture*—she practically hectored her audience on the importance of footnoting. Why was there no class on this in grad school? At Berkeley, much of what was expected of us was implied. It was our job as students to pick up the clues as to which historians were doing it right and which were doing it wrong. None of our professors ever came out and said, "So-and-so is an embarrassment," but it became obvious after a while. Straightforward lessons on how to avoid becoming an embarrassment were unforthcoming. If you have to ask, you'll never know: the pet phrase of the privileged classes.

As I listened to Mills I felt a wistful pang about what might have been. "When people tell you 'they've looked at everything . . .'" she said, cocking her head like a puppy, "well, there's looking and there's *looking*." She was talking about researching land deeds, and she insisted that we look at the actual deed in question—not just the deed index (which usually includes all the relevant information. Usually). As far as I can tell, this is the definition of integrity: if you're going to do something—even if it's tiresome and unpleasant—why not do it well?

The rest of her lecture drew on family history case studies. Instead of using real names, she substituted "Pernilia Pickleheimer," and when she discussed the case of "Pernilia Pickleheimer's poppa," it sounded cute in her juicy southern accent. Here, drawn from the files of Pernilia Pickleheimer, are some of

Elizabeth Shown Mills's Best Tips

- No man is an island—you will hit a brick wall unless you study your more distant ancestors—and their neighbors, co-workers, etc. (And in case you were wondering: no, there is no end to this list.)
- Many babies were named after the midwife who assisted the birth—not after a blood relation.
- Records do not exist in a vacuum—when you're copying a

page from the archive, copy a few pages before and after because you might find info about neighbors, and all those other Important People.

- All records naming individuals are genealogical records, whether they're birth certificates or land deeds.
- Don't trust your relatives' stories—dis/prove them.
- Don't explore without a map—and by this, she means an actual map. Genealogists must begin with geographical charts and maps in order to understand county lines, geographical features, and the like.

By this point, forty-five minutes into her lecture, we were all overwhelmed and fearful of the tasks before us. Mills was still, as ever, smiling.

Niall of the Nine Hostages

It was cocktail hour now, and I'd already learned more about genealogy in the past twenty-four hours than I'd ever dreamed existed. But there was one last lecture that caught my interest: John Grenham's "The Naming of the Green: Irish Surnames and Place-Names."

My own two-minute analysis of my paternal DNA test had suggested to me (maybe?) that I might be a descendant of Niall of the Nine Hostages, an early Irish "king" (aka, leader of a clan or tribe) who died around 450 A.D. and was the father of the Ui Neill (later "O'Neill") dynasty. If true, this would link us to approximately three million others with a similar DNA signature, mostly centered in northwest Ireland, Scotland, and the east coast of the United States, where so many Irish immigrated.

The case of Niall of the Nine Hostages is one example of a new trend in genetic genealogy: celebrity ancestors writ large. Or maybe that should be writ long, because geneticists are now able to link people living today all the way back to our prehistoric ancestors. One of the first cases of this occurred in the 1990s, when Brian Sykes, a genetic scientist at Oxford University, analyzed the DNA of Otzi the Iceman, a five-thousand-year-old man who was found in a melting glacier in the Italian Alps. As someone who'd spent his career identifying DNA markers, he immediately recognized Otzi's haplotype as one he'd seen before: it was the same as that of Syke's lab colleague, Marie Mosely. She was happy to claim Otzi as a long-lost uncle, and thus a new genealogical pursuit was born: the search for prehistoric patriarchs and matriarchs.

The next big discovery along these lines was the identification of what became known as the Genghis Khan gene. The rosy-cheeked American geneticist and anthropologist Spencer Wells and his team of fellow scientists identified a genetic marker common to about 8 percent of men living in a remote part of Asia ruled by Genghis Kahn in the thirteenth century. That fact alone would not be enough to link these men to Khan, but they combined this information with genetic analysis performed on the DNA of a tribe in Pakistan called the Hazaras—a relatively isolated group with an oral tradition identifying Genghis Khan as its patriarch. The markers matched, and so did the time frame: Well's team estimated that the genetic marker probably originated with a great-grandfather of Genghis Khan. But there was more than molecular biology at work in the perpetuation of the marker; human culture played a large role, too, for the Mongolian warrior's practice of mass slaughter of the vanquished populations (thus extinguishing the unique genetic heritage of the conquered), mass rape, and the cultivation of huge harems (both of which allowed Khan and his male relatives to pass on their genetic signatures on a mass scale) provided uniquely ideal conditions for the propagation of a single genotype. The only absolute test of this theory, of course, would be to dig up the corpse of Genghis Khan himself (or his father or brothers) and test that DNA. But the tomb of Genghis Khan has never been found. Nevertheless, Wells's theory of the Khan haplotype is widely accepted by the scientific community. The latest calculations estimate that approximately 16 million men, or 0.5 percent of the global male population, now carry the so-called Genghis Khan gene.[5]

You don't have to know anything about Niall of the Nine Hostages to have an interest in Irish genealogy. Between the middle and end of the nineteenth century, Ireland lost almost four million people to migration, and most of them came to the United States. This room was packed with genealogists looking for clues to their Irish heritage.

John Grenham is a one-man Irish genealogy industry. He is the author of the book *Tracing Your Irish Ancestors* as well as many other works on Irish family history. He runs a genealogy service through the *Irish Times* newspaper's Web site, using software he wrote himself. Bottom line: John Grenham *is* Irish genealogy.

Today's lecture focused on Irish surnames. Grenham began with some fun facts about surnames. As it happens, surnames have only been used in Europe for approximately one thousand years. Compare that with China, where they've been around for five thousand years. They've been around so long that the Chinese used them up, apparently: in Shanghai today there are 11 million people and only twenty-two surnames. Is that really enough? Grenham thought so. Ireland has about six million people and over 26,000 surnames. "Why do the Irish need so many surnames for so few people?" Grenham asked the audience. We didn't have a good answer.

European surnames fall into categories. Some are based on occupations, such as cook, smith, and baker. Some are locational, such as da Vinci (one who is from the town of Vinci). Some are descriptive: Longfellow evoked a tall man. And some are patronymic, honoring a patriarchal line. Patronymic names include: Jones (son of John), O'Brian (grandson of Brian), and, of course, Jackson (son of Jack or son of Jacob or even son of James). Most Irish surnames are patronymic: *O'* means "grandson of," *Mac/Mc* means "son of." And although I always thought Macs were from Scotland and Mcs from Ireland, apparently that's not true: the names are found in both countries.

This brings up the old problem of defining Irishness. According to Grenham, "Irish" does not connote a single race, ethnicity, or (obviously) religion. Ireland was invaded and settled by so many different groups from 8000 B.C.E. on that such distinctions don't mean much. Before the tenth century B.C.E., Irish society was tribal, described in terms of ancestry. And that's where surnames—and Niall of the Nine Hostages—come in. The Ui Neill tribe consisted of people who claimed descent from Niall of the Nine Hostages—grandsons of Niall. But according to Grenham, these are tribal names, not true surnames. A cursory exploration of the surname O'Neill will reveal the various and extravagant claims made on behalf of it. According to many researchers, the O'Neill name is not even Irish, but originates in Egypt. Well, who did you think they named the Nile River after? Don't go down this road, I urge you.[6]

The first person to grant what we now recognize as a surname in Ireland was Tigherneach Ua Cleirigh (that surname is now often pronounced O'Cleary; I'm not even going to try the first name), lord of Aidhne in County Galway in the year 916. After this point the Irish acquired surnames gradually over the next few centuries, as did the rest of Europe. In the seventeenth and eighteenth centuries, Irish culture—a mix of Norman and Gaelic traditions and languages—collapsed, and English took over as the language of choice for record keeping. All those Irish surnames were transcribed and translated into English, and guess what? We have another case of the Damn Clerks, because all continuity with the medieval Irish surname tradition was lost, thanks to those English-speaking desk jockeys. According to Grenham, the spelling of surnames in Ireland was "completely fluid" up to 1900. This meant not only the various spellings of O'Brian/O'Brien/O'Bryan ad infinitum, but also an ongoing problem of dropping and adopting prefixes such as *O'* and *Mac/Mc,* depending on the whim of any given ancestor.

"Irish genealogy is easy," Grenham reassured us "given the fact that so much of it was blown up."

He's referring to the destruction of nearly a thousand years of public records in Ireland, which were incinerated in the Battle of Dublin in 1922 during the Irish Civil War. Irish Republican forces opposed the signing of the Anglo-Irish Treaty (which would establish Northern Ireland as part of the United Kingdom) and barricaded themselves inside the Four Courts, a complex of buildings comprising the country's highest courts of law. According to some, the Republicans booby-trapped the public records building, setting bombs timed to explode after their surrender. Some Republican defenders deny this, saying that incoming shells from the Irish army detonated the Republicans' ammunition stores. In any case, virtually every scrap of information in the Irish public records building burned. The only exceptions were those documents that had been recently requested in the reading room.

As Grenham explained, "most of the census data between 1821 [the first Irish Census] and 1920, Anglican Church records before 1870, wills going back to the fifteenth century . . . it was all gone." As a matter of fact, the census records for 1861, 1871, 1881, and 1891 had been destroyed even earlier, by order of the government when a cabal of—you guessed it—Damn Clerks in the central Irish government decided to destroy the census data in order to preserve the privacy of respondents who had been asked to name their religious affiliation. We'd reached the heavy-sigh segment of Grenham's lecture, in which every few minutes he simply stopped, shook his head, and silently lamented the impenetrable nature of Irish bureaucracy.

Grenham eventually gained the emotional strength to move into a new topic, that of the townland, the smallest officially defined geographical unit of land in Ireland, defined by social and economic issues rather than plain geography. Townlands are the basis for land records, census returns, baptismal records, marriage licenses, and the like. Here's his point: if you want to know where in Ireland your ancestor came from, you need to know the townland he came from. But understanding townlands is incredibly difficult. There can be many repeated townland names within one county alone. More sighing—this time from the audience.

Grenham had a classic Irish sense of humor: dry, self-deprecating. He felt our pain; it was his own. It can't be easy being the foremost Irish genealogist. "And the future of townlands?" he asks. "There is a place on one of Jupiter's moons, Europa: an ice field named Conamara Chaos." That seemed to sum up Irish genealogy right there. Chaos.

Questions?

There was one conference attendee who loved to ask crazily specific questions in group discussions; she'd done it at the Lambert talk the night before. I suspected she wanted to demonstrate how far back she'd gotten in her family history, since Grenham had already made clear he'd answer personal questions at any point on the cruise. He tolerated her question, then addressed the rest of the crowd, which remained silent.

"If you don't want to admit your Irish heritage," he joked, "I understand. Just come talk to me after the speech."

I did. Grenham was politely unimpressed by my self-identification as a relation of Niall of the Nine Hostages. "DNA is better at telling you whom you're descended from than whom you're related to," he told me. (Is this a zen koan? I wondered.) "Of course, the two are connected," he allowed. "But maybe thirty percent of Ireland is descended from Niall. Does that tell you who your cousins are?" I began to see his point.

I offered to buy him a beer that evening in exchange for his insight into the Niall business, and he accepted. It was a date.

5

Beaches and *Burke's Peerage;* or, the Genealogy Cruise, Part II

No, it wasn't that kind of date.

It was Formal Night. The Princess Cruise Line was not kidding about it, either. I'd read about Formal Night in the Princess brochure as well as in the horrified prose of David Foster Wallace, but it was still a mind-blower.

It seems unfair or at least too obvious to say that Formal Night feels contrived, because all events requiring formal attire are by nature contrived. I enjoy dressing up as much as the next gal. Yet something about doing it on a cruise ship just seemed silly. It would make more sense to ask passengers to dress up in period costumes from the *Titanic* era if we were going to go to the trouble at all. The first-class guests on the *Titanic* and other ocean liners of that era got dressed up for dinner on board because they got dressed up for dinner when they were on land. Here on the *Caribbean Princess,* passengers were getting dressed up for dinner because . . . why? I suppose we all desire a few more formal events in our day-to-day lives, and cruises recognized a need. People were having fun doing it, so who was I to complain? Clearly, I belonged in steerage with Leonardo DiCaprio.

I found Crooners Bar on the Promenade level and there was John Grenham about to take his seat. Another man sat with him: same age, short salt-and-pepper hair, his features all angles, as opposed to Grenham's softer, kinder features. The man was reading *Lolita*.

It had not occurred to me that John Grenham might be gay.

"I brought a friend along, I hope that's okay," Grenham said. "Of course," I responded. I was thrilled to meet a gay couple here—finally. The unexpected sight of Nabokov's masterpiece, one of my favorite books, I took as an auspicious sign.

"This is Paul," John said, "a drinking buddy from Dublin." *Drinking buddy?* I thought. Maybe this was a euphemism that hadn't made it across the Atlantic yet.

"Hello," said Paul, smiling and shaking my hand. I liked him immediately. "Just so you know," Paul said, still grasping my hand, "I don't give a fuck about genealogy."

We all laughed. I instantly fell in love with my two new Irish friends in the way that only a lonely person can. Up until this point I hadn't realized how isolated I'd felt—a novice genealogist among experts, a skeptical cruiser among the tuxedoed keepers of the faith. We ordered a round of beer and started talking.

It seemed like the right time to introduce them to a neologism coined by David Foster Wallace himself: *bovoscopophobia,* the fear of being mistaken for a cow. DFW invented it while watching his fellow cruisers march off the ship and plod along the dock toward their tropical island destination. The Irishmen loved *bovoscopophobia*. We all related to it, watching our fellow passengers stroll by in their finery, oblivious as livestock drawn to the abattoir. Then we looked at ourselves and laughed: we may not have dressed in formal wear, but we sure as hell were on this boat, drinking and eating and escaping reality. And yes, we were having fun on this cruise ship, just like the rest of them. In the words of the immortal Pogo: "We have met the enemy, and it is us." We toasted to *bovoscopophobia,* this time implicating ourselves.

At some point a creeping realization began to invade my

consciousness: John and Paul were not gay. They were, in fact, actual drinking buddies—old friends from high school who met regularly at the pub back home. Paul was a professional photographer who worked on film sets and did commercial work. Also, they were both married. To women. Why did I think they were gay? *Lolita.* It's not a gay book; in fact, it's the opposite, but somehow the combination of Paul's close-cropped haircut + his erudite choice in reading material + his unexplained appearance for cocktails led me down the wrong path.

I confessed my misunderstanding.

They laughed. In fact, they had each brought a copy of *Lolita* on board because they were reading it in their book group at home. "It's a bit weird, though, two grown men reading *Lolita* side by side on the sundeck," John admitted. They agreed that only one of them would read it in public at any time. We made a toast to Vladimir Nabokov and bought another round. It was now almost eleven o'clock and a windy night but sometime that day we had slipped into the Gulf Stream and the wind now felt warm and supple. Suddenly it felt like a vacation.

Strangely, we seemed to be the only guests enjoying the alfresco drinking experience, and the outdoor bars began to close on the early side for lack of customers.

"What the hell?" asked Paul. "Aren't people supposed to be drinking all night on these barges? Where is everyone? What happened to the conga line?" The bartenders just shrugged and smiled, no doubt exhausted from their heightened state of vigilance in the face of the Norovirus situation. Personally, I clung to a belief that the consumption of alcohol would act as a disinfecting agent on behalf of my immune system, so I lobbied for one last drink, a move supported implicitly by my Irish brothers.

I hung on the edge of the bar—the rough weather was causing my unsteady footing, I was sure—and started chatting with the only other customer, a blond-haired, blue-eyed, Jean-Claude Van

Damme look-alike with a strong Eastern European accent who was speaking Russian with one of the bartenders. Van Damme told me he was from the Ukraine but now lived in Queens, where he ran some kind of import/export business. I told him I myself had ancestors from the Ukraine area—Galicia, to be specific. He was thrilled to hear it.

"Is beautiful, Galicia!" he exclaimed, waiting for me to concur.

"I've never actually been there," I admitted.

"Oh, is beautiful. I take my children there. Mountains! You have never seen such mountains! Rivers! Trees!"

I nodded and smiled. I grew up on the shores of Lake Tahoe and in western Montana. I now lived in the foothills of the Rocky Mountains with fourteen-thousand-foot peaks visible from my driveway. I'd seen mountains and rivers and, yes, trees. What really stumped me, though, was the fact that I'd never heard a single good thing about Galicia before this. My grandparents didn't just leave Galicia; they fled under pressure of conscription and death. Fairly or not, I associated Galicia with one thing: anti-Semitism.

Van Damme smiled. He didn't know any of this. He was a little bit drunk and happy to meet someone who shared his roots. He seemed like a nice guy. "You must visit Galicia!" he said.

In fact, my mom had considered it. But a few minutes of Googling convinced her that Rovno, her mother's hometown, was now known primarily for its dangerous proximity to the Chernobyl nuclear facility and for its heavy concentration of neo-Nazi groups. Thus ended her investigation into a journey to the old country, however ill-informed. I liked Van Damme and I wanted to feel connected to him, but I couldn't see how explaining the Galician history of my Jewish ancestors would bring us closer, at least not in this vodka-soaked moment at the bar. It seemed that Van Damme and I were not from the same Galicia. This is one of the paradoxes of genealogical research: sometimes what you find connects you to people, but other times it pulls you apart.

One of my family's closest friends is a man named Tom, whose ancestry is pure White Russian czarist loyalist. "My family oppressed your family," Tom says, and we all laugh. His family was finally forced out of Russia during the Bolshevik Revolution. After spending much of his childhood in a Japanese POW camp, he and his mother and sister arrived on the west coast of the United States right around the same time my mother's parents gained citizenship in Detroit. Decades later Tom and his wife, Joanne, met my parents when they were all in graduate school in Iowa. It's those thirty-five years of friendship between our families that has brought us together—not our "shared" Russian past.

Van Damme and I had a few things in common: same blond hair, same blue eyes and a shared historical point of origin, but it wasn't enough, somehow. At least not in my current state of mind. Although I'd only begun to investigate my maternal Jewish heritage, the few facts I'd learned had made this history much more personal. It wasn't Van Damme's fault. Blame genealogy.

I returned to the table. I started to explain my encounter to the lads but was interrupted by a glare from Paul. "Oh, right," I apologized. "You don't give a fuck about genealogy." He smiled. He didn't want to hear my family story. We made plans to explore the islands together once we got past the high seas. Apparently, that's where we were. Four drinks later, all I was sure of was that my stateroom was a long way away.

After spending the evening with a self-proclaimed genealogical skeptic (Paul eventually explained his position, saying that in his opinion, the pursuit of genealogy was simply a waste of time), it was refreshing to return to the enthusiasm of the Wholly Genes gang for the next day's round of lectures. I was reminded of high school: Paul was the cynical tough kid smoking a cigarette behind the school and the genealogists were the student-council kids, all eager and full of team spirit. I thought back to the reunion a month earlier and realized I'd always gotten along well with both.

Old Iron Butt

Elizabeth Shown Mills returned, this time with a new topic: "Identity Crisis: Right Name, Wrong Man? Wrong Name, Right Man?" Here she was again, so polished, so completely together. Together, Mills and Smolenyak defined competence.

Mills began by listing all the reasons why the ancestors you're searching for may have gone by a different name. Listening to these lectures, I was once again struck by the key to genealogy: stick-to-itiveness. Yes, it takes creative thinking and knowledge of available resources, etc., but basically it takes a willingness to just keep at it and never give up. Being an optimistic idiot helps. That's really what it comes down to—an unflagging desire to solve the puzzle. It's the same quality that earned Richard Nixon—though he was never mistaken for an optimistic idiot—the nickname "Iron Butt" in college: the ability to sit in the library and keep studying. Great genealogists have Iron Butts. It's what distinguishes them from the other members of their family who claim to be interested in the family history yet never get around to going through the scrapbooks.

I've exhibited an Iron Butt from time to time; a lust for undiscovered archives is part of what drove me to genealogy. I remember the first time I entered UC Berkeley's hallowed Bancroft Library, home of precious documents from the Egyptian Tebtunis Papyri ca. 300 B.C. to the works of Galileo, Mark Twain, and Langston Hughes. Not being a religious person, I can only imagine that the feeling I had upon walking into the Bancroft Reading Room was similar to what others might feel as they first enter the sanctuary of Lourdes: profound respect, curiosity, and gratitude.

At the Bancroft and at many other archives—the National Archives, for example—once you figure out what item you want to request, a librarian delivers it to your reading table. Once delivered, it's up to you to do something useful with it. This is where an Iron Butt comes in handy, because this type of research is all about you, the papers, and time. Unless photocopying or photographs are allowed (only sometimes, depending on the material), it's your task to analyze what's in front of you and transcribe it as quickly and legibly as possible. I talked to Megan Smolenyak Smolenyak about this experience and she concurred: "I'm one of those who thinks bathroom breaks are for wimps when you're trying to snag all you can in a short amount of time." That's Iron Butt talk, right there. No bathroom breaks, no snacks, no daydreaming. Just reading, transcribing, and trying to stay organized.

Among all the professional genealogists I met on the cruise, Smolenyak and the Irish genealogist John Grenham seemed best adapted to maintaining their senses of humor about the whole endeavor.

Grenham, in particular, always displayed a strong sense of the absurd as it related to genealogy. He gave a second lecture on Irish records and began it by saying, "Irish research is not complicated, in the way that finding a needle in a haystack is not complicated." This time the bombing of the Irish national archives was not the problem.

"The first item on the agenda of any Irish organization," Grenham said, "is, 'how are we going to split up?' It's a bit of a stereotype, but it's true." Irish bureaucracy is apparently its own special flavor of aggravation. There are few public-access indexes to Irish genealogical records and no plans by the Irish government or anyone else to offer it. "If you know the minister of health in Ireland," Grenham said, ". . . or you know her cousin, please talk to her."

Months later, when I spoke with the chief genealogical officer of the LDS Church in Salt Lake City, David Rencher, he pounced on the topic. Of all the records the Mormons have not yet collected, Rencher would most like to get his hands on church records in Ireland. None are available in the United States. "As a culture, the Irish don't really do genealogy—they live genealogy," he said. "They're very family-oriented, very social, and most people know their family stories going back generations. But Ireland's had such a big diaspora over the centuries, and it's those people who do genealogy. The diaspora does genealogy and so many of their people just cannot get to the church records they need."

"Why not?" I asked. "Well, you can get them," Rencher said, "but they're all in Ireland. And just recently they gave a copy to the British Library. So now there are two places you can see those records." Rencher shook his head sorrowfully: Irish/Anglo genealogy is his area of specialization.

"The Irish authorities don't understand how many of their people want this information," he said. "Every Irish-American I talk to wants to go to Ireland, but first they need to know where in Ireland their family is from so they can plan their trip around it. The Irish model is: we want you to come to Ireland and *then* discover where your people are from. That may take months or years! You can't plan my trip around that model. If they'd just open up their records, their tourism would explode exponentially." This was precisely John Grenham's point, too. But no one in a position of archival authority appeared to agree.

After his second lecture, I approached the stage to speak to Grenham and somehow ended up winning a raffle prize: a pen in the shape of a femur inscribed with the phrase "I collect dead relatives." I was thrilled: perhaps this was how my shipmates felt about their glass (ahem, crystal) figurines.

That evening we finally came in sight of land: tomorrow we would dock at St. Kitt's.

The best reason for beer

Long before the cruise left Brooklyn, I'd made a few reservations for onshore activities, usually bus rides to the beach (lunch not included). In the meantime I'd become pals with the Irishmen, who had the brilliant idea of specifically avoiding all cruise-based activities and instead planned to find less touristy beaches on their own. I was all in.

I hurried over to the excursions desk first thing in the morning to try to cancel my beach reservations. What do you know? Those reservations must be canceled weeks in advance. I was out at least seventy-five dollars with not a single piña colada or a bouncy bus ride to show for it. It's those little, trifling expenses that drive cruise goers crazy: the not-free soda, the overpriced Bacardi, the four-dollar M&M's. It's always the "package" in the package vacation that gets you.

But we were at a Caribbean island, after all: how annoyed could I be? John, Paul, and I met on the dock and began the first true test of *bovoscopophobia* as we trudged alongside our humongous white cruise ship toward the small town of Basseterre.

Thus began what would become our daily ritual upon arriving at each island: find a cab, request passage to a remote beach, then swim and drink beer. This was the only aspect of the cruise that I'd been able to imagine before debarkation, and thanks to the fun-loving influence of John and Paul it met all my expectations. The three of us emerged from our land-bound sabbatical waterlogged, happy, and tanned. Well, the Irishmen were pink. "That's what the Irish do in places like this," John said, gesturing to the beach and the palm trees. "We get pink."

After two days away from genealogy (I refrained from seeking special tips from John while he was off duty), it was time for the last official genealogical lecture of the trip, this one by Cyndi "Cyndislist" Howells, the doyenne of genealogy Web sites. As I walked down to the lecture I realized it must also be the final Formal Night: the bejeweled flip-flops gave it away.

Broken links

Cyndislist (www.cyndislist.com) is a legendary genealogy Web site, a sort of archive of archives: a massive compendium of almost every known genealogical Web site, with categories that start at "Acadian, Cajun, and Creole" and end with "Writing Your Family History." What started in 1996 as a list of a few hundred Web links now features over a quarter-million links and growing. If genealogy is now in its Web 2.0 mode, Cyndislist was there when it was still Web 0.8. Remember that in 1996 America Online was assigning numerical passwords that resembled pi solved to the 364th decimal place. Of course, only four hundred or so people had e-mail back then. Cyndi Howells was one of them.

The notion of sitting down to talk with Cyndi of Cyndislist was something akin to sitting down to talk with Mr. McDonald of McDonald's. You mean there actually is one? Yes. And there she was, sitting at a small table in the Café Caribe, waiting for me.

Cyndislist began in 1995 when Cyndi Howells, of Puyallup, Washington, thrilled with her new computer and its 9,600-baud modem, printed a one-page list of Web sites she found useful and made copies of the list for everyone at her fall genealogical society meeting. They wanted more. A few months later, Cyndi drew up a five-page list and included it in the society's newsletter. They wanted more. She decided to add the list of genealogical Web sites as a side page to her family's personal Web site. People began to seek it out, this list of Cyndi's . . . this Cyndislist.

"I wouldn't call it that now if I were starting today," she admitted. "But it does give the site a personal feel." It does have a personal feel—possibly because it is still a very personal site.

"How many people work on Cyndislist?" I asked her. "Me," she said. "Just me. I still see it as basically a volunteer position for the genealogical community." Once you visit Cyndislist, you realize that working on such project alone is akin to single-handedly staffing Ticketmaster.com. Everyone wants something from you, simultaneously. It seemed impossible to me. She made money off the few ads posted on the site, but not a lot of money. Not enough to hire help.

"So what happens to Cyndislist while you're on this cruise?" I asked.

"Nothing. It just sits there. I do go on every night and scrub links because hackers have figured out how to post inappropriate links. I've been going into the Internet café every night at eleven-fifty and doing that." (That's dedication. Not only because it's tedious work, but because it costs twenty-five cents a minute to use the onboard Internet connection.)

"When I first started," Cyndi continued, "I worked on the site two to three hours a day. Then it became the whole morning. Then . . . I don't think we understood where this whole thing—the Internet—was going. I kept thinking, 'If I work harder, I'll catch up.' Around 1998 I thought, 'We're going to max out on genealogy,' but we haven't. It's like I'm the Coyote and it's ["it" being the ongoing explosion of genealogical data online] the Road Runner. It's constant. It mocks me. It throws boulders down the hill at me, and I just keep trying and trying. That's the situation I'm in."

Was she ever. I knew that she knew that neither genealogy nor the Internet was going to "max out" anytime in the next century. In fact, more than most people, Cyndi grasped the past, present, and future of the Internet and its possibilities.

"I believe that the Internet was created for genealogy," she said with a wink. "Everything you need for genealogy is there: education; tips on getting started; communications; publishing . . .

"I have twenty-eight third and fourth cousins who've found me—they're distant cousins, and they're all interested in genealogy! In the old days, you might have gone to a library and found a copy of an old genealogy newsletter in which someone from that family put out a query about looking for relatives; ten years later you can try to contact them—did their address change? Are they still alive? Now you just e-mail them.

"There's a time machine effect happening [thanks to the Internet]. Time is no longer an issue. It used to cost sixty dollars to send all the family group sheets to some cousin, who was then supposed to send me a check." She shook her head. "That old story. You did it because you hoped they'd send you something back.

"So I believe the Internet was created for genealogy. I've heard that it's useful for other things as well, but . . ."

"I've heard it's popular for pornography," I said.

She nodded. "Well, we're supposedly the second most popular use for it. Which makes sense, since you need to have sex in order to have genealogy."

So true. She had a good sense of humor, Cyndi Howells. Which probably helped make her Sisyphean task more bearable. Apart from humor, if Cyndi had a strategy for the approaching information tsunami, she wasn't sharing it with me. Cyndi's attitude struck me as a balance of selfless obligation, resignation, and denial. Millions of people relied on her to maintain her links (over 264,000 and growing). Her site is so helpful that people constantly overestimate what it—and she—can do.

"I always give the same advice for beginners: you can't find everything you need online. And even if you find it, it's not all free. People make assumptions—about the Internet and about me."

"What kind of assumptions?" I asked.

"Well, people assume I know literally everything. One gal wrote me personally to ask how to spell her husband's name in Cherokee. She wanted to get it tattooed on her body. Cyndislist contains links to Cherokee genealogy sites, so she assumed I must know. Then there was the guy who didn't know his father's name—his mother had never told him—so he e-mailed me to find out 'where the database was . . . the one where everybody's family is.'"

"Oh, the Big Database," I said. I'd harbored that fantasy myself, even though I knew it existed only in the imagination of Jorge Luis Borges and his wonderful, impossible Library of Babel.

"Yeah, the Big One," Cyndi said, shaking her head. "It's hard for people to see the big picture. And, of course, it's growing all the time."

"But you do help people see the big picture," I said. "That's what Cyndislist is, isn't it?"

"Well," she said modestly, "I may not provide the big picture, but I do try to provide links to it."

And links are her biggest headache. "The biggest problem I

have is broken links." She sighed. People will forward her their personal link and then a few months later make some kind of minor adjustment to their page or change their server address, and suddenly the link is broken. "Keeping up with the randomness of human nature is impossible," Cyndi said, shrugging.

Yes, it's impossible. Broken links. The randomness of human nature. These, I thought, were both Cyndi Howells's bêtes noires as well as the meat and potatoes of genealogy. Were it not for broken links (divorce, death, disaster) and the randomness of human nature (immigration, shotgun weddings, unplanned pregnancies), there would be no need for genealogy. If human beings were predictable and logical creatures, our ancestral past would lie behind us like a ledger sheet, each birth, marriage, and death neatly filled in exactly where it should be. But we're not, and it's not. And that's Cyndi's problem and every genealogist's challenge. This was why she still saw herself as a "volunteer" for the genealogical community: because no one would ever do what she does for the money. It could only be love.

She presents herself as just plain old Cyndi: self-deprecating, warm, easily approachable. For a while Cyndi received six hundred e-mails a day. She finally added a lot of obstacles between her global Web audience and herself, but she still gets about two hundred a day. "I have a standard reply for the people who contact me looking for help with their research," she said. "Four words: 'I'm already doing that.'"

Cyndi's generosity of time and spirit was, of course, admirable. Yet as I ventured further into the world of genealogy I began to see that such openhandedness was a hallmark of this culture. There was a Golden Rule quality to it; the idea that we should do unto others because ultimately we'd like them do unto us, someday, too (just as Cyndi had hinted in her story about mailing boxes of data to distant cousins). I started to see that the magnanimity of genealogists was both an expression of their kindness and decency and also an acknowledgment that, in fact, this was the only way the enterprise could possibly work.

I thought of a story that Elaine, a BGS member, had told me about a research trip she'd taken to Ontario, Canada, a few years earlier. She'd traveled from Colorado up to a tiny town in Ontario, Canada, whose name she'd once seen on some genealogical records pertaining to the Craig line of her ancestry. She stopped in at a small historical society and inquired about their holdings on local history. When she mentioned the name Craig, the staffers consulted with each other for a moment, and then told her that a few weeks earlier someone else had been in, also looking for Craigs. They rummaged through their desks and found a note with a phone number on it, called it, and spoke to someone on the other end. It was a man who lived sixty miles away. He was also a Craig descendant. After speaking to Elaine for a few minutes, he told her to wait for him at the historical society. An hour or so later, he showed up with a stack of papers and a CD-ROM filled with, as Elaine described it, "my entire Craig family history going all the way back to Scotland." He and Elaine were distant cousins. They'd never met before. They never met again, although Elaine did mail him as much information about her side of the family as she could.

The material Elaine received that day spurred her to travel to Scotland the following year, where she made contact with many distant Craig relatives and was able to visit many of the sites where her family once lived before emigrating to North America. The credit for this genealogical jackpot goes not only to the man with the CD-ROM, but also to the historical society staffers who understood that this man would, in fact, want to be summoned from his home with no notice to meet a woman from Colorado he'd never met before. They recognized that this is how genealogy works. When you're looking for information about other people, you have to rely—to some extent, anyway—on the help of other people.

I liked the mix of pure intentions and pragmatism. Although I'd walked onto the cruise with a looming sense of unworthiness about my own fund of knowledge, five days into it that not-ready-for-primetime feeling was gone. I was still a beginner. But the enthusiasm of my genealogical colleagues was an inspiration.

Writing the dictionary

In this state of grace I signed up for the following day's final official genealogical activity of the cruise: the Wholly Genes Caribbean Genealogical Society Tour of St. Thomas, U.S. Virgin Islands. A dozen of us, weighted heavily toward the professional genealogists, showed up on the dock the next morning and boarded an open-air bus that drove us past the usual genealogist hot spots: cemeteries.

Our guide was Myron B. Jackson, a genealogist and candidate for the local legislature. His presence on this tour demonstrated that life on a Caribbean island really was different from life on the mainland, because what local politician on the mainland would spend the Saturday before an election driving a bus around town filled with a bunch of tourists who weren't even eligible to vote? Myron was suave, funny, and knew the ins and outs of every cemetery on the island. Secretly I hoped Myron and I were related.

My seatmate on the tour was John Titford, an expert in British genealogy and a speaker on the cruise. I asked him what he was working on and he mentioned that he'd just handed in his latest manuscript. "What is it?" I asked breezily.

"*The Penguin Dictionary of British Surnames,*" he answered.

"Sounds . . . long," I ventured.

"It'll probably run to eight hundred pages by the end of it," he said, shaking his head. With Elizabeth Shown Mills, Cyndi Howells, and now John Titford, I was surrounded by one-person reference libraries. How many people can say they single-handedly wrote a dictionary? I was impressed.

When we finally arrived at the St. Thomas Genealogical Society, where the majority of our crowd lunged for the books on local history and privately published genealogical works, not knowing how to best take advantage of this far-flung archive, I pulled out a book I could easily have found in my local library: *Burke's Peerage and Gentry: The Definitive Guide to the Genealogical History of the Major Royal, Aristocratic and Historical Families of the United Kingdom, Ireland and the United States of America.* I saw an opportunity and tugged on Titford's sleeve.

Burke's Peerage is the preeminent A-list of who's who among royal families of the United Kingdom. First written in 1826, *Burke's Peerage, Baronetage & Knightage* was originally the work of genealogist John Burke. The book was a sensation, provoking an interest among "commoners" in the details of royal lineage that contributed to the ongoing popularity of the British Royal Family today.

Less well known but arguably more influential was the *Almanach de Gotha* (in English, *The Almanac of Gotha*—Gotha being a town in what is now central Germany), a pan-European list of royal families first published in 1763. Here, in the salad days of the European Enlightenment, we see the flowering of enlightenment's constant companion: bureaucracy. Well, someone needed to keep a record of all those marriages. In fact, *The Almanach de Gotha,* with its heavily researched, in-person verifications of title and peerage, became an indispensable tool for those seeking to ratify their status as heirs in later generations. The *Almanach* was the original Paris Hilton playbook. It also contained diverse articles of interest to royals, including, for example, the care and feeding of hamsters and the practice of something called *arithmétique politique,* though, strangely, nothing on how to detect a pea hidden underneath twenty mattresses and feather beds. The history of *The Almanach de Gotha* offers a fascinating look at the intersection of the personal, the political, the sexual, and the ideological in human history. Couplings, divorces, truces, invasions—all these contribute to the forking narrative of the *Almanach,* culminating in the dramatic destruction of the entire archive of the *Almanach* in 1945 at the hands of the monarchy-intolerant Soviet army. Archives or no, the *Almanach* lives on, its extant (and recently updated) copies still recognized as the single best source of royal lineage.

The *Almanach* did not appear to be present in the St. Thomas

Genealogical Society but *Burke's* was, no surprise since it pops up everywhere English-speaking people plant their flags (the island was first claimed by the Dutch in 1657, followed by the Danes in 1666, and finally the United States in 1917). "Can you explain the peerage system to me?" I asked Titford. The man had literally written the book on English surnames; I figured he must know everything else.

John smiled. "If you go back to William the Conqueror . . ." he began. Twenty minutes later I'd heard a detailed, if rushed, explanation of everything from the meaning of *writs patent* to the coup enacted by Margaret Thatcher when she managed to secure the title of baronet for her husband, thus ensuring a hereditary aristocratic status for her descendants (prime ministers are traditionally granted life peerages, which are not hereditary). In case you were wondering: Sir Elton John? "Sir and lord—these are generic terms," explained Titford. Sorry, Elton: not a peer.

This was another thing I appreciated about genealogists: despite Cyndi's denials, a surprising number of them really did seem to know everything.

The conversations

When the tour ended I skulked around the cobbled streets of St. Thomas for about half an hour until I couldn't take it anymore: the heat, the tourists, the bizarre proliferation of jewelry stores. I almost thought I saw Freddie and ducked into a café in a moment of animal terror. I returned to the ship three hours before departure and realized I felt not a shred of guilt for sitting on boat rather than "exploring" St. Thomas.

That evening I found out the Irishmen had done the exact same thing. We'd intended to meet up onshore but couldn't reach each other; they spent the afternoon attempting relaxation on a beach while a monstrous desalination plant just offshore roared at dangerous decibel levels every two minutes. So much for our island paradise. We drowned our shared sorrows at the Wholly Genes farewell party, where we were treated not only to complimentary drinks but also to John Titford performing a little ditty about divorce, death, and incest—an apparently (in)famous song in genealogical circles—"I'm My Own Grandpa." That's genealogy humor.

I also ran into Millie and Patsy, the New Englanders I'd met on the very first day of the cruise. At that time they'd been excited, if a little skeptical, about the prospects for the upcoming week. Now, here at the farewell cocktail party, they were full of horror stories about the indignities of cruising. Their complaints about the experience were not related to the Wholly Genes conference, which they found interesting and well run. They were simply stunned and appalled by the cruise culture.

Patsy lived on an island off the coast of Maine accessible only by a small ferry. It sounded as though her lifestyle was not exactly rugged but had its share of daily inconvenience—which I suspected she rather liked. She had the lean, attractively weathered look of an N. C. Wyeth portrait sitter, so I wasn't surprised when she revealed to me the single most shocking thing she'd seen on the cruise: "the obesity." Millie agreed. It did seem possible that cruises, with their all-you-can-eat ethos, probably attracted a certain kind of traveler: one who likes to eat a lot. I suspected the ferries to Patsy's island attracted a different crowd.

I ended up running into Millie in the Puerto Rico airport on the day we flew back to the States. She was sitting at a Starbucks surrounded by the Sunday *New York Times* and she looked happy. She confirmed that there would be no more cruises in her future.

The Irishmen and I left the party. It was our last night together. I knew I would miss these two, and I told them so. The feeling was mutual; although they had each other for company, my presence had kept them from getting at each other's throat because of an excess of togetherness. They were guys, after all. Straight guys. There was only so much caring and sharing with each other they could take.

We had The Conversation all travelers must at the end of their shared voyage: Would we ever see each other again? I started to utter all the usual clichés: Where are you going next . . . If you're ever in the States . . . Here's my contact info . . . and I meant them.

Paul, a world traveler, nodded, smiled, and then said, "You know, I've met Americans everywhere. And the thing I hate about them is that you meet them in a bar in Thailand, talk to them for a while, and tell them to look you up if they ever come to Ireland—and they do! They come to stay with you!"

Noted. I wrote down John's contact information (not Paul's), gave them each a quick kiss, and said good night.

Back to the real world

I finally made it onto the airplane, where I scored an exit-row seat and a good view of the movie screen. Once I was settled in, a melancholy sensation began to feather the edges of my psyche. The genealogical aspect of the cruise had been solid. I'd gotten more helpful research tips than I could remember. Which was, perhaps, the problem: how to implement the many, many pieces of advice I'd just received. How to emulate these genealogical gods and goddesses, that shipload of Encyclopedia Browns?

I couldn't compete with the experts, nor did I want to. That wasn't the point. Yet my ego was pushing me: surely I, a trained historian, didn't have to start at the last starting block? I only had one ace, the single point on which my stance might possibly advantage my position over a veteran genealogist: DNA. Rather, my belief in DNA as a genealogical asset versus their (some of them, anyway, if Megan Smolenyak Smolenyak was to be believed) skepticism.

I'd swabbed my cheek. Now I just had to collect some dead relatives. I already had the femur-shaped pen.

6

Information Wants to Be Free: or, How I Learned to Stop Worrying and Love DNA Testing ◀

I'd attended a serious genealogy conference with a scrawny, sparsely populated family tree, which is sort of like seeing the dentist when you only have three teeth: everyone's nice and you're treated with professional courtesy, but the experience itself is mostly theoretical. If you want a real dental exam, you need a full set of choppers. If you want to do serious genealogy, you need to find some ancestors.

I started looking—really looking.

Not Niall

Most of what I knew about the Jackson family tree came from a pedigree chart sent by my aunt Nancy. She'd researched as far back as her mother's grandparents: John Hartsfield (1857–1930) and Johnnie Talitha Skinner (ca. 1864–1899)—my great-great-grandparents. That was four generations back, the same time frame I'd reached on my mom's side. I was grateful to get that far, but I knew that from a genealogical standpoint it was, as my Jewish great-grandparents Chaim and Teizi Marienstraus might have put it: *bupkis*.

Four generations of Jacksons? That only got me to the nineteenth century. The nineteenth century was not going to help me get my hand in the air at the military records seminar, waving to signal my ancestors' participation in King Philip's War. I didn't even know if any of these folks served in the American Civil War, though the fact that I had relatives in Alabama during the nineteenth century suggested they probably did.

As I'd confessed to John Grenham, I'd jumped into the DNA testing before I knew much about my ancestry. Grenham was not impressed. I was starting to see his point. It was one thing to think you shared a genetic marker with Niall Noigiallach, aka Niall of the Nine Hostages (d. 455 A.D.); it was something else to try to connect the dots between a fifth-century tribal leader and a nineteenth-century Alabama merchant John Hartsfield. That's a lot of genealogical ground to cover. Still, that's what I had, so once I got home from the cruise I began to try to understand what my genetic information meant.

It only took me a few minutes of close reading to make my first major discovery: I was not, in fact, related to Niall of the Nine Hostages. How had I gotten that one so wrong? I blame the fine print. That is to say, I blame myself for not reading it. The testing company did its part: it ran the test and then sent me the data. Interpreting it was my problem. Over time I discovered this is everyone's problem.

There are lots of DNA testing companies specializing in genealogical services. Once I got excited about testing, I looked into most of them. I was entrusting my genetic information to a for-profit company, after all. Although I wasn't aware of any scams or fraud in the genetic genealogy industry, I had heard of people who tested with a start-up DNA company that promptly folded. This is not good. Their biological information may have remained safe, but then again, maybe it's sitting in a Dumpster in the back lot of a research park somewhere in Virginia. Not ideal. I wanted to find a company that would be around for the long term, so I chose one that had already been in existence for a while: Family Tree DNA.

Founded in 2000 by Bennett Greenspan, an obsessed genealogist who'd finally hit the dreaded brick wall in his family history, it was one of the first genetic genealogy companies and today has processed a half-million genetic tests. The anonymous data from each one of these tests becomes part of Family Tree DNA's proprietary database, and the bigger the database, the better to compare one's own tests for possible matches.

Other reputable DNA testing companies exist. Some have developed their own databases focused on geographical origins (for example, some concentrate on helping those with African heritage pinpoint the specific tribal origin of their ancestry), but most offer all-purpose genealogical tests that can reveal in what part of the world, generally speaking, your ancestors lived.

Even the most skeptical genealogists admit that DNA testing has the potential to break through genealogical brick walls in ways that traditional genealogy simply can't. Personally, I hadn't even reached a brick wall yet. I just wanted data. Most experienced genealogists advise people to do traditional research before doing DNA, but I think this is mainly because some people go into the genetic testing with the wrong expectations, hoping a DNA test will somehow provide them with a list of names of relatives and ancestors. It won't. I wasn't sure what my DNA test would tell me, if anything. I just wanted in.

I had no idea—no expectation at all, I swear—that DNA testing would rock my genealogical world. I was just a closet science geek. Better living through chemistry . . . er, molecular biology, and all that. I loved the concept of DNA but I hadn't actually reviewed its principles since college. It was less complicated and more fascinating than I remembered.

Most of us remember learning about DNA in a high school biology class: the building blocks of life, the double helix, the way fellow researcher Rosalind Franklin was denied her share of credit when they gave Watson, Crick, and Wilson the Nobel Prize. In case you don't remember, here's an extremely brief refresher.

Chromosomes

DNA is a molecule. This molecule contains a person's (or any organism's, but we'll stick to humans here) complete genetic code. Most of that genetic material lives in the nucleus of each cell in the form of chromosomes: twenty-two pairs of chromosomes and two chromosomes that determine sex—arranged as XX for women and XY for men. When the male's sperm, which has twenty-three unpaired chromosomes, fertilizes the female's egg with its twenty-three unpaired chromosomes, their DNA pairs up to form twenty-two new pairs plus the XX or XY pair. The result of this combination is a single cell containing genetic information from both the father and mother, and this unique cell begins to replicate itself, eventually growing into an embryo, a fetus, and ultimately into an infant human being.[1] That would be you. And me.

Geneticists have identified (and continue to identify) genetic markers, which are segments of DNA located in places along the DNA sequence that correspond to heritable traits such as blue eye color or hemophilia. Markers are present in all DNA, and one of the easiest places to test for them is in the DNA present in the Y chromosome, which is passed exclusively from father to son (because women do not possess a Y chromosome). There are four types of inherited DNA: Y chromosome, mitochondrial DNA, autosomal DNA, and X chromosome. Only the first two factor into most genealogical DNA tests, though, so we'll focus on those.

Why genealogists love the Y (male) chromosome

The presence of a Y chromosome determines that a person's sex will be male and, in being passed down from father to son, it reflects inherited genetic similarities for many generations. This absence of female genetic material makes Y-DNA testing a natural choice for genealogists, because the nature of most human surnames follows the same inheritance pattern as Y-chromosome markers. (There are some human societies in which surnames are passed down on the mother's side, but not very many.)

What do I mean by this? Let's use our genealogical laughing-stocks, the Smiths, as an example. Andrew Smith's son, Ben Smith, inherits both the last name Smith and also a Y chromosome from his father. If Andrew Smith has another son, Caleb Smith, by a different mother, Caleb will carry the same surname (Smith) and the same Y chromosome as his half brother Ben, despite the fact that they have different mothers. When it comes to Y-DNA testing, mothers just don't enter into the picture. The similar Y-DNA pattern possessed by Andrew, Ben, and Caleb Smith is called a haplotype, and like their surname (Smith), the Y chromosome haplotype can be traced back through the male half of the family line for thousands of years.

Groups of related haplotypes are bunched together as haplogroups and haplogroups help geneticists track the geographic diversity of human populations over time. In the longest view of human history, people who lived in a particular geographical location, especially if they were isolated, tended to share similar genetic markers, thus similar haplogroups. (Here we're talking about groups of humans thousands of years ago.)

Sometimes haplogroups are referred to as the branches of the human genetic tree. Scientists have identified over twenty (and counting) Y-DNA haplogroups and assigned each of them a letter or letters to differentiate them.

Why genealogists are starting to like mtDNA (the female stuff), too

There is one other part of the cell where genealogically significant material is located: mitochondrial DNA, or mtDNA. Unlike the male Y-DNA, mtDNA is not found in sex-determining chromosomes or even in the nucleus of the cell. Instead, it's found in the mitochondria located within the cell membrane.

MtDNA is not part of the sex-determining chromosomes. Women pass along mtDNA to both female and male children. But there's a catch: sons cannot pass down the mtDNA, only daughters can. This means that when geneticists trace mtDNA back through the generations, they're only looking at the moms. Y-DNA reflects no influence of women ancestors; mtDNA reflects nothing about the dads.

The surname–Y-DNA link makes genealogical sense. But why would genealogists care about mtDNA? It comes down to time. MtDNA mutates much more slowly than Y-DNA. This makes mtDNA useful for scientists who study the earliest origins of human development—like tens-of-thousands-of-years-ago early.

By the way, if all this talk about genetic variation is suggesting to you that there's a lot of genetic difference among individuals, then let me clarify: there's not. Over 99.9 percent of the human genome (which means the complete set of genetic material in a person) is exactly the same across the species and around the world. All human variation, from height to hair color to freckles, comes down to just the 0.1 percent of our genetic makeup that differs. It's a small world after all.

By analyzing the information from haplogroups, Y-DNA, and mtDNA, those clever geneticists have been able to trace the origins of human beings back to two genetically specific human beings who lived tens of thousands of years ago. Allow me to introduce your ancient ancestors: Y-Chromosomal Adam and Mitochondrial Eve.

The genetic Adam and Eve

These two do not have anything to do with the biblical Adam and Eve, but their names were chosen to represent the parents of all people living today, for that is indeed who they are: the oldest known ancestors of everyone on earth.

The funny thing is, while Y-Chromosomal Adam lived in eastern Africa about 60,000 years ago, Mitochondrial Eve lived there about 150,000 years ago. So they were not an actual couple. Then how were they our "parents"? Although these two were the earliest known ancestors of all living humans today, they left their genetic imprint at different times in history.

Mitochondrial Eve is the direct female ancestor of every living person today—she left her mark about a hundred thousand years earlier than Adam. By the time Y-Chromosomal Adam showed up, Eve's mtDNA was already established in the genetic material of lots of Adam's friends. Keep in mind: there were only about ten thousand human beings on earth during Adam's time (and even fewer during Eve's) and they were all living in Africa, probably somewhere around the Rift Valley (present-day Tanzania, Kenya, or Ethiopia). By having children, Adam added his genetic material to the mix, and the genetic lottery played out in such a way that their descendants survived to the present day.

Y-Chromosomal Adam is the direct male ancestor of every living person today. Although there were other human beings alive at the time Mitochondrial Eve and Y-Chromosomal Adam respectively lived, none of those humans have a direct, unbroken ancestral line to humans now.[2]

Homo sapiens first branched off from the rest of the hominid family around 40,000 to 200,000 years ago, but we didn't start spreading out across the globe for a long time. Evolutionary biologists and geneticists now believe that humans only began to move out of Africa about 60,000 years ago (bear in mind that there is a large margin for error here, perhaps tens of thousands of years, and new data is constantly challenging these figures), around the time Y-Chromosomal Adam showed up.[3]

Extreme genealogy

Everything we know about human evolution and migration comes from archaeology and genetics: bones and DNA. One of the most ambitious attempts to track the migration of early humans is the Genographic Project, a global study of human DNA that's unraveling the story of how our species grew in number and spread across the globe. Run by National Geographic, the Genographic Project is collecting DNA samples from the world's most isolated peoples, such as the Yagnobi of Tajikistan, the Kuranko of Sierra Leone, and the Shuar of Ecuador. Not only are these groups isolated geographically, but so are their unique languages and their distinctive DNA. "Different populations carry distinct [genetic] markers," explains the Genographic Project Web site. "Following them through the generations reveals a genetic tree on which today's many diverse branches may be followed ever backward to their common African root." In other words, the genetic tree is the biggest possible family tree there is or ever was. It's all genealogy.

The processes of globalization in the twentieth and twenty-first centuries are creating a much more migrant human population, though. While human populations have always mixed, it's now happening faster than ever, and as it does, these unique keys to the history of our origins disappear. The Genographic Project is working against the clock to create a library of DNA through which we can read the story of our origins.

And they needed my help.[4]

In fact, they need everyone's help. In addition to gathering the genetic code of far-flung tribes in the Amazon, the Genographic

Project is also asking people around the world to donate their DNA (anonymously) to the project. This prospect was almost more exciting to me than the genealogical part—although, in fact, this was still genealogy. Call it extreme genealogy. In any case, I went for it.

As an official partner of the Genographic Project, Family Tree DNA offered a fifteen-dollar add-on to send the results of my genealogical DNA tests to the Genographic folks, and that's what I did.

The truth is in there . . . or, rather, in here

As I found when talking to some of my friends at the Boulder Genealogical Society, even people who find this DNA stuff kind of interesting on the level of cocktail-party chatter may not be moved to apply it to their genealogical research.

I felt differently. You might say DNA testing was my gateway drug to genealogy. It fascinated me in its own right, and if it turned out that there were genealogical advantages to be gained through the testing, so much the better. DNA testing seemed like cheating, almost: all this hidden genetic information was trapped inside my body and I only had to swab my inner cheek to reveal the traces of ancestors long gone. The futurist and cyber-philosopher Stewart Brand famously said, "Information wants to be free." That's how I felt about testing for DNA: set that genetic information free! Or, to paraphrase Agent Fox Mulder: "The truth is *in* there." Why not find it?

As excited as I was about DNA testing before I did it, I found the experience itself to be a series of thrills and disappointments. If you're like me—and from what I've read on the genealogy listservs, lots of people are—your DNA testing journey will feel something like watching a Japanese movie with subtitles in Danish (assuming you speak neither). You can sort of understand what's going on by watching the actors and you can occasionally pick out a word at the bottom that jogs your memory, but if you really want to comprehend it on a deeper level, you're going to need a translator. I did.

Know your haplogroup

The most important and most useful bit of information most people get from a DNA test is the knowledge of which haplogroup they fall into. Here's how you get there.

First, I swabbed my own cheek with the little plastic Q-tip thingy provided (a painless process), then slipped it inside a test tube and mailed it off to the lab. Because I'm female, this produced a sample of mtDNA, providing a direct link back through my mother's female ancestors.

The results of my mtDNA test did not surprise me, but they did confirm what I thought I knew about my mother's heritage. My mtDNA haplogroup turned out to be K, a haplogroup shared by almost a third of Ashkenazi, or Eastern European, Jews. K is a haplogroup that's been present in Europe for about twelve thousand years and is common today in the Alps and the British Isles. My first task was to scour the Internet to find out which celebrities shared my K haplogroup. I found that our old pal Otzi the Iceman (ca. 3300 B.C.) was a K. So are Katie Couric and Stephen Colbert. Not that this tells us much beyond the fact that the four of us shared European heritage.

All this haplogroup-K information was fascinating, but it didn't tell me anything about the Jackson family, because mtDNA only reveals information about the female line, and I am a Jackson through my dad. So I bought my dad his own test. Getting a sample of my dad's Y-chromosome DNA (or Y-DNA) was the only way I, as a female, was going to get access to the haplogroup associated with the men with the Jackson surname. I could also have asked any other male Jackson in my family, but it was easiest to ask my dad.

With a name as popular as Jackson, it's not surprising that different Jacksons have different haplogroups. When my dad got his test back, we discovered that our Jackson Y-DNA haplogroup is I1a. Apparently there are a lot of other Jacksons out there who descend from Niall of the Nine Hostages, but those folks all share a haplogroup of R1b. How did I screw that up? I'm still not sure.

So, no Niall for us. The most famous historical personage from the I1a haplogroup is United States Founding Father Alexander Hamilton (1755–1804), the first secretary of the Treasury. Several months earlier, back on the Caribbean island of St. Kitts, I'd had no idea that I was enjoying the same balmy clime that had once cosseted my (extremely distant) ancestor Alexander Hamilton (who was born on the neighboring island of Nevis and moved to St. Kitts before heading to North America).

My dad and I found our DNA results fascinating, but not because they revealed anything specific about our heritage. They did not, for instance, uncover anything surprising about our ethnicity, which was clearly European, just as we expected.

Notice I said European, not white. I'm choosing my words carefully here, not because the issue of race is politically sensitive (although it is), but because genetic testing cannot tell us anything about race per se.

Race is not a scientific category; it is an artifact of society and culture. Racial categories have not only changed over time, they are also inconsistent across national borders. Someone deemed "black" in the United States for example—a person with both African and European heritage, such as President Barack Obama—would be considered *pardo,* or brown, in Brazil, according to the five racial categories that appear on its current census forms. So while DNA testing can reveal the migration path of one's earliest African ancestors (everyone's ancestors originally lived in Africa, beginning their migrations to other continents roughly seventy-five thousand years ago), it cannot definitively tell you what those people looked like and certainly not their race. It's confusing—sometimes it even confuses the experts.

The strange case of Dr. Watson

Consider the controversial life of James Watson, the scientist who, along with Francis Crick, Maurice Wilkins, and Rosalind Franklin, first decoded the double-helix structure of DNA in 1953. Watson's Nobel Prize–winning research established him as one of the world experts in genetics. Despite his deep understanding of the power and the limits of human genetics, Watson often confused socially constructed notions of race with scientific findings, as in 2000 when he suggested that dark-skinned people have higher libidos. In 2007, Watson told a reporter that although he liked to believe that everyone was equal, "people who have to deal with black employees find this not true."

This and other statements equating dark skin with lower IQ scores provoked a furor in the scientific community and among most everyone else who heard them. Francis Collins, the director of the National Human Genome Research Institute, called Watson's statements "both profoundly offensive and utterly unsupported by scientific evidence." In effect, Watson was trying to link scientific data (genetics) to unscientific, culturally specific outcomes (IQ tests). A lifetime of inflammatory comments against women, minorities, and even fat people ("Whenever you interview fat people, you feel bad, because you know you're not going to hire them") suggests that Watson's own very human, yet unscientific prejudices often clouded his interpretation of the science he helped create.[5]

It was an astonishing irony, then, when the results of Watson's DNA analysis were published. Watson had offered to share his genome—a map of a person's genes, a much more intimate data set than the simple haplogroup produced by genealogical DNA tests—with the world as a step toward decoding the genetic basis of disease. But along with the announcement that Watson was, for example, 31 percent less likely to suffer from asthma than the average person, his genome also revealed that 16 percent of his genes were inherited from a relatively recent ancestor of African descent—about sixteen times more "African" genetic material than the average European. "This level is what you would expect in someone who had a great-grandparent who was African," said Kari Stefansson of deCODE Genetics, who conducted the mapping. Does this mean James Watson is black? Well, it depends on whom you're asking. Results such as Watson's can be confusing, but they are also instructive in revealing the limits of racial categorization.

Are you who you say you are?

Now consider the case of Wayne Joseph, a self-identified black American "on the lighter end of the black color spectrum," descended from a Louisiana Creole family. In 2002, Joseph decided to take a DNA test to determine the exact amount of African genetic material his genome contained. He was stunned to read the results: "57 percent Indo-European, 39 percent Native American, 4 percent East Asian—and zero percent African." Joseph found himself questioning his identity as a black man, an issue he never thought he'd face. "The question ultimately is, are you who you say you are," Joseph said, "or are you who you are genetically?"[6]

What happened next is what often happens next, after a surprising genetic test: questions were asked. Joseph began querying his older relatives about their racial identity. His mother was unmoved by the results. "I'm too old and too tired to be anything else [other than black]," she replied. One of his aunts, on the other hand, confessed that the test results were no surprise. Joseph eventually discovered that various mixed-race ancestors in Louisiana had most likely made a conscious choice to identify as black. This may have been motivated by ideological reasons or simply because of an affinity for black culture, but in Creole Louisiana his family was dark enough to pass for black, and they did.

In the end, Wayne Joseph regretted taking the DNA test. "It's like a genie coming out of a bottle," he said. "You can't put it back in."

Wayne Joseph's question—"are you who you say you are?"—has haunted the United States for generations, long before anyone got a genetic test or James Watson published his first paper on DNA. I was disturbed to find that when I entered my paternal haplotype I1a into the Google search bar, up popped the Web site for an international white supremacy group, apparently offering haplotype I1a as an example of a "pure white" genetic marker. Gross.

This is the dark side of genetic genealogy: the quest to divide the human family according to its DNA. Variations on this theme can also be found in standard genealogical practices such as lineage societies that try to separate royalty from the rest of society. As we've already seen, race is not a scientific concept. Royalty is an accident of history. Yet some people don't want to let this stuff die. They should.

Are you who you say you are? Well, that depends. I know I don't want to be a part of the Aryan pride group claiming my haplotype for its own purposes; based on the gaps in logic and spelling mistakes I saw there, it's pretty clear they're far from a "master race." I wanted nothing to do with them. As Wayne Joseph discovered, you may not be able to choose your genetic ancestry, but you can choose to define your own personal identity, DNA be damned.

The one-drop rule

So what does all this have to do with traditional genealogy? In contrast to genetic genealogy, traditional genealogy relies on written records. Written records are artifacts of the era in which they were created, which means they reflect the values and standards of their day. Those change over time, which can lead to interpretive challenges for genealogists, especially when it comes to race.

Before the double helix, there was the family tree. In theory, individuals inherit the racial status of their parents. But what if each parent belongs to a different race? By the early twentieth century, the one-drop rule, a tradition of racial classification with its roots in slavery, had become law in many American states. Race matters. And definitions of race can have a big impact on genealogy.

By the post–Civil War Jim Crow era, when the infamous U.S. Supreme Court case *Plessy v. Ferguson* (1896) first established the federal policy of "separate but equal" facilities for whites and blacks, the one-drop rule was becoming the new standard. The one-drop rule, as it is still known and practiced (but only by the United States) today, decreed that any person with at least one African ancestor (i.e., "one drop" of African blood) was no longer considered white: that person and all his descendants were to be considered black, no matter the actual color of their skin. By the 1930s, nineteen states, from South Carolina to Nebraska, had one-drop rules on the books.

Although slaves were enumerated (though they only "counted" for three-fifths of a person) in the very first U.S. Census in 1790, racial categories per se did not become a feature of the census until the nineteenth century. At this point, census takers visiting each household were responsible for assigning the racial identity of each person they encountered. The available options changed from decade to decade, at various times offering "Indian," "black," "mulatto," "Chinese," "Japanese," "quadroon," and "octoroon." Racial designation was based solely on the judgment of the census taker, based on the appearance of the inhabitants in question. In 1920, the U.S. Census officially dropped the mixed-race category "mulatto" and replaced it with "black," the federal government's official recognition of the one-drop rule and its good-bye to any acknowledgment of multiethnic heritage until 1960, when individuals were offered the option of self-defining their racial status.

Changes in census forms are, of course, of great interest to gene-alogists. Despite their admittedly ignominious implications, the dis-appearance of categories such as "mulatto," and, as the 1880 Census offered, "deaf and dumb," "blind," "insane," "idiotic," "pauper," or "convict" meant the loss of vast amounts of interesting information for future genealogists. (In the end, even if one disputes the judg-ment of the census taker, it's still interesting to know what he or she thought of these folks.) By 1960, the ascent of the one-drop rule was total; even when given the option to acknowledge a mixed-race heri-tage, almost all Americans with at least partially African ancestry continued to identify themselves as black.[7]

Such self-identification highlights one of the ironic conse-quences of the one-drop rule. Although originally enacted for the promotion of white supremacy, the one-drop rule ended up reinforc-ing a sense of ethnic solidarity among Americans of (full or partial) African descent. This imposed group identity, linking those with African heritage despite the vast spectrum of skin, eye, and hair color they as a "people" displayed, was essential for the emergence of the black pride and black civil rights movements of the twenti-eth century. That sense of shared ethnicity, no matter how bogus its foundation, eventually led to the revocation of *Plessy v. Ferguson*. It also led to Exhibit B in our history of unbelievably appropriate case names: *Loving v. Virginia* (1967), in which the U.S. Supreme Court ruled that laws forbidding interracial marriage were unconstitu-tional. Virginia is for lovers, after all.

The Pocahontas Exception

Although the one-drop rule has been most consequential to mixed-race Americans of African descent, in theory it applies to all races in the United States, even those no longer considered races at all, such as Irishmen (considered "black" in America until the late nineteenth century) and Jews.

An interesting distinction, however, was made early on for one racial category, if only in Virginia: Native Americans and their genealogically inclined descendants. During the nadir of the Jim Crow era (itself the nadir of U.S. race relations, so that's really saying something) in 1924, the Commonwealth of Virginia enacted the Racial Integrity Act. This legislation (ultimately overturned by *Loving v. Virginia*) outlawed interracial marriage and strove to be as encompassing as possible, listing as nonwhites: "negro, Mongolian, American Indian, Asiatic Indian, Malay, or any mixture thereof, or any other non-Caucasic strains" (which leads one to wonder where all the Mongolians and Malays are today, apart from Mongolia and Malaysia . . . those still insisting that race is an unchanging, purely scientific category can stop reading now).[8]

Even though American Indians were included in Virginia's list of one-drop violators, the definition of "white" in the statute included one fascinating outlier. "For the purpose of this act, the term 'white person' shall apply only to the person who has no trace whatsoever of any blood other than Caucasian; but persons who have one-sixteenth or less of the blood of the American Indian and have no other non-Caucasic blood shall be deemed to be white persons."

This is classic genealogy territory. Because if you've only heard one tall tale from an aspiring genealogist, it was probably the one about the legendary Indian princess in their ancestry, that long-sought great-great-grandmother of yore. Ah, the Indian princess. If everyone who claimed ancestry from an Indian princess were right, we'd be living in the United States of Indian Princesses. We'd all be royalty. Apparently this Indian-princess thing has been going on a long time, though, at least in Virginia. The Pocahontas Exception wouldn't exist otherwise.

Just weeks before the 1924 introduction of the Racial Integrity

Act, State Senator James S. Barron voiced an objection. Like quite a few powerful and established Virginia families, the Barrons were proud of their family trees demonstrating their descent from America's earliest celebrity, Pocahontas. As the daughter of Powhatan, chief of the Powhatan Confederacy, Pocahontas (1595–1617) was one of the few legitimate Indian princesses. Her marriage to the Virginia Company employee and tobacco-planting enthusiast John Rolfe (1585–1622) produced one child: Thomas Rolfe (1615–1675). Single-child families always make genealogists worry about the perpetuation of the family name; thus the phrase used for the two-child strategy: "an heir and a spare." Thomas Rolfe must have held up his end of the bargain, however, because four centuries later genealogists estimate that there are now over 100,000 descendants of Pocahontas and John Rolfe alive today.

Senator Barron was one of them. Realizing the impending Racial Integrity Act would define him as nonwhite, Barron persuaded the legislators to make an exception. It worked; Barron and his fellow Pocahontas-claiming brethren could relax in their official whiteness. But the Pocahontas Exception did not make life any easier for contemporary Native Americans in Virginia. The point was not to make Native Americans white, but to honor the white descendants of an almost mythological native mother. One wonders what Pocahontas would have made of this: her own heirs waging political battles for the right to be distinguished as separate from brown-skinned Indians. It's such an American story.

Out of Africa

As a Jackson, I've always been interested in the fact that so many African-Americans share my surname. Although, genetically speaking, we are 99.9 percent identical, the fact is that our inherited phenotypes—our differences in skin color, for example—have had a huge impact on our family histories and they continue to influence our distinct experience of the world.

While I was awaiting my Y-DNA results I imagined how I would react if they revealed a significant African influence. I think some part of me would have felt proud, but I'm not sure why. I don't actually suspect I'm African-American, after all. But as someone who looks back with disgust at the history of black oppression in this (and other) countries and also takes pride in her heritage as a Jew—another group subjugated on racial and ethnic grounds—I suppose I would have felt proud to be a part of such a courageous, resilient group of people.

The Jews would have to carry that load. While my mtDNA haplogroup confirmed the Jewishness of my maternal line, my dad's Y-DNA revealed this about my ancestors: they originated in Africa and they never went back. Most recently (which, in this context, means fifteen thousand to twenty thousand years ago), nearly half of the people carrying the I1a haplotype were located in Scandinavia, leading some to refer to haplogroup I1a as a "Viking haplogroup."

The Y-DNA results I obtained through Family Tree DNA and the Genographic Project were able to tell me a great deal about the earliest history of my ancestors—people whose names we will never know, but whose migration patterns are becoming clearer over time. Here, for example, is a brief outline of the history of my I1a ancestors, as told through the identifying genetic markers unique to my haplogroup (arranged here in chronological order): M168 → M89 → M170 → M253.

M168: Time line: approximately 50,000 years ago. Location: Africa. The end of an Ice Age allowed my ancient ancestor and his community to follow his animal prey to new hunting grounds. Scientists note that this period also coincided with a revolution in human intellect, leading to the creation of new tools and more so-phisticated thought processes and cultural expression in the form of art. At this time, there were probably only ten thousand humans on the entire planet—and they were all in Africa.

M89: Time line: approximately 45,000 years ago. Location: northern Africa or the Middle East. This ancestor was part of the second wave of migration out of Africa (the first took the coastal route to Australia, where Australian Aborigines today carry a distinct genetic marker distinguishing them from later waves). Another cold snap hit, making passage back to Africa impossible. The herds of game—antelope and woolly mammoths included—were heading north, and so were the humans who lived off them. By this point there were tens of thousands of humans on earth. They were adapting to their new environments rather well.

M170: Time line: 20,000 years ago. Location: southeastern Europe. This great-great-great . . . *very* great-grandfather lived during the height of the great Ice Age. Despite the challenging climate, human culture flourished in this time and place, giving rise to sophisticated toolmaking and art, including the famously voluptuous "Venus" statuettes that are attributed to the Gravettian culture of the period. Some geneticists believe that these people, who numbered in the hundreds of thousands, were early ancestors of the Vikings.

M253: Time line: 15,000 years ago. Location: Iberian Peninsula. Driven south by massive ice sheets covering much of the European continent, this guy and his community sought refuge on the Iberian Peninsula, in what is now Spain. As the ice gradually retreated, these people—now numbering around a million—slowly moved northward, leaving evidence of their culture in the cave paintings of Altamira and Lascaux.[9]

That's the Stone Age history. After this, my I1a ancestors continued northward as the melting continued. This haplogroup eventually made it as far as Finland and Sweden before heading back down to the British Isles.[10]

So. Scandinavia, Vikings, Britain . . . nothing in the Jackson DNA was bringing me any closer to Bill Cosby's warm embrace (remember "We are a proud people"?).

Yet it was still possible that I could have African-American relatives. Although none of my paternal ancestors had recent African heritage, some of them may have had relations with African or African-American women and produced biracial children. Those children and their descendants would be my relatives; they just wouldn't show up in the Jackson Y-DNA. I knew that my Jackson ancestors lived in Alabama during the slavery period. The historical record shows that sexual relations between white male slave owners and their female black slaves, whether consensual or (more often) forced, were common. The genetic record also supports this.

In the several years since the DNA testing company African Ancestry began offering its services, over a third of African-Americans who took the test discovered that they descended from Europeans on the male side and Africans on the female's. This was not always welcome news to those seeking to substantiate their black heritage. Phenotypes support this history as well, as many African-Americans have discovered upon visiting Africa for the first time, expecting to be embraced as family. In the eyes of black Africans, most African-Americans are quite obviously racially mixed. African-Americans visiting Africa often find themselves described as brown rather than black.[11] As it happens, about one in twenty "white" American men who test their DNA find that they have a relatively recent African ancestor.

In any case, I now had more evidence on hand were I to encounter an African-American Jackson. We could compare DNA, assuming they'd been tested themselves. It wasn't much, but it was more than I had before.

Caz's story

Clearly, knowing a little bit about one's DNA signature can reveal a lot about one's ancestry. Of course, there's another side to DNA data: medical information. But a genealogical DNA test is different from a medical DNA test. There was nothing in my report from Family Tree DNA that was going to help me predict future diseases, apart from the fact that, as someone with Ashkenazi Jewish heritage, I was statistically more likely to carry a gene for Tay-Sachs disease (about one in twenty-five Ashkenazi Jews carries the faulty gene while about one in three hundred in the general population does).

The benefits of combining genealogy (e.g., a knowledge of family medical history) with genetics (modern DNA medical testing) became incredibly relevant to me when my cousin Tim had his first son, Caz.

One spring day in 2006 I received a shattering e-mail from my cousin Tim and his wife, Julie, in Nashville, Tennessee. Julie gave birth to their second child, Caz, a month after I had my son, Jackson, in 2005. At this point, both boys were almost a year old.

It had been a challenging year for me. Sometime during the extreme sleep deprivation that naturally follows the birth of a child, it occurred to me that I had not fully prepared myself for this whole parenting thing. Whether it's actually possible to be prepared for parenting is a question I will leave in the rhetorical state for now, but I now realize that I was suffering from postpartum depression. So when I saw the e-mail from Tim and Julie, I was probably not, in the words of Oprah, my "best self." Instead, I was muddling through and sneaking a few delicious moments to check e-mail as an escape from Babyland. How I craved those moments. I wondered how parents dealt with more than one child at a time. Then I opened the e-mail from Tim and Julie:

> Caz has been diagnosed with a condition called "Severe Combined Immune Deficiency" (SCID), which means he was born without a functioning immune system . . . They call this the "Boy in the Bubble" syndrome; there was an old movie in the '70s with John Travolta and also a Seinfeld episode about this! I don't know how Caz made it to ten months of age

before this was discovered . . . and they're not just telling me he'll grow out of it. It is an extremely rare disease caused by a recessive genetic defect that Tim and I both carry . . . He is the third case in the WORLD that has this particular type of SCID. The other two cases didn't survive. Caz is breaking new ground!

The only way to treat these kids is to do a bone-marrow transplant.

Allow me to reiterate: I thought I'd had a hard year. This e-mail finally snapped me out of my self-pity. I was blown away by what I read, trying to imagine how Tim and Julie were coping with such a terrifying situation. It was as if my own worst nightmare appeared in my in-box, daring me to confront it. Postpartum depression can express itself in many different ways. Some women feel alienated from their children and unable to bond. My problem was the opposite: I felt so totally bonded to Jackson that I suffered almost constantly from anxiety, imagining graphic, detailed scenarios in which my son was taken from me, either by abduction, disease, or my own negligence. And now here were Tim and Julie. Their son's first year of life had been an unending series of illnesses, worry, and doctor's visits, which finally resolved itself in the discovery of a disease so rare only two other people had ever been diagnosed with it.

I reread the e-mail trying to understand how Tim and Julie managed to retain their composure long enough to write it. What I gleaned was this: Tim and Julie were incredibly, incredibly busy dealing with all the facets of Caz's situation, from the basic (Caz vomited all day long) to the exotic (Tim and Julie learning about the specifics of CD45-deficient SCID) to the mundane (would their insurance cover Caz's care at Duke University Medical Center?). It seemed that the busyness, combined with some kind of instinctual parental protective instinct, enabled them to focus simply on what needed to get done on a day-by-day basis. I could only imagine, really.

One detail caught my attention right away. It was in Julie's explanation of the disease when she wrote, "It is an extremely rare disease caused by a recessive genetic defect that Tim and I both carry." Back to genes.

I was familiar with this whole recessive-gene concept from my own pregnancy, when I was surprised by the news that I was a carrier of the Tay-Sachs genetic disorder. Prenatal screening for Tay-Sachs disease is one of the great success stories of genetic epidemiology. First detected (independently) in the 1880s by the English ophthalmologist Warren Tay and American neurologist Bernard Sachs, Tay-Sachs disease is a rare but fatal illness that kills most of its victims by age five. In 1969, Dr. John S. O'Brien discovered a way to screen for the disease, and by the mid-1970s, Tay-Sachs had been nearly eradicated.

In my case, my husband was tested and found not to be a carrier: we were out of danger. In Julie's case, neither she nor Tim was ever screened for SCID because its occurrence is so rare. When I later spoke with Dr. Rebecca Buckley, the remarkable immunologist at Duke University responsible for Caz's successful bone-marrow treatment, she told me that SCID is probably underdiagnosed because of this lack of infant screening.

As Julie indicated, the fact that Caz survived undiagnosed for ten months was incredible. The fact that he held on beyond that is largely due to the amazing work of Dr. Buckley, whose extensive work with SCID patients (123 of them over twenty-seven years) and mastery of a bone-marrow transplant technique in which "nonperfect" bone-marrow matches may be used essentially saved his life.

Dr. Rebecca Buckley was born in 1933. She wears a string of pearls and she can talk about T cells, autosomal genes, and the future of gene therapy in language that is friendly and, at the same time, extremely comforting in its subtlety and intelligence. Dr. Buckley has four grown children. Her father was a physician, and as a child in Hamlet, North Carolina, young Rebecca would hear him talk to patients on the only phone in their house, right outside her bedroom. It was through listening to him that she decided she wanted to be a doctor, too. When she applied to medical school at the University of North Carolina in the early 1950s, she was asked only two questions: 1) Why did she want to take a man's place in the program?; and 2) How soon was she planning on dropping out to get married? Rebecca Buckley did not drop out, though she did get married. She earned her M.D. in 1958 and is now the division chief of pediatrics/allergy and immunology at the Duke Medical Center.

As a physician with fifty years' experience, Dr. Buckley told me that the single greatest change she's witnessed in her field is the genetic revolution. She saw her first SCID baby in 1965. There wasn't much she could do to help. Today, thanks to advances in genetics, 80 percent of her SCID transplant cases go on to healthy lives. For those few potential SCID babies screened at birth (such as Caz's little brother, Bennett, whose umbilical-cord blood was FedEx'd to Dr. Buckley at Duke within an hour of his birth in Tennessee), those testing positive for the defect can be treated with stem cells and enjoy a 98 percent success rate. And this, Dr. Buckley says, is just the beginning of a new era of genetic therapy.

Caz's little brother, Bennett, did not carry the SCID marker; he was "normal." Ever since Caz's birth, Dr. Buckley has been testing and retesting my cousin Tim's DNA samples, trying to find evidence of X-linked SCID in his body. So far she hasn't found it, but it must be there or Caz wouldn't have the disease. "It could be a new mutation in Tim," Dr. Buckley said, but that would be extremely rare. Most importantly, though, four years after Caz's birth and three years after his bone-marrow transplant, he was quite healthy and his prognosis was very good. I felt I needed to meet him, this little blond cousin of mine, this sweet survivor. And I wanted to see Tim and Julie, too, my cousins. My heroic cousins.

If my cousin Tim carries this marker, I might, too. We are first cousins, after all. Getting a genetic genealogy test to discover your ancestry won't tell you much about the future of your health. But knowing your genealogical medical history might.

God bless Judy Bennett

I was happy with the results of my genetic genealogy test. To be honest, I felt that just learning about the prehistoric history of my DNA-linked ancestors was enough. When I realized "my" people were responsible for the incredible cave paintings of Lascaux (though I admit it's a bit of stretch), I was thrilled! Studying my DNA testing results also helped me understand Caz's diagnosis. My crash course in DNA had paid off in significant ways.

Throwing myself into the DNA stuff also had another effect: I was finally starting to feel like a real genealogist. I'd finally found my niche among the genies: genetics. While I wasn't an expert, I was interested and engaged in this new front of genealogy—while many of my fellow genies were still skeptical. I wouldn't say I became an evangelist for genetic genealogy, but I did find myself advocating for DNA tests during the coffee break at BGS meetings. Most of the really experienced among them just nodded politely but weren't really interested. I think that's because they'd already had so much success with traditional research methods that they couldn't imagine what good would come of this newfangled DNA stuff.

Until I told them about Judy Bennett.

It all started on the genealogy cruise. I'd interviewed so many of the pros on board that apparently word got out about me and the fact that I was writing a book. Suddenly, in the genealogical echo chamber of the *Caribbean Princess,* someone wanted to point the microphone at *me.* It was Dick Eastman, creator of the well-known and eminently useful blog Eastman's Online Genealogy Newsletter (www.blog.eogn.com).

I was soon squashed on a settee next to him as Megan Smolenyak Smolenyak videotaped my responses to questions about what I was doing, and why. Smolenyak posted the resulting video to her own site, www.RootsTelevision.com within a few weeks of our debarkation in Puerto Rico. And there, online, is where Judy Bennett saw me.

"We were very interested in your interview with Dick Eastman," Judy wrote. "My husband and I are both retired and genealogy is now our second 'occupation' outside of our family."

So far, so good. She liked the video. Then it got personal.

"My husband's mother was a Jackson and when we started investigating the Jackson line, we were overwhelmed." I knew the feeling.

"I do not know which Jackson line is yours but if I can help in any way, I would be delighted. One of the marvelous attributes of genealogists is their generosity in sharing their knowledge and I like to continue that tradition with anyone that I can help."

It sounded good. I needed help. Her husband was a Jackson. So I wrote back.

I thanked her. I told her I didn't have much information to offer, but I'd do my best. I offered her the names of the furthest-back Jackson ancestor I could prove: my great-grandfather William Daniel Jackson (1856–1924). By genealogical standards, this was laughable. She wrote back.

"I have attached a Word document showing your Jackson ancestors back to John [Jackson] b. ca 1670s . . . This doc is just a *bare* outline. I just wanted to get it to you and see what access you have to the documents that 'prove' this line . . . I feel very comfortable that this is your line but will let you draw your own conclusion when you get all of the documentation. My husband's line is from Ambrose [Jackson, d. 1745] and yours is from his brother, John [Jackson, d. ca. 1713]."

Here are your ancestors back to the 1670s . . . ? Could it possibly be true? I didn't know where to begin.

"I had a Eureka! moment when I put it all together!" Judy wrote. "Love to do that!!"

I loved it when she did that, too, if "that" meant sending me three hundred years of documented Jackson family history. And it was well documented, most of it published in a series of articles from the respected journal *The Virginia Genealogist.* There were footnotes and everything. Still, I was skeptical. How did I know these were "my" Jacksons?

DNA, of course.

I wrote back, politely asking if Judy's husband, Kent (who was apparently my distant cousin), had tested his Y-DNA so that I could compare it to my father's. He had not. But, Judy suggested, why not check the Family Tree DNA Jackson Surname Project Web site? On it is a listing of the proven DNA signatures for all the Jackson lines so far discovered. No, they didn't dig up the bodies of these long-dead Jackson progenitors but living descendants who can prove their ancestry (via documentation) from them have had their DNA tested, and they all matched.

"If we have found the right line," Judy explained, "your Dad should probably match the Ambrose/John 1713 box. If he does, that is a clear indication that we are on the right track."

Okay. I went to the Family Tree DNA Jackson Surname Project Web site. I scanned the "Y-DNA Test Results for Project Members" page. And there it was:

JOHN JACKSON / 1713 VA: HAPLOGROUP I1

Just like my dad's. Other Jackson lines were listed, each with different haplogroup signatures. It was a done deal. In five minutes I'd confirmed that the genealogical data Judy had sent me—names, dates, vital record information, marriages—the entire paper trail—was real.

These really were "my" Jacksons.

This was a genealogical jackpot. It doesn't always happen this way. But it happened to me. "One of the marvelous attributes of genealogists is their generosity in sharing their knowledge," Judy had written. It was true. I'd seen variations on this genealogical generosity before and now I was experiencing it firsthand.

"Can I call you?" I asked in an e-mail. Judy said sure.

Judy lives in Texas. I know no one in Texas. But now I knew Judy. I called; we started talking and didn't stop for an hour.

"I hope you don't mind my accent," Judy said.

"What do you mean?" I asked. She sounded like my idea of a Texan, but I didn't see any problem with that.

"I know it's strong," she said bashfully.

"I love it!" I said. "You probably think I sound like a Valley Girl, being from California," I said.

"No!" she exclaimed. "Yours is nice!" We'd established one thing right there: we liked each other.

Our conversation eventually moved on to genealogical matters. Judy told me about the trips she and Kent had taken to Virginia to see the land where our ancestors lived. "It's still called Brunswick County," she told me. She'd studied all the place-names in the documents before going on the trip. "I study maps; I love maps," she said. "I found the Monk's Neck area mentioned in the land deeds. We almost gave up at one point, but thank goodness we have a good GPS." Sometimes she found a spot in present-day Virginia by closely reading the description of what the place looked like in the eighteenth century. "That's how I found Reedy Creek," she said.

"Brunswick County is very poor. The land has been farmed out," she said. This was where our Jackson ancestors lived and owned property—property originally granted by King George III when Virginia was still a colony. "Around the creeks it was lush and nice. That's why they went there." She was full of details about the place, as well as opinions about who the first Jackson to come to North America might have been (she'd like to think it was John Jackson of the Jamestown, Colony, but she's not sure).

Much of what Judy had learned about these early Jacksons she'd gleaned from following the movements and genealogy of others who lived near the family at the time, or whose names appeared in the records with them. "At first you just trace your own line," she said, "then you find out later that the only way you're going to make connections is to trace everybody's name in the records because generally people moved in groups."

Judy's comment reminded me of one of the more remarkable things I heard on the genealogy cruise. I'd attended a lecture on English genealogical sources by John Titford in which he suggested that, as long as we were looking up our ancestors' wills in a particular English village, why not look at them all? And by "all" he really did mean all the wills in an entire English village. I heard a collective gasping for breath in the auditorium.

"It was the sixteenth century," he hedged, sensing his audience's trepidation. "There was a much smaller population in England then, so we're only talking about a few hundred wills." Oh, only a few *hundred* wills. Judy Bennett traced "everybody's name" in the early Brunswick County records. Titford's advice seemed absurdly ambitious at the time, but I now realized it was simply a matter of desire: How badly did you want to know your family history?

Many times as we talked I expressed my amazement at her dedication to the research. "Oh," she said, "it just gets my juices flowing when I get into all this!" Her enthusiasm and her kindness were overwhelming. I really did feel as if I'd met a relative. That conversation started an online correspondence and occasional phone calls that continue to this day. I still don't receive many family Christmas cards from the Jacksons, but now I get them from Judy Bennett.

The connection with Judy reminded me of one of the peculiar aspects of genealogy: the research is always pulling you into the past and the present simultaneously. It's easy to get lost in the archives or in the history of a haplogroup, but it's also important to connect with the living—whether they're relatives whose memories need to be preserved on paper or acquaintances whose research can lead you to new branches of the tree.

Overall, it felt as though my genealogical journey was entering a new, supercharged phase of activity. Not only did I now better understand how DNA played into genealogical research; I also had three centuries' worth of names to investigate. I wanted to learn more about these Jacksons: Who were they? Why did they move when they did?

I was also struck by a funny feeling, something like regret. I looked back on the years I spent in school learning about America's colonial history, from kindergarten Thanksgiving pageants to graduate seminars at Berkeley, never ever suspecting my ancestors were part of the early history of this country. It had never occurred to me. I did remember one moment, in the midst of college applications, when my mom read aloud a list of potential scholarships and stopped on the listing for the DAR: Daughters of the American Revolution.

"Do you think there's any chance you might qualify for that?" she asked. "You know, on your father's side?" I shrugged. "It's possible, I guess," I said. But the odds of tracking down that information seemed impossibly remote, so we let it go. Now, twenty years later, I reconsidered it. I put DAR on my genealogical "to-do" list.

Genetic genealogy had led me—thanks to Judy Bennett—back to colonial Virginia, and beyond, even further into a nameless prehistory that stretched tens of thousands of years back to the great Rift Valley of Africa. Given all that, my next destination was self-evident.

Alabama, of course.

7

Get Back to Where You Once Belonged; or, Hitting the Road to Alabama with Cousin Mooner ◄

Yes, Alabama. The mother ship.

And not Virginia? It was true that the Judy Bennett Genealogical Jackpot e-mail successfully shifted my definition of "Jackson homeland" to colonial Virginia, where our ancestor John Jackson (d. ca. 1713) was the earliest substantiated ancestor to live in North America. Yet Alabama still held a special place in my imagination as the home of our Jackson kin. My grandfather, Jabe Cook Jackson, was born and raised there before moving on to Michigan, and his father lived there, and . . . well, until Judy's e-mail, that was about all I knew.

I'd always wanted to do it: go to the South, see the old homestead, but it was all very vague. Judy's e-mail changed that. Before Judy, I knew only two names beyond my father's. Now I knew nine. Nine more generations of Jacksons! Learning these names meant that I knew who to look for when I hit the archives, the cemeteries, and the homes of my relatives down south.

I'd been talking to my friends at BGS, who had plenty of advice.

"Check out the archives in advance, so you know what they have and what you want to ask for."

"Take photographs of every document you find—don't just make photocopies."

"Bring change for the copiers."

One BGS member, Betty Youngblood, took me aside at the end of the meeting just before I was to leave for my trip. Betty and her husband, the Reverend William Youngblood, always reminded me of a pair of doves atop a wedding cake with their white hair and delicate features. The Youngbloods were longtime genealogists and veterans of many long car trips in search of old graves. They were also natives of Louisiana, so they knew I needed a heads-up.

"When you're down south," Betty said in her gentle voice, "people will give you directions?" She made it sound like a question, but it wasn't. "They'll give you directions that will just go on and on? They'll tell you, 'Turn left at the old Bailey place, then right where the old bridge used to be'—and none of it will make any sense." I nodded, sensing she knew what she was talking about.

"So what should I do?" I asked.

Betty gave me one of her sweetest looks. "Oh, honey. You just smile and ignore them? And bring a map."

The itinerary was this: fly to Nashville and meet Cousin Mooner, who was flying in from San Francisco. We would stay in Nashville for two days, just long enough to stop in and see Cousin Tim and his wife, Julie, and their kids, including, of course, little Caz. I wanted to see him with my own eyes, after hearing so much about him. We'd then drive south, through Alabama at first, in order to get to Jannelle, my dad's cousin (therefore my first cousin once removed) in Hattiesburg, Mississippi, not far over the state line from Alabama. There we'd meet her and her husband, George, as well as her daughters, Janet and Jackie, and their families.

We'd spend the next three days in and around Sumter County, home of at least three of our Jackson ancestors. We planned to hit the University of Western Alabama in Livingston, where the local history room of the library purported to be fully stocked with materials we needed. I called the local courthouse to make sure they'd be open when we arrived. I discovered that most of their records were also available by mail and e-mail from the centralized Alabama records office. Good to know, should we run out of time.

We also intended to track down as many graves as we could.

I went online and immersed myself in the world of virtual cemeteries. The Association of Graveyard Rabbits (www.thegraveyard rabbit.com) is one of the most notable names in this field, a group dedicated to the preservation of cemeteries and education about rituals of death and burial. I began with the Graveyard Rabbits and eventually came across thousands of listings of cemeteries on US GenWeb.com, RootsWeb.com, and even personal Web sites.

I finally tracked down the approximate locations of two cemeteries in the Emelle area where we might find some Jacksons waiting for us: Old Side Baptist Cemetery and the Sumterville Methodist Church Cemetery. I printed out two fairly featureless maps courtesy of Google and packed them for the trip. While on Google Maps, I checked out the Satellite View, just to get a sense of the landscape. As far as I could tell, this place was flat. And green. And flat. Hard to get a handle on it, really. There were very few landmarks. Emelle was rural. And apparently only thirty-one people still lived there.

When I first Googled Emelle, I encountered this line, the very first Web site offered: "Emelle, Alabama: Home of the Nation's Largest Hazardous Waste Landfill." Super. Isn't that what everyone wants to read when they begin researching their ancestral homeland? In some sense, however, I relished the horror of it. My notions of the South were heavily influenced by the writing of William Faulkner and Flannery O'Connor, along with the disturbingly vivid photographs of William Eggleston—all equally strange depictions of southern weirdness.

Studying the history of African-Americans also left me with a deep curiosity about southern life. One of the first things I learned about my eighteenth-century Jackson ancestors was that they had owned slaves. Thanks to Judy Bennett, I'd read various wills of my earliest Jackson ancestors stipulating the dispersal of their property with lines such as:

> "He left the tract of land on Reedy Creek where he lived to his son Thomas Jackson, along with a Negro woman after his mother's decease . . ." (Will of John Jackson, 1739/40).[1]

> "To prevent disputes between us and my son Thomas over the will of my late husband John Jackson and for love and affection," my tenth great-grandmother Rebecca Jackson bequeathed "a Negro boy, Ben" (Rebecca Jackson, 1749).[2]

And so on. Every succeeding generation seemed to hand down at least one slave to its descendants. This news didn't exactly surprise me; the Jacksons were white farmers in colonial Virginia, after all, but it was shocking on a more subtle level. All these years I'd been studying American history I'd known it was possible that my family had played a part in slavery, but I'd never seen proof. Here it was. I wasn't sure what to do with this information, except think on it. Sleep on it. And think some more.

Homecomings and horse thieves

For people like myself, born and raised after Emancipation and north of the Mason-Dixon Line, the everyday reality of Jim Crow laws was simply an abstract concept. Racism is found everywhere, of course, but in my own personal experience as a child in Northern California and Montana, I simply did not live near many people of color, so whatever latent racism existed never found much of an outlet. As my trip to Alabama drew closer I realized that I was waiting to see what the South was "really" like—racially speaking.

I'd spent five years of graduate school as a research assistant to my dissertation adviser, Leon F. Litwack, during which I'd read through the entire collected correspondence of the NAACP as well as thousands of other documents related to race relations in the American South. The book Professor Litwack eventually published, *Trouble in Mind: Black Southerners in the Age of Jim Crow,* was a brilliant and devastating account of the struggle blacks faced to build lives of dignity in a climate of violence and oppression. All this was present for me as I booked my tickets. I realized I was embarking on this trip with northern prejudices, so I resolved to try to keep an open mind. I was, after all, curious. And I knew my southern relatives probably had their own suspicions about me.

I found this out on Inauguration Day, 2009. I'd spent a lot of energy campaigning for Barack Obama, so January 20 was a happy day in my house. As I watched the festivities, I giddily updated my Facebook and Twitter profiles, thrilled to be sharing this moment with the rest of my network. Not everyone was a supporter. I knew that, of course. But I was ignoring it for the day. Suddenly there on my Facebook page I saw a comment from a southern relative, someone I'd introduced myself to via e-mail but never met:

(10:02 A.M., January 21) After reading all your posts of the last 24 hours, I am not certain you are ready to meet the rest of the Jackson crowd.

Ouch. I was shocked. But why? As a close watcher of the presidential campaign, I was well aware of the political divisions in this country. I had no expectation that my family members—particularly those I'd never met—would share any of my values, political or otherwise. This particular cousin wasn't a fan of Barack Obama. Fine. But I think there was something else at play, as well: it's one thing to be contacted by a relative you've never heard of (in this case, my cousin being contacted by me), and another to hear that this new cousin (me) is coming to your part of the country to visit.

Many of us have a suspicion of relatives (and doubts as to whether they really are our relatives) coming out of the woodwork. My zealous pro-Obama posts only strengthened those fears. My cousin was entitled to them.

So I was heading south with my own fears and expectations and my relatives were probably awaiting my arrival with their own. This is why doing the dead-people part of genealogy is often easier than the alternative: fewer interpersonal issues.

I called a family friend from North Carolina, Allan Gurganus, to get some tips on what to expect on my southern sojourn. Two of Allan's books, *The Oldest Living Confederate Widow Tells All* and *The Practical Heart,* directly address issues of family history. I asked him what role genealogy played in southern culture.

"It's almost a religion," Allan said. "The South was very under-populated for the first century or so and people were very prideful about family, whether they were rich or poor. If you had money, you spent summers on the plantation and learned about family history. If you were poor, well . . . you had to be proud of something."

I told him about what I was hoping to find on the trip: a connection to some of my living relatives, as well as clues to how and why my ancestors moved to Alabama from Virginia. I hoped to learn something more about their lives, but I wasn't too hopeful about that. Allan laughed.

"We all have a hilarious tendency to imagine that we're related to William Pitt the Younger—instead of a convict," he said. "Yet how often the horse thief turns up . . . This is particularly true in the antebellum South, which was a feudal society. Sir Walter Scott was the favorite writer, and so many held delusions of knightly grandeur."

I knew all about it. The Indian princess. The Pocahontas Exception. The lost line to royal succession. Personally speaking, I'd given up on those dreams a long time ago, if I'd ever held them at all.

"The first question you have to ask yourself," Allan said, echoing Pat Roberts in the beginners' genealogy seminar six months earlier, "is what do you hope to find? Because whatever it is, you aren't going to find it. You might have to combine relatives to get there."

I doubted Pat Roberts would approve, but I liked the idea. My conversation with Allan eased my mind a bit: at least I knew I wasn't entering into this with fantasies doomed to disappointment. If anything, I was going with a sense of apprehension: What would my relatives think of me? What would I think of Alabama? And, crucially, would the barbecue really be as good as everyone said it would be?

Meet Mooner

Like all great adventurers, I brought one secret weapon: Mooner. Mooner Jackson, my first cousin. Four years younger than me, Mooner (her nickname) had eventually left Michigan and Jabe Mountain and settled in the San Francisco Bay Area, where she was now a chef and catering director at a catering company. They did big swanky weddings and bar mitzvahs and also hosted the occasional weird San Francisco foodie bash.

Mooner and I were enjoying pretty dissimilar lifestyles, and it wasn't just the menu options. I was working from home, married, with a small child, and she was single in the city, staying up late, and working her ass off at functions all over Northern California. Our only chance to talk was during her morning commute across the Bay Bridge; a harmonic temporal convergence during which (a) she had a few spare minutes before work and (b) I was awake (I had a much earlier bedtime than she did). Mooner was excited about our trip. She'd already begun researching our dining and thrift-store options, creating interactive online maps displaying all the possibilities for fried okra and undervalued vintage clothing available within a hundred miles of the Natchez Trace. It was my job to get her excited about the genealogy.

I'd known all along that Mooner would make a great companion: she's smart, funny, and able to drive a stick shift if necessary. We inherited the same Jackson hair phenotype: fine, straight, blondish brown stuff that is thankfully immune to humid frizziness—thus we could probably share hair products if needed. I also felt the trip would be a good opportunity for us to bond; she'd grown up so far away from me that although we'd always felt affectionate toward each other, we'd rarely had a chance to just hang out. Our fathers are brothers. This bond alone would provide hours of good conversation, comparing their distinct brands of Jackson weirdness. This was our chance.

Nashville

Dolly Parton tote bags. Hank Williams baseball caps. The famed local chocolate confection, the GooGoo Cluster. Nashville is a town that knows how to market itself. Somehow it managed to seem welcoming instead of obnoxious, but maybe that's because I liked everything they were selling: hillbilly music, American history, and chocolate. Not five feet from my gate, I bought a GooGoo Supreme (caramel + marshmallow + pecans + chocolate) and ate it while listening to a remarkably good singer, accompanying himself on an acoustic guitar in the airport lounge. Both the GooGoo Cluster and the singer were terrific. This is what a surfeit of showbiz talent provides: excellent entertainment everywhere, for free. I already loved Nashville. When I found Mooner at the car-rental area, she had discovered the GooGoos, too, and she shared my instant crush on the city. It was an auspicious start.

When visiting relatives, it's best to think carefully about the lodging options: Will they have room for you? Will your daily habits clash? Will you be able to find an escape route? In Nashville we opted against imposing ourselves upon Tim and Julie; with their three young kids, they probably had enough excitement in their home already. Also, we were interested in getting some sleep. So we stayed instead with my husband's aunt Carol and uncle Howard, who were incredible hosts, indulging every one of our Nashville whims, from peeking at the solar panels on Al Gore's house to getting a palate-scarring yet delicious chicken dinner from Prince's Hot Chicken Shack in a run-down strip mall in north Nashville.

Prince's Hot Chicken Shack was the first stop in Mooner's Stations of the Southern Food Cross. She'd brought a list of all the local restaurants and specialties she wanted us to experience. Her "Foods on the Must Try List" included: a "Meat and 3" lunch or dinner, chess pie, banana pudding, sorghum with corn cakes, country ham, biscuits, fried chicken, and grits. I vowed to help her in this quest.

My friends at BGS had advised me about this aspect of a genealogical road trip: keeping your genealogically dispassionate companions happy while you pursue the family history trail. Cari, one of the younger BGS members, told me about the many times she'd dragged her toddlers along to cemeteries, enlisting them as helpers by asking them to find every gravestone with the letter *M*. This bought her a little bit of time. One day, as Cari, her mother, and her kids drove by a business with a large carved limestone sign, her son called out from the backseat: "Stop! Grandma, is that a tombstone? My mom stops at anything that looks like a tombstone!" Cari laughed. "That's when I thought, 'Maybe we've been doing too much of this cemetery stuff.'" But she's still doing it.

"Mooner and Buzzy! Mooner and Buzzy!" We heard the shrieking before the door opened. This was the place: Tim and Julie's place. Curly-headed Ava (aged five) threw open the door and then stepped back with a shy smile. Her little brother Caz (aged three) hid behind her. Julie walked up holding six-month-old baby Bennett on her hip. "They are so excited you guys are finally here," she said as Ava pulled us out to the backyard to show off her cartwheels. Mooner followed but I stood back, watching the kids—especially Caz. He was beautiful. Just about the same size as my son, Jackson, with the same blond hair and blue eyes. You'd never know he'd been so sick. I looked at Julie, who knew what I was thinking.

"Amazing, isn't it?" she said.

"Amazing."

In fact, Tim and Julie were the amazing ones. As we spent the next few hours in their beautiful house, I began to see little hints of the odyssey their family had been on. The upstairs playroom was covered in a festive barnyard mural: a surprise gift from a foundation for sick children and their families. Next to the couch, some kind of feeding-tube contraption stood—this had been Caz's primary source of nutrition for the past three years, through a tube attached to his belly. He was just beginning to eat solid foods like other three-year-olds.

Julie, with her cute flip hairdo and huge smile, managed to be upbeat and energetic despite the many, many demands on her time and attention. She had a sense of the absurdity of it all—the trials of Caz's illness, but also the everyday demands of parenting and trying to stay connected to her own interests—singing in choir, teaching piano, and trying to have a life beyond the toddler set. I admired her, though she didn't want to be admired—she just wanted a few more hours of child care every now and then. "I really never imagined I'd have three kids . . ." she said at one point as we stared at them whirling around the backyard. She looked and me and laughed: "I swear to you, I didn't!" I asked if it was hard having a new baby amid all the ongoing challenges facing Caz.

"It's been a gift, actually," Tim said in a quiet voice. "That's why we named him Bennett: it means blessing. He's just a joy, and he's healthy, and he reminds us of everything that's blessed about being here right now. He brings us out of our sadness, when we're in it. The kids just love him, too."

Sweet Tim. I hadn't seen him in over a decade. I suddenly saw his father's face in his in a way I'd never noticed before. Was it just my genealogical obsession or a function of aging? Probably both.

Tim took us out that night to some of Nashville's famous honky-tonks. The first two were a disappointment: bad cover songs (no one comes to Nashville to hear "Don't Stop Believin'") and a fratty crowd, but the third was fantastic. Robert's Western World, just across the back alley from the hallowed Ryman Auditorium (home of the *old* Grand Ole Opry), functions as a western-wear store by day (cowboy boots line the walls) and as the home of classic country-and-western music by night. The godheads of Robert's were easy to peg: Hank Williams and Johnny Cash. Their influences were everywhere, from the songs played by the supertight band to the dress style of the patrons: lots of plaid shirts buttoned up to the neck (Hank) and all-black ensembles (Cash). Robert's also seemed to nurture a younger rockabilly crowd; the place was full of men in their twenties who looked like a cross between Buddy Holly and Morrissey of the Smiths. Mooner and I loved it.

So, we drank a few beers. We were seriously bonding with our cousin Tim. We asked him how things were going. "It's hard," he said, shaking his head. "It's getting better—Caz is getting better—but it's still a mess." He and Julie had fought with their insurance company over Caz's expensive and lifesaving treatments for almost Caz's entire lifetime. Now they were dealing with the local school district to get a few accommodations for Caz's needs once he started kindergarten (because of his susceptibility to germs, even post-bone-marrow transplant, every surface of Caz's classroom must be wiped down with sterile solution before he can attend—this is something Julie would probably end up doing before class every day). "We're a mess," he said, half laughing and half crying. But they were holding it all together beautifully, Mooner and I said. "We hold it together," Tim agreed. "We hold it together. But it's hard."

Did I mention we were standing in a parking garage? By now it was two o'clock in the morning. We were supposed to be saying good-bye, but we didn't seem to be able to do it. Instead we cried, talked, hugged, talked some more. We were three true cousins locked in a bond.

Forget, hell

Nashville was such a nice way to start our southern sojourn. Friendly, pretty, great food, great music. Staying with Carol and Howard had been a good choice: while they were family to me (through marriage), they weren't implicated in the whole southern roots thing (they were from Philadelphia) and their gracious home was thus neutral ground. A good launching pad. Staying with Carol and Howard and enjoying the cultivated pleasures of Tennessee's capital, Mooner and I started to believe that we'd been misled about the South. What was so different about it, anyway? we remarked as we drove past its independent bookstores, nature preserves, and Al Gore's aforementioned solar panels. We were so innocent then.

As we approached the border of Alabama and Tennessee two huge billboards confronted us, daring us to make a choice. On the west side of the highway we read this charmingly open-ended question:

WHERE WILL YOU SPEND ETERNITY?

And on the east side, this:

BOOBIE BUNGALOW—
ADULT DANCING EMPORIUM—NEXT EXIT.

"I'm guessing Boobie Bungalow is not one of our eternal options," Mooner remarked. "Or is it?" On we drove. We got about twelve miles into Alabama before we began to see the Confederate memorabilia.

"Look at that," Mooner said, pointing to the bumper of a

passing sedan. "Is that a Confederate flag?" It was. And then they were everywhere: on billboards, on car-radio antennae, on clothing. We'd seen a few items of Dixie kitsch in Nashville, but there it seemed to be offered up to tourists almost as a curiosity: *Well, you came to the South to see it, so here it is.* Here in Alabama, it felt much more real. My associations with the Confederate flag were unambiguous: secession; the Klan; race-baiting. All solidly located in the "bad" category. It was a shock to see this symbol everywhere.

We stopped for gas at a nameless pit stop and parked next to a pickup truck featuring at least a dozen versions of the flag. One in particular caught my eye. It was a bumper sticker featuring a caricature of an old hillbilly—ripped overalls, crumpled hat, chewing on a piece of straw—with the phrase FORGET, HELL!

"What's that supposed to mean?" Mooner asked.

"I guess he doesn't want to forget . . . the Civil War?" I answered. Mooner shook her head. We both knew that wasn't the real story, but the whole thing depressed me and I just wanted to move on. Alabama's license plates themselves featured an homage to Lynyrd Skynyrd, with the phrase SWEET HOME gracing the top of each one. It was an improvement on the state motto that used to adorn its plates: ALABAMA: HEART OF DIXIE. Which is functionally equivalent to FORGET, HELL! if you stop and think about it. I've never understood how celebrating the South's secession could coexist with such supposedly patriotic fervor, and I suppose I never will.

There was no respite from the sentiment, however, as we were venturing deeper into Dixie by the mile. Now, lots of African-Americans live in Alabama; they make up over a quarter of the state's population. They, too, drive by the Confederate gewgaws and I wondered: What do they think when they see the "Forget, Hell!" bumper sticker? Or the "We Don't Call Them Yankees, We Call Them TARGETS" mottoes? It was hard to tell. This Confederate miasma simply floated in the air everywhere we drove, and I suppose those who didn't appreciate it did the same thing we did; averting their eyes, swatting it away like the smoke from a cheap cigarette or one of the ever-present mosquitoes. You could ignore it, but that didn't make it go away.

I asked my friend Allan about it, thinking that as an outsider I might be misinterpreting the symbol or missing some of its context. "Are there any southerners who offer any defense of the flag apart from 'states' rights' issues?"

"In a way, these days, the Reb flag stuff is more like sports branding paraphernalia than it is some true symbol of a fallen nation," he responded. "That state existed only in relation to its declaration of war. So there was nowhere left to go—once the cause was lost. 'Not Hate, Heritage' is one bumper sticker [you see in the South]. That is like the great-grandkids of the SS wearing the S-shaped lightning bolts on their collars."

It didn't sound like I was missing anything. This was our homeland, Reb flag and all.

We practiced our powers of Confederate kitsch avoidance on down the highway and eventually stopped in Birmingham at another of Mooner's food finds: Niki's West Steak and Seafood, which served neither. It was definitely a locals' spot, way off the highway, wedged next to a produce depot near a block of truck stops. Niki's offered approximately seven hundred options in its lunch buffet and we were able to knock at least four items off our must-try list. The food was incredible. But the jig was soon up. Our waitress stopped by with her pitchers of sweet and unsweet tea and asked us point-blank: "So, where y'all from?"

"What gave it away?" I asked.

"Y'all are takin' pictures of the food," she said, nodding at my camera. It didn't faze her. Niki's might not be on the general tourist route, but it had already been discovered by the foodies and their blogs. We were just part of that subculture, the People Who Take Pictures of Their Food.

Real live Jacksons

We made it through Alabama and into Mississippi early that evening, arriving at Jannelle and George's house in Hattiesburg around
eight o'clock. I had never met Jannelle, never even seen her photo
until a few weeks earlier, when she mailed it to me. She was about
my dad's age. He had never met her, either. But my aunt Nancy,
Tim's mom, had, and she assured me that Jannelle would welcome
us with the proverbial open arms. And so she did.

We had barely made it out of the carport before the first course
arrived: chicken-noodle casserole, followed by butter beans, dinner
rolls, green salad, and lots of that good southern iced tea to wash it
down. So much food was placed before us, it was difficult to speak.
That was okay; Jannelle was great at speaking. By the time we got
to the two dessert options, pecan pie and Italian cream cake ("I can't
believe y'all never tried Italian cream cake!" Jannelle exclaimed),
we'd already heard the story of how Jannelle and George first met,
the story of how Jannelle's parents first met, and the story of how
both their daughters, Janet and Jackie, met their husbands.

Jannelle was a family historian's dream. With her, there was no
prompting, no wheedling or cajoling to winkle out a story. Jannelle
was a one-woman stream-of-consciousness epic audiobook of family
lore. As Mooner and I pushed our chairs back from the table to accommodate our expanding waistlines, Jannelle urged us to repair to
"where it's soothing and pretty," so we moved into the formal dining
room. There followed another hour of the Jackson family epic.

As the exhaustion of the day's drive and the evening's food
coma settled over us, Mooner and I felt ourselves slip into a disori-
ented state of consciousness. Jannelle's conversational turns veered
from tales of her father's jewelry store to direct questions about our
relationship with Jesus (neither Mooner nor I had one). Slowly, the
two cultural bubbles in the room—mine and Mooner's, floating in
from the West, and Jannelle and George's, surfacing right here in

Mississippi—were bumping up against each other. Something had to pop.

George, who'd been almost silent until now, though friendly, took the opportunity to present us with some pages he'd printed off the Internet. One featured a national map divided by color (red and blue) according to which counties had voted for McCain and which for Obama.

"You see, McCain got a lot more counties than Obama. So how'd he 'win'?" George asked me—rhetorically, I assumed.

"Well, as I understand it, the issue's not counties, it's votes. And there aren't many people in most of those rural counties." George just shook his head.

"He wasn't even born in this country," George said, looking back at me. "You know that, right?"

"Who wasn't?" I asked, though I unfortunately knew what he would say.

"Barack Obama," George said with a nod. "He wasn't even born here."

I sighed. Audibly. We really were going down this path. "Actually, George, he was born here. Though I believe even the Republican Party acknowledges that John McCain was born in Panama."

"On a military base!" George replied. I nodded.

"I'm just saying—" I started, and then was cut off.

"I hope you didn't vote for him," George said with a smile. He must have known.

"Barack Obama?" I asked. "Not only did I vote for him, I campaigned for him. I'm a big, big supporter." I could feel my eyes widening and my throat going dry, fight-or-flight style. I really hadn't wanted things to go this way—certainly not on our first night. But I wasn't going to pretend to be someone I wasn't, either. I looked across the table at Mooner. She offered a smile.

Were we back in Facebook territory? George had welcomed me into his home, so I played along politely. I'd already resolved not to discuss politics or religion with any of my relatives—I didn't really see the point—yet here we were, not two hours into our visit, and already up to our voter registration cards in it.

George next showed me an e-mail he'd received that warned all American citizens about the need to arm themselves in the face of an encroaching antigun Obama administration. Then he asked me to confirm that I was from California. I did. "Well, as far as I'm concerned," George said, "California can just break off the continent and float away into the sea. And we've gotta do something about that Ninth Circuit Court."

I was baffled. How had we gotten to the Ninth Circuit Court so fast? And why?

"Well, George, I may not live in California anymore," I said, "but my mother and my brother still do—"

"Like I said"—George cut me off in his polite, friendly tone— "the whole thing could just float away and that would be fine with me."

It was so interesting. I felt as if I were sitting in the midst of two massive clichés: that famous southern hospitality, with all its good food, good humor, and good manners; and the southern hostility to northerners ("We Don't Call Them Yankees, We Call Them Targets!"). It was all right here in the formal dining room. And in the guest bedroom, where Mooner noticed the family photo I'd mailed to Jannelle—my husband, son, and me—propped up right next to a framed portrait of George, Laura, Jenna, and Barbara Bush. We were all together now and we were going to have to figure it out.

And yet. Almost as soon as he'd started, George stopped. He put all the handouts away and offered to show us our rooms. Then he offered to drive me to the drugstore to pick up a few supplies I needed. So I went. And we had a lovely conversation there and back. George was tickled by my interest in the local candy bars, an interest stoked by my experience with the GooGoo Cluster and Nashville's other native chocolate treat: Colts Bolts (a hockey-puck-shaped disk of chocolate + peanut butter + almonds). He was determined to find me his favorite candy bar, the Heavenly Hash. Chocolate: bringing politically polarized families together.

Having staked out our positions, we were now free to simply enjoy each other's company. The next thirty-six hours were filled with warm family togetherness for all of us. We met Jackie, Jannelle and George's daughter. "Has she been telling you stories?" Jackie asked, looking over at her mother. We nodded. "She knows a lot of 'em," Jackie said.

She surely did. Just as my BGS mentors advised, I spent hours with Jannelle in her parlor, going through photo albums (I made copies and took photographs of them, natch), recording her memories on a digital recorder, and making notes as we went along.

I did encounter a situation no genealogist had warned me about, though: the proprietary nature of some family memories. Jannelle greatly admired her parents, both as individuals and as a sort of ideal of marriage.

"Everybody thinks their parents were the best, but I'll tell you this: mine really were." After telling me another glowing story of their relationship, she stopped herself and looked at my recorder.

"Now, are you going to write all this down eventually?" she asked.

"Maybe not all of it," I said.

"Well, I just want to say something about that. My momma and daddy's marriage was so beautiful. The story of their love for each other would make a wonderful book, that's what I've often thought."

I nodded.

"And I've often thought of writing that book myself. So I need to ask you not to put in the stories of their love affair into your book, because I want to save them for mine."

I was surprised, but when I thought about Jannelle's propensity for storytelling, it started to make sense. "Sure, of course," I told her. "I won't steal them."

"Okay, good," Jannelle said, smiling. "I already have a title for the book, too: *Jewels of Love*. Don't you think that's just perfect?"

I did.

The home place

I'd asked Jannelle for clues about how to find the old Jackson homestead in Emelle, Alabama. She'd been there many times, earlier in her life; her father, John R, had grown up there with my grandfather, Jabe. She referred to it as "the home place." Although she could picture it in her imagination, it had been so long since she visited that she couldn't exactly give me directions.

"There's a lot of acreage," she said. "And a pond. Just ask around Emelle for Isie Joyner's place."

Isie, aka Isaphena Jackson Joyner, had been my great-aunt, sister of my grandfather. I'd never met her. According to my dad, her brothers gave her their share of the house and property after their parents' death as a dowry present. She lived there until her death in 1986. None of her children lived in the state anymore, nor had I ever met them. The Jacksons, as far as I knew, had abandoned Emelle completely. But if we wanted clues about their lives and how they'd gotten there in first place, we'd still have to visit Emelle to find out.

I was sad to say good-bye to Jannelle and George. But once we on our way back to Alabama, we felt energized: this was where the real genealogy was going to happen.

We crossed the state line and began looking for the smaller roads that would lead us to Emelle. The landscape was gentle, green, and agricultural. We passed very few people, buildings, or even cars. When we saw the "Waste Management" sign, perched on a grassy hill above what must have been the giant toxic waste dump, I knew we had to be close.

Generally speaking, it's a very bad sign when, in the course of researching your ancestral homeland, you keep running across a history of the place written by Greenpeace. In this case, "The Greenpeace History of Emelle," in *Waste Management Inc.: An Encyclopedia of Environmental Crimes & Other Misdeeds, A Greenpeace Report* by Charlie Cray. A very bad sign. I'd read a bit about the history of the landfill and the town. Of the thirty-one souls left in Emelle, twenty-nine were African-American. More than 60 percent lived below the poverty line. One hundred percent of the children lived in poverty.

The satellite view of Emelle on Google Maps hadn't revealed much about the place when I'd inspected it on my computer screen. Now I was driving ten miles an hour along the very same stretch of road and finding that this wasn't much more edifying, itself. We'd seen a sign announcing the existence of Emelle but where was it?

Mooner needed to find a ladies' room but there was nowhere to go. It seemed inauspicious to begin our visit to Sumter County with an alfresco pit stop, but we saw no good alternatives.

"Just . . . hold on," I said. "We'll find something. We have to . . . right?" Mooner shrugged and crossed her legs. No gas stations meant more than no restrooms: it also meant no gas. I checked our tank nervously.

We finally saw a scattering of run-down buildings on the small road parallel to Alabama State Highway 17, so we pulled in. The road was called Martin Luther King Boulevard—another sign of the change in these parts over the past century. The first building looked like a variation of every photo I'd ever seen of a southern grocery store: a single-story cinder-block structure with a shaded porch and screened windows. The windows were barred. This establishment was closed, and it appeared to have been that way for a long time. The sign said STEGALL GENERAL STORE. Stegall—I recognized the name. I'd seen it in my family research: Joseph Stegall was the author of several books on the genealogy of Sumter County. I'd actually e-mailed him with a question, but never heard back. This was his family's store. It looked as if it had been out of operation for a decade, at least.

The only building that appeared to host live human interaction was a small brick structure, the Emelle Post Office. I was surprised Emelle could still support it. We pulled in, if only in the hope of finding a bathroom.

I tapped on the service bell and a tall African-American man walked out of the back office. This was William Dunsmore.

"Hello," I said. "We're not from here—" That much was obvious. He laughed.

"Are you from here?" I asked. He shook his head.

"I'm from Chicago," he said.

Bad luck. I really needed to find a local, someone who might know something about our family, who might remember the Old Jackson Place. This was not the right guy.

"I see," I said. "We're here trying to find some information about our family, the Jacksons, who used to live in Emelle."

"The Jacksons, you say?" Dunsmore looked interested. "They lived around here?"

"Yes, supposedly. We're just trying to find their old house—"

"What were their first names?" he asked.

"Isa Jackson Joyner was the one who lived here most recently," I offered.

"Isie Joyner?" he repeated, smiling. "You're looking for the Joyner place, then?"

"You know it?" I asked.

"Sure," he said. "I lived in Chicago for thirty years, but I was born here in Emelle. Just moved back a couple years ago. I remember Isie and Melvin Joyner. Lived right down the road," he said, pointing south.

So he *was* from Emelle. I was confused. But mostly I was happy to hear he knew something about the house. He drew us a little map and we saw that we were only a few blocks from the house. He even gave us the names of the current occupants and encouraged us to stop and say hello. We thanked him up until the point when we felt we might be embarrassing him, and then we headed off down Highway 17.

Two minutes later we were there. A long dirt driveway led to a one-story brick ranch house—not the original home, obviously, but there was the pond Jannelle had mentioned, as well as a lot of undeveloped acreage. According to my dad, there used to be a dairy farm here. No sign of a barn or cows now.

One day on the phone I asked my dad to tell me what he knew about the place. He'd heard descriptions of it from his father, of course; they mainly followed the script Jannelle knew: a pond, a few acres of land, and not much else. Except the story of the ghost train and the tale of Bullwhip Jackson.

The first was a story about my great-great-grandfather John R. Jackson (1831–1924), who'd served as some kind of local official in Sumter County. There had been an election, and John R. Jackson was responsible for keeping the ballots safe overnight. He was riding through the woods on a lonely road toward home when his horse balked and wouldn't go any farther.

He got off the horse and tried to lead it, but just as he did he heard a tiny tinkling sound coming from the surrounding darkness. Suddenly a tiny railroad train emerged out of the woods, rumbled across the path in front of him and the horse, trundled across the road, and disappeared into the trees on the other side.

John could see tiny people inside, all lit up in the dining car, drinking from tiny glasses and talking in tiny voices, unaware of his presence. Stunned, he walked out of the woods and suddenly saw his neighbor there in his nightshirt, walking along the road. This was strange, too. It was the middle of the night, after all. John called to his neighbor, who began to run. John followed him across the road and through a field. His neighbor kept running until he came to a tree, which he climbed. John ran to the tree but the neighbor had disappeared.

First the train, then the neighbor: John was dumbfounded. He went home and told his wife, Rebecca, what he'd seen. The next day they learned that the neighbor died that night—at home, well before John "saw" him. None of it made sense. What about that train?

"This story grabs your imagination," my dad said, "but it doesn't really have any point. And the neighbor dying—that just seems added on." I suppose. My dad is a novelist and a serious skeptic, so his interest in stories such as this are mostly focused on aesthetics. He'd once told this ghost story to his friend the writer Raymond Carver. "Carver was impressed by the modernism of these stories," my dad said, "because they made no sense. The main concern was to convince the listener with the notion that they were true, and who knows or cares what it means?" Sort of like Carver's own stories, I thought. One other aspect interested my dad: the fact that these stories had no overt religious significance, "which was unusual for these people," he said. The only point seemed to be to persuade the listener that ghosts were real.

The other tale was that of Bullwhip Jackson. This one concerned my great-grandfather William Daniel Jackson (1856–1924) and how he got his nickname: Bullwhip, or just "Bull" Jackson (nicknames really do run in the family). Thanks to his work as a teamster, he was adept with a whip. According to the story, there was a haunted house in the area and a standing dare that went with it: anyone who could survive an entire night there alone would earn a dollar. Bull Jackson stuck it out. When his friends came by in the morning to check on him, he invited them in to see for themselves. Inside the otherwise empty house, the floors were strewn with the bodies of dead bats, which he'd spent all night killing with his whip. Or so the story goes.

The ghost train, the bullwhip, the bats. My grandfather's visitation from Jesus as his father lay dying or dead. These were the stories illustrating this unseen place. And now it was early afternoon and sunny, just a beautiful March day, about seventy-five degrees and low humidity. Not a ghost in sight. Just a one-story ranch house with a long dirt driveway.

We drove toward the house and three scruffy, barking dogs greeted us. No cars were in the drive. We parked and just looked. The dogs kept barking. They didn't seem friendly. Apart from the barking, it was quiet. We took photos. I pulled out my audio recorder and made a tape of the ambient noise: barking, birds, and the very occasional passing car. This was it: the home place.

Ghost stories notwithstanding, neither Mooner nor I had expected to see much, so it wasn't an anticlimax. We were just happy to have found the right spot. And we were moved in some subtle way. As we drove off, we noticed the sweet-smelling wisteria and the vines creeping over every telephone pole and fence post. It was a pretty place. Nothing about it seemed haunted, which might be another way of saying that we barely felt attached to the place at all.

The bees were a-humming

One town in Sumter County was still prospering: Livingston, Alabama, home of the University of Western Alabama, pop. 3,000. I'd planned pretty seriously for this part of the visit. Livingston is the county seat and the home to its archives. The official documents—wills, land records, and the like—were held in the county courthouse. I'd called ahead and spoken with a clerk there about the hours, the cost of copies, and all the other logistics.

I'd also come across a potential treasure: UWA's Alabama Room and Special Collections in the Julia Tutwiler Library. Its Web site seemed designed to make a family historian salivate: right there on the home page it offered a special subcategory for genealogy. As I scanned through the Alabama Room's holdings it became clear that I'd found a gold mine: local histories, collections of letters, photographs, and much more. I resolved to prioritize the library over the county courthouse if I had to, simply because most of the materials from UWA could only be viewed on-site, whereas documents from the county courthouse could be sent by mail if I needed them.

"I spoke to a librarian here," I told Mooner as we drove through Livingston toward the university the morning after visiting Old Side Cemetery. "She's expecting us and she said we don't need a parking permit—we'll just have to find a place wherever we can." We pulled into the parking lot and there was an open spot, right in front of the library's front steps. I'd obviously spent too much time at huge, urban universities where parking spots are only available to star athletes, school trustees, and academic superstars (UC Berkeley has a special parking area reserved solely for Nobel laureates). City mouse, meet your country kin.

We were met by Christin Loehr, who will one day be honored in the Librarian Hall of Fame under the "Most Friendly and Helpful" banner. A slender blond woman in a long dress, Christin was quite familiar with genealogical inquiries. "We get a lot of folks coming in here looking up their family history," she said.

After we provided Christin with some names, dates, and locations of interest to us, she left the room and returned wheeling a double-decker cart filled with books, folders, and boxes of materials that might be of help.

What followed was the most efficient library research, ever. As a graduate student, I'd often fantasized about the luxury of hiring a research assistant. How many days had I descended into the basement stacks of UC Berkeley's Doe Library and emerged with more books than I could reasonably carry home or read in a timely manner? Too many. But this day was different: I had Mooner.

I did a quick once-over of all the materials, prioritizing anything featuring a Jackson or a location that looked promising. Triage completed, I gave Mooner a list of names, dates, and concepts to look for, then pushed a stack of archival materials her way. We didn't waste much time with careful reading or time at the photocopier;

anything of interest got photographed on my digital camera, from which I could later post images to my computer, to the Web, enlarge and refine the picture, and print or scan copies. We were a two-woman data-processing machine, Mooner and I.

"This is fun," Mooner said. She'd been dreading the research. "I love the Scooby-Doo of it all." And it *was* fun, combing through old books and papers for recognizable names. Suddenly Mooner let out a shout.

"Oh. My. God. Check this out!" She handed me a local history, *Pioneer Families of Sumter County, Alabama,* by Nelle Morris Jenkins. Right at the bottom of page 128, our great-aunt Isaphena Jackson's name popped off the page, telling Jenkins the story of her grandfather, John R. Jackson—the same John R who'd seen the tiny ghost train.

Isaphena, who would have been about sixty-two years old when Jenkins's book was published, told a story about how John, a Confederate soldier home on furlough, had escaped roving Union soldiers. "He knew if they found him they would take him prisoner," she told Jenkins, who wrote, "he ran around the house looking for a place to hide. The most likely place was the bee hives which were alive with bees. He scraped the bees out of one of them and into the hive he crawled." Said Isaphena, "The bees were a-humming and Yanks were a-coming but they could not find Grandpap."[3]

Gold. Mine. This is exactly the kind of thing you hope to find in a local history archive, but rarely do: a funny, first-person family story told by your own great-aunt Isa. From a purely genealogical perspective, it also provided helpful information, confirming, for instance, John R. Jackson's service in the Civil War (with this tidbit, I could now search military records for muster rolls, pension records, and more).

We were running out of time. As the light of the spring afternoon waned, Mooner and I faced a choice: we could go to the county courthouse or find the Sumterville Methodist Cemetery, but not both.

Logistical concerns and the Scooby-Doo of it all won the day.

Thanks to our day in the library, we knew that an index to the county archives existed. While it's always better to look through the materials for oneself, an index by a reliable researcher (in this case, our old friend Joseph Stegall, of Emelle's Stegall General Store) is the next-best option.

The Sumterville Methodist Cemetery, on the other hand . . . seeing that with our own eyes was an experience not to be replicated by mail or the Internet. No Graveyard Rabbit had yet documented the cemetery, as far as I could tell, so there were no online records of who was actually buried there. We'd have to see for ourselves . . . if we could even find it.

We thanked Christin for all her help. Although Mooner was ready to leave, I felt the pang that every researcher feels upon leaving a far-flung archive. There's always more research one could have done, and a few more files one would have liked to examine. But it was time to go. Headstones beckoned.

The inevitable "No Trespassing" sign

What do you do if the only roadside sign is a "No Trespassing" sign? You stop and check it out—at least, that's what we did. Mooner and I had been cruising the back roads (not that there were any front roads) of Sumter County for forty-five minutes, studying the extremely unhelpful Google Map I'd printed out and trying to figure out where the Sumterville Methodist Cemetery could be.

I knew Mooner would be a great traveling companion and, indeed, she'd proven that already, but in addition to her good manners, charming hostess gifts, and sparkling conversation, she'd also brought her Google Phone along for the ride. This was invaluable. As we cruised the southern byways she provided directions, and pointed us toward good restaurants, questionable flea markets, and places to avoid.

"It should be right around here," she said, staring at the tiny map on her phone as we slowed our rental car to a walking pace along a featureless rural road. That's when we saw the "No Trespassing" sign. We pulled over, got out, and pondered our options. I'd read online that the cemetery we were looking for was in bad shape. I pictured a moldering, overgrown graveyard straight out of a Halloween diorama, so I didn't expect to find a shiny sign showing us how to get there. This "No Trespassing" sign might be it.

What was once a road stretched beyond a cattle fence where the "No Trespassing" sign was posted. We could just barely make out the twin runnels of tire marks from some car or truck now long gone, passing over the hill.

"Well?" I asked.

Mooner shrugged. "Let's do it."

I grabbed my camera, purse, and notebook from the car, locked it, and then we climbed the fence. We walked to the top of the hill and saw before us . . . not much. More hills. A few clusters of trees. We stopped to listen, but heard nothing, just birdsong and a distant generator.

"Maybe we're standing on the Waste Management landfill," I ventured.

"Maybe."

"Maybe they dug up the cemetery," I said.

"Maybe."

We walked around for about fifteen more minutes, exploring the trees and hidden vistas of the place, but saw no trace of a cemetery or anything else. We tromped back to the gate and clambered back over. "Well?" Mooner asked.

"I don't know," I said. "This map is so bad. And the cemetery might not even exist anymore." It was about four-thirty and the slanting sunlight only enhanced my feeling that the window of opportunity was closing, fast.

We got back into the car and drove down the road about half a mile when we saw a house with—gasp—actual people present in the driveway. They were the first people we'd seen since leaving Livingston. "I'm pulling in," I told Mooner.

The two men in the driveway regarded us with friendly curiosity. Two African-American men in their thirties, standing by their trucks, just chatting. Both wore baseball caps, T-shirts, and jeans.

After a few minutes of passing the tattered Google map back and forth, they showed us the way back. We followed one of them men in his truck, past the "No Trespassing" sign and straight through the tiny, almost totally abandoned Sumterville, where I never would have thought to look. We drove through the little ghost town, passing its defunct post office (a sign on the empty wooden building read 1935–1968), and then started down a dirt road shrouded in a canopy of tall trees and hanging wisteria—a road I never would have considered otherwise. After fifty feet, the road turned to mud and I steered us to the shoulder so we wouldn't get stuck. We kept going. The truck finally stopped about a half mile down the road, but I couldn't fathom why, exactly. I certainly didn't see any graveyard. "Keep your wits about you," my mother always told me when I'd go out in the evenings in high school. I tried to do that now.

The driver of the truck got out and smiled, pointing up a small hill to our right. There was, in fact, what looked like an old path leading up the hill toward a thicket.

"That's it," he said. "I don't know if it's what you're looking for, but this is the place where they say there used to be one. I've never been up there, myself." He and his friend shrugged, smiling, just looking at us. Mooner was wearing a nice summer dress and Mary Janes; I was in white jeans and white sneakers, standing in the mud. I think they may have believed we (okay, maybe just me) were insane. I felt a little insane.

"Great!" I said, perky as a six-year-old who's just been deposited at the front of the line at the Teacup Ride on her first trip to Disneyland. "Thank you so much!"

"You're welcome," the driver said. He gave us one last look. "Y'all be careful out here, now. Don't get stuck in this mud."

"We'll be careful!" I assured him. They maneuvered their truck around and waved good-bye, leaving us standing at the foot of the hill, alone.

"Well?" Mooner asked. "Should we try it?"

"Let's go," I said. We began to climb.

After a couple minutes we saw it: another "No Trespassing" sign. By now I was starting to associate these signs with progress, if for no other reason than they indicated the presence of human beings at some point in the recent past. We kept clambering and then, suddenly, we saw something else.

On the crest of the hill, intermingled with the trees, we saw the looming, tilting forms of a half-dozen headstones. We walked closer. A rusting line of barbed-wire fencing halfheartedly threatened interlopers; we stepped over it and walked on.

We'd found it. No sign remained to name the place, but we knew where we were. The ground beneath our feet sank into a litter of decaying organic matter with every step. Trees, big and small, grew everywhere, as did thorny brambles and wildflowers.

"Let's split up," Mooner said, now a veritable Graveyard Rabbit herself, and we headed in different directions. I walked toward a small square in the center of the cemetery where an iron gate still stood guard around a family plot. An oxidized lock in the shape of a heart held the gate fast. I peered over it and saw a dozen headstones, large and small. It appeared as though no one had visited this place in decades. Suddenly Mooner called out.

"Jacksons here!"

I looked back and saw her peering at a group of stones clustered in the southeast corner of the cemetery and walked back to see for myself.

She was right. Seven Jackson tombstones sat there, and thanks to Judy Bennett, I recognized all the names: Jacinth; Prudence; J.T.;

Sarah; James; Elizabeth; and, the jewel in this genealogical crown: Randle Jackson: BORN IN BRUNSWICK, CO., VIRGINIA/OCT 17, 1763/ AND DEPARTED THIS LIFE MAY 17, 1839 AGED 75 YEARS AND 9 MONTHS.

This was it: the missing link between the seventeenth-century Jacksons of Virginia (Randle's established ancestors) and the Jacksons of Alabama. His wife Elizabeth's headstone provided even more unexpected information: B. SOUTH CAROLINA/MOVED TO GEORGIA AT AN EARLY AGE AND REMOVED TO ALABAMA IN 1818. SHE DIED JUNE 1854, 78 YEARS OLD. Well. It's not every day you find the migration history of an ancestor written on her headstone. You're lucky if you get clear birth and death dates, really. This was something else.

Thanks to Judy, I knew that several of the Jackson brothers in Randle's generation had moved to Georgia from Virginia. Many of them stayed there, but it seemed likely that Randle had met Elizabeth in Georgia, married her, and then moved to Alabama with his wife and family in tow. In 1818! This part of the world was still part of the Choctaw Nation then, and would remain so until 1830 and the Treaty of Dancing Rabbit Creek, one of the first and biggest land transfers under the United States' newly established Indian Removal Act. I didn't know much about what life for the newly arrived Jacksons would have been like in 1818 (one guess: tough), but it had now become a new area of inquiry to pursue.

This, in fact, is what genealogists most hope to find. Answers, yes. Facts, yes. But ultimately they're looking for new leads, because the research never ends. Standing among my ancestors' headstones in the Sumterville Methodist Cemetery that day with my cousin Mooner, I felt that elusive thrill of accomplishment, of finding exactly what I'd hoped to—and more.

We were thrilled. We took photos, took notes, and used sticks, leaves, and the soles of our shoes to scrape away the mud and mold that covered some of our family's headstones. It was so quiet there. Somewhere over the hill we thought we heard the sound of mooing cows. Other than that, it was just the breeze in the trees. It was a lovely place. The most recent headstone I saw was dated 1920.

"Time for a short-order prayer," Mooner announced. I laughed. This was a Jannelle thing. As soon as we'd arrived at her home in Hattiesburg, she'd gathered us together in the carport with George in a football huddle. With our arms on each other's shoulders and heads bowed, she told us she wanted to do a "short-order prayer" before we went inside, and then said a quick thank-you to the Lord for delivering us safely to her home. Although Mooner and I were nonbelievers, it felt sweet and welcoming. Mooner and I appreciated the sentiment.

As we assumed the familiar huddle, we heard a rustling in the leaves. A black-and-tan puppy burst into the clearing, wagging its tail so hard its entire body shook. We stared at it, and then each other.

"Is this some kind of sign?" I asked Mooner.

"Maybe," she said. She had experience with this kind of thing.

"When I was eighteen, I visited my mother's grave just before I left for college," she said. "I went out to the tree on our property in Michigan where she was buried and I was choked up and teary. I'm not a religious person, so I didn't really know what to do. I wasn't going to pray. I stood in silence for a while and finally I just looked up and said, 'Well, Mom, I'm here. But I'm gonna be going soon.'

"Then I heard something." Mooner stopped. "This sounds like one of Jannelle's stories, doesn't it?" She laughed.

"Keep going," I said.

"Okay. I heard something, so I looked down. And there was a coyote about twenty yards away from me. And there it stood . . . with the head of a faun in its mouth. It just stopped there, looking at me with this severed head."

"A faun?" I asked. "As in, a baby deer?"

"Yep," Mooner said. "I mean, 'show me a sign,' right? Man. I felt my heart fall and I just started bawling and the coyote ran off. I was so tripped out by it. I didn't try to give it any significance for a while, but in retrospect I think maybe it was a sign of severed youth. The end of youth. I was going off to college, I was saying good-bye to my mother, and that was it."

"Wow," I said. "When you look for a sign, you probably expect a beautiful white dove alighting in the tree."

"Yeah," Mooner said. "Or maybe a double rainbow. But this was pretty much like: fend for yourself."

I knelt to pet the puppy, which suddenly seemed extremely benign, as far as graveside animal symbolism goes. "Maybe its tag will say Jackson," I speculated. No dice. It had, however, been recently vaccinated for rabies. Could that be construed as a sign?

Maybe not, but nevertheless the puppy lightened both our spirits. It's not that I was sad, exactly. But the thought occurred to me that I would probably never visit this place, and these ancestors, again. Honestly, when would I ever be back in this part of the world? None of my living relatives were anywhere near here; not anywhere in the state of Alabama, as far as I knew. I'd seen everything I'd come for: the old home place, the cemetery plots, the woods where the ghost train once ran. Would any of our descendants visit this spot? And if they did, would this cemetery remain? And even if it did, would our ancestors be as lucky to meet a friendly local to drive them down this old road? Maybe not.

So we stayed longer, even after we'd noted all the information from the headstones and taken multiple photographs of each one. I tried to appreciate the moment, to be here now, as it were, trespassing. Who are gravestones for? I wondered again. For the living, I suppose. Mooner and I had discussed this during our long car rides. She wondered if the new world of data made possible by the Internet and Web sites and all the rest would change the nature of family history.

"Do you think these new technologies will preserve ancestry longer by making it more accessible?" she mused.

"I don't know," I said. "But, ultimately, it doesn't matter if it's a tombstone or a Web site; the only thing that matters is whether any of your descendants are interested. That's what it always comes down to. Lots of genealogists have done amazing family trees that no one else in their family has ever asked to see. I think the most you can hope for is one person from every generation who's interested in it."

Well, we were there in the cemetery for a few more minutes, in the presence of our ancestors. J. T. Jackson, son of Jacinth and Prudence, WOUNDED AT RESACA, GA. ON THE 15TH OF MARCH 1861/ WHILE BRAVELY DISCHARGING HIS/DUTY AS A SOLDIER. AGED 25 YEARS 3 MO 2 DAYS. Two other children of Jacinth and Prudence died before their parents: Sarah E. Jackson, eighteen years old, and her brother James, twenty-eight. J.T.'s stone featured a biblical inscription from the story of Job that surely applied to all their children: MAN THAT IS BORN OF WOMAN IS OF FEW DAYS AND FULL OF TROUBLE. HE COMETH FORTH LIKE A FLOWER AND IS CUT DOWN.

"Ready for that short-order prayer now?" Mooner asked.

"We want to take a moment to reflect on the history of our kin here and acknowledge their presence and the hardships that they faced on the very land that we're standing on," Mooner said. "We want to acknowledge their final resting place, and the struggles they must have faced in that time; coming to this new land; the suffering they faced losing children to wars and disease. We acknowledge how grateful we are to have the opportunity to be here and be present in the moment and feel the dirt that they felt, smell the air they smelled."

"Should I say 'amen'?" she asked.

"I think it's okay as is," I said. The nameless puppy wagged its tail. We climbed back over the barbed wire, took one last look at the place, and then we left.

8

The Mountain and the Cloud; or, A Pilgrimage to Salt Lake City's Family History Library

I have always imagined that Paradise will be a kind of library.

—Jorge Luis Borges

Yo también, Jorge. I'm a total library geek. A book junkie. An archive addict. This explains seven mostly happy years in graduate school, I think. It also explains my admiration for genealogists: they're just grad students without the Pell Grant funding or a degree waiting for them at the end. Dedicated researchers doing it for the thrills, not the grades. Is it any wonder I wanted them as students whenever I taught a college course? There's no surer way to win a history professor's heart than by confessing a crush on interlibrary loan.

I was thus pretty hyped for my visit to the Family History Library, the Mecca of genealogical research. Now that I'd finally seen Alabama, the FHL was the last major stop on my stations of the genealogical cross. Religious metaphors kept popping up as I considered the FHL, and not just because it's funded and operated by the Church of Jesus Christ of Latter-Day Saints, also known as the Mormons or just the plain old LDS Church. Aside from Mecca (which every genealogist cites when talking about the FHL), my first thought upon approaching the venerated structure was Vatican City.

I've never been to Italy, so this is conjecture. But most of us know the basics: Vatican City is a sovereign city-state ruled by a theocracy. Salt Lake City may not technically be a theocracy but it only took a few hours of being there to realize I needed to stop asking, "Does the LDS Church own this park/building/bank/parking lot?" because the answer was always yes. Over half the population self-identifies as Mormon, as do a majority of Utah's legislators.

I'd heard about the LDS Church's proscription against caffeine and remembered it again as I stepped off the plane in Salt Lake City: Was I about to embark on yet another genealogically related voyage sans quality coffee? Memories of the cruise and its vats of beige Sanka sloshed over me (metaphorically speaking). I began to panic. In my experience, archival research depends upon large quantities of caffeine. It was a huge relief, then, when I discovered a Starbucks in the lobby of my hotel, along with a bar (alcohol is prohibited for Mormons and until recently one needed to join a private club in order to drink).

Obviously, a hotel is going to be a magnet for out-of-towners. Normally, being among one's own kind is a comforting feeling, but when the category is this broad—everyone who isn't a Mormon— the likelihood of bonding shrinks to a pinpoint. On my last morning in Salt Lake City, I encountered a woman from Florida in the hotel's Starbucks. Her eyes locked on me as soon as I walked in, and as I approached the pickup station she leaned toward me.

"Are you from here?" she asked in a stage whisper.

"Nope," I said.

"Are you a . . . Mormon?" she whispered. About halfway

through her four-word sentence, she tried to make herself sound friendly. It didn't work.

"Nope," I said. She relaxed.

"Well," she said, as if revealing a classified bit of intelligence, "there are a *lot* of Mormons here!"

I hated to give her an inch, but I had to admit she was right: there are a lot of Mormons in Salt Lake City! Who knew? Aside from everyone, I mean. So much for bonding with a fellow gentile. (Mormons refer to non-Mormons as Gentiles—but not the Jewish version of gentile, which means non-Jew. As a Jew, I guess this made me both a gentile and a nongentile.) Religion is funny.

Based on my conversations with official LDS Church public-affairs staff, the church seems to own most of the real estate in Salt Lake City, including the hotel I stayed in, the convention center across the street, and the mall under construction next door. Oh yeah, and that giant temple in the middle of town and all the park-land surrounding it. Like I said: Vatican City.

Why do you do it? And who pays for it?

And just like the Vatican, and Fatima, and Varanasi, the Family History Library (FHL to its fans) pulls pilgrims from all over the globe. I was there, sure. But every morning—every *single* morning, according to the FHL staff—a line of hopeful genealogists sets up camp in front of the FHL, forming an orderly line of middle-aged bodies stretching around the perimeter of the library from about six-thirty A.M. on, waiting for the doors to open. If you didn't know what you were seeing, you might think you stumbled across the ticketing line for an Andrea Bocelli concert. The folks in line are excited. Some of them plan their trips for years. I didn't see any fights breaking out but perhaps that's just because there's nothing to scalp at the FHL.

Admission is free at the largest genealogical library in the world. The FHL contains over two million rolls of microfilm; over 350,000 books; more than 4,500 periodicals; and it's staffed by seven hundred volunteers and about 150 paid employees.

"The questions we get most often are 'Why do you do it?' and 'Who pays for it?'" FHL staff member Laurie Hilliard told me. The second question is easier to answer: LDS Church members pay for it. All of it. Use of the library is free, as is the use of the 4,500 Family History Centers located around the world, each staffed by LDS volunteers ready to help you with your genealogical research. There's one about a half mile from my house and it's open almost every day of the week, with twenty new computers and ten microfilm readers ready to go. It's all funded by the tithing of LDS Church members, who are expected to give 10 percent of their income to the church for its various efforts. At the FHL, the only thing you'll pay for are photocopies, and even those are only five cents apiece.

I've met genealogists who explain their passion for family history by saying something along the lines of, "In our house, genealogy is a religion." In the LDS Church, that's a fact. That is to say, genealogy is essential to one of the holiest sacraments of their religion: the sealing ceremony, in which family relationships are united for eternity. LDS Church members are required to research their family history in order to provide the names and pertinent vital information for their ancestors so that their sealing ceremonies may be performed by proxy; that is, by the living on behalf of the dead. Because the LDS religion only emerged in 1830, a lot of pre-nineteenth-century folks missed out on the sealing ceremony, not to mention baptism in the faith. Thanks to the genealogical holdings of the FHL, they get a chance to participate anyway.

As impressive as the genealogical work of contemporary LDS Church members is (Brigham Young University offers degree programs in genealogy), the church believes that most of its genealogical work will be done in the future, after the Second Coming of

Christ, "during Christ's thousand-year reign here on earth prior to the end and the final judgment," as the FHL's chief genealogical officer, David Rencher, explained to me. "That, in fact, is the great work of the millennial period . . . the church (and therefore, we believe, Christ's) ultimate goal is to make the opportunity to be baptized and to have other temple ordinances performed available to all who have lived on the earth. We believe that we are acting under Christ's direction to begin the work now and that it will ultimately be completed under His direction and in accordance with His plan."[1]

As Rencher pointed out, current estimates of the total number of people who have ever lived on earth run from 106 to 125 billion people, so divine assistance plus a thousand years of workweeks will surely come in handy.

The LDS Church's decision to offer postmortem enrollment in its faith has not been welcomed by all. Although proselytizing is common to many religions, most of them focus on the living—people who can actively say yes or no when a missionary knocks on their door. Not the LDS.

Jewish groups, in particular, were outraged when they discovered that Mormon baptisms had been performed on behalf of thousands of Jewish Holocaust victims—people killed expressly because of their religious and ethnic identification as Jews. Jewish groups were also concerned that the addition of Jewish names to the LDS Church's International Genealogical Index (IGI), a list of several hundred million names of people who have been named in church baptism and sealing ceremonies, would confuse future generations by providing the false impression that these Jewish people were actually Mormon.

"We want to say this to all well-meaning Christians," wrote Bernard I. Kouchel, a prominent Jewish genealogist. "We don't want to be saved, redeemed, forgiven, reincarnated, resurrected, or enraptured. We just want to be left alone. After 2000 years—is it so much to ask? If everyone has free will, or 'free agency' as Mormons say it, why bother with baptizing the dead who chose not to accept Christ? It takes the spiritual hounding of Jews to new lows; not even the grave is a refuge from over-zealous missionaries!"[2]

The LDS Church took this issue seriously and in 1995 it agreed to remove the names of Jewish Holocaust victims in the IGI. But nine years later Jewish groups again called on the church to abide by its agreement after discovering that many new Jewish names had been added to the IGI in the intervening years. The onus is on Jewish groups—and any other group interested in stopping the practice—to find the names in the IGI and ask for their removal.

According to the LDS Church, its members are encouraged to submit only the names of people they know to be relations—thus the emphasis on doing genealogical research before performing temple ceremonies—but the church itself does not fact-check the submissions of its millions of worldwide members, nor, probably, could it. It's an ongoing public-relations nightmare for the church, though; when I was planning my trip to Salt Lake City, I was asked about the Jewish baptism issue by a few people—most of them assumed the stories of baptized Holocaust victims were urban legends, along with the stories they'd heard about the baptisms of Adolf Hitler, Joseph Goebbels, and Benito Mussolini. As far as I could ascertain, there was some truth to all of them, just as it was also true that the LDS Church did not approve.

The church gets it—they've apologized for the unauthorized baptisms multiple times. They removed the names and they've tried to prevent it from happening again. But it's probably going to happen again. I asked Ellen Shindelman Kowitt, president of the Jewish Genealogical Society of Colorado, about the issue. She told me that in the Jewish community opinions ranged from outrage to total disinterest, with folks like Bernard Kouchel representing the most vocal segment. There are lots of Jewish folks whose distaste for the baptismal practices are outweighed by the knowledge that these are the actions of individuals, not the church itself, and they're grateful to the church for providing such a wealth of genealogical information to the public. "They negate it," Kowitt said, referring to the fact of these unauthorized baptisms, "because they don't accept the reasons the church does it in the first place."

This was the FHL's chief genealogist David Rencher's assumption, too. The FHL is more than an archive; it's a central part of the church. As Rencher put it, "All roads lead to the temple in this church, where ordinances are performed on behalf of deceased individuals. Whether you believe that or not, the efficacy of that ordinance depends on your faith. For those who don't believe it, it basically doesn't matter. For those who do, then it matters. This is why we originally began trying to assist people in identifying family members."

The FHL so totally dominates the world of genealogical archives that some genealogists harbor a secret fear that the church might one day close its doors to nonmembers, as Ellen Shindelman Kowitt's remark suggested. I don't think they have much to worry about. That's because the scope of the church's genealogical goals require an open-source strategy; that is to say, compiling genealogical information on 106 to 125 billion people cannot be completed by Mormons alone.

"We invite the public because it's all based on shared ancestry," Rencher said. "We're trying to reduce the duplication of effort. We try to underwrite our side and to make those resources freely available, in the hopes that people will share their information . . . and then everybody wins." I'd encountered this "sharing" mentality before in my genealogical explorations, of course, but it hadn't occurred to me that the massive FHL would face the same issues I did. Yet all genealogists encounter the same challenges, whether they're fourth graders trying to complete their first family tree or professional researchers hoping to prove a connection to Charlemagne: it's just a matter of scale.

This was the first of several surprises I encountered at the FHL.

The place is more than a repository of information; it's an icon. And the fact was that I'd put off visiting the FHL as long as possible, simply because I felt I wasn't yet ready to go. Thanks to Judy Bennett, I'd leapfrogged from twentieth-century Jackson family history to the seventeenth, but because I hadn't actually done all that research myself, I felt that I was somehow not yet worthy of the FHL's riches. Months went by until finally I realized I simply had to do it, even if I'd be the sole beginner genealogist in the joint.

I wasn't.

Wait here while I get my family history

The FHL is really two libraries: the online version, FamilySearch. org, with 10 billion searchable names in its database and one million pages on its Web site viewed each day, and the physical building, a modernist gray, five-story library on North West Temple Street in Salt Lake City, nearly in the shadow of the quasi-Gothic spires of the Salt Lake Temple across the street. Fifty thousand people visit the FamilySearch Web site every day. About two thousand people pass through the doors of the FHL on an average day, and a few hundred of the most hard-core of this group can be found each morning from 6:30 A.M. on, forming a well-mannered line around the building, waiting for the doors to open at eight.

"We're open from eight A.M. to nine P.M. most days," a library staffer told me, "but I think we should stay open twenty-four hours a day, because the demand is there." (When I mentioned this comment—the personal opinion of one FHL employee and not necessarily an indication of future FHL policy—to a genealogist friend, she nearly squealed in excitement. If the FHL is soon barraged with petitions for longer hours: I'm sorry. But, hey, maybe you should consider giving the people what they're squealing for!)

In fairness, the FHL is already giving a lot. All five floors of the library are constantly abuzz with activity, from the huge octagonal reference desks on each floor to the banks of computers, stacks of books, and endless, *Citizen Kane*–like storerooms filled with millions of rolls of microfilm.

The overall vibe here is one of hushed frenzy. As I walked through its floors—divided by geographical regions of the world—I soon discovered that I was not the only relative ignoramus in the place. While some researchers appeared to work with monkish concentration, surrounded by books and notes, others wandered around, merely browsing. Several BGS friends had told me about the way they prepared for an FHL visit and I saw that they shared a common strategy: one dedicated, experienced genealogist will often bring a family member along to help with menial tasks—as a book runner or photocopy maker—while the expert focuses on amassing as much raw data as possible. The actual data analysis could be done at home, later.

I witnessed at least one minor skirmish taking place at one of the long reading tables on the third floor as a daughter admonished her mother for wanting to take a lunch break (of all things!) instead of powering through her hunger in the name of family history. I was prepared for this. Megan Smolenyak Smolenyak confessed to me that she was "one of those who thinks bathroom breaks are for wimps" at the FHL "when you're trying to snag all you can in a short amount of time." I noticed two women napping in chairs in the lounge area of the fourth-floor bathroom—probably trying to escape the surveillance of their taskmaster daughters, I thought. A sign in the lounge read NO FOOD PERMITTED IN LOUNGES. Take that, wimps.

The FHL is set up to meet the needs of both its intense, no-bodily-needs-breaks patron as well as the casual visitor. "We had one woman run in here a few months ago," a staffer told me. "She rushed up to the visitors' desk and told us that she was 'here to get her family history' but she was in a hurry, so she'd left the taxi waiting outside for ten minutes while she gathered the information." The staffer shook her head. "It happens more than you think."

And here I'd thought I was unprepared! At least I'd brought a list of names, questions, and appropriate expectations.

As I prepared for the trip I decided to focus on just a few areas of potential research. The first was nineteenth-century Alabama. My visit with Jannelle and the information I gleaned from the headstones at the Sumter County cemeteries had provided a truckload of new information. The one thing I hadn't uncovered, though, was any sense of the relationship my family had with the enslaved population of Sumter County.

I was curious about this not only because of my general interest in the relationship between America's black and white Jacksons, but also because I knew that my branch of the Jackson family had owned slaves in Virginia in the eighteenth century. The earliest mention of slave owning in my family dated from 1749, when my tenth-great-grandmother Rebecca Jackson (?–1758), the widow of John Jackson (1670?–1746/1747) gave her son Thomas a slave named Ben "to prevent disputes between us . . . over the will of my late husband John Jackson and for love and affection."[3] Thomas Jackson (?–1751) in turn left three slaves, Dick, Wingo, and Gaffy, to his sons Ralph, Daniel, and Peter, and many similar mentions of human property populate the wills of other Jackson ancestors.[4]

I also knew that my third-great-uncle Jacinth Jackson (1786–1869) was one of the biggest slaveholders in Sumter County, Alabama; according to the 1860 U.S. Slave Census, he owned fifty-five. Were there still descendants of these slaves living in Sumter County? Was it possible that, as in the case of Thomas Jefferson's family, some of his descendants shared parentage with Jacinth's slaves? I didn't know, but it was worth investigating.

I was also interested in the broader history of Jacksons in seventeenth-century Virginia, particularly the issue of whether my line was related to the John Jackson who lived in the original Jamestown Colony. I loved the idea that I might be able to find some kind of clue that would prove helpful to Judy Bennett as she researched this mystery.

Oh, that our ancestors might have given their Jackson sons names other than Thomas or John! Later in the genealogy a few more unusual names do pop up: Seaborn, Ambrose, Jandox, even Ralph is a welcome change. But in seventeen generations of American Jacksons in my line, seven of the patriarchs were named either John or Thomas. Two were Williams. It could have been worse: historians of the medieval period estimate that in the fourteenth century over a third of all men were named John! This is why surnames were invented—though if everyone ends up as John Smith and John Jackson, perhaps a third surname is called for. In any case, I didn't expect to get much further than Judy had in the search for "our" John Jackson, but I brought along my notes just in case.

Donny Osmond and Emily Dickinson: yep, they're cousins

Once you begin doing genealogy, the concept of cousinhood becomes pretty ho hum. That's because you soon discover—and actually comprehend in a meaningful way—that everyone is some kind of distant cousin. So it takes a pretty special cousin connection to break through this blasé attitude. Leave it to the FHL to find a way.

Upon walking into the main-floor reference room of the library, I was confronted by a huge mural of a family tree covering the entire back wall of the computer room. At the bottom were the names and vital dates for an otherwise unremarkable married couple: Robert White and Bridget Allgar, husband and wife who lived in Essex, England, ca. 1558–1623. They had eight children, four of whom went on to produce the following descendants—all cousins: Philo T. Farnsworth (inventor of TV), Lucille Ball, Joseph Smith (founder of the LDS Church), Donny Osmond, Steve Young (San Francisco 49ers quarterback), Emily Dickinson, William Williams (a signer of the Declaration of Independence), Shirley Temple, Orville and Wilbur Wright, and Ulysses S. Grant. Yep. All distant cousins and all descended from Robert and Bridget. It was stunning to see it all laid out in this way, and I think the point was that with enough genealogical research, everyone is going to find someone notable in the extended family.

I, for example, had already discovered that I was a distant cousin to Kate *Charlie's Angels* Jackson. This, thanks to the research of Judy Bennett. So, while I may not be able to claim Emily Dickinson or the inventors of the airplane; as cousins, I do share an intellectual heritage with the one I always thought of as "the smart Angel." Small victories count, too.

The FHL family tree mural also reinforced another impression I was getting from the FHL in general: a surprising lack of Mormon-centricity. Sure, Joseph Smith was one of the cousins on the chart, as was Gordon Hinckley, a former president of the LDS Church, and Mormon superstars Donny Osmond and Steve Young. But not much else on the walls of the FHL shouted "Mormon!" no matter how hard I looked. One entire conference room was filled with individual photo portraits of individuals from around the world; every possible ethnicity was represented in the panorama. When I asked about the identities of these people—famous Mormons I didn't recognize, perhaps?—a staffer told me they were stock photos chosen for their diversity to represent the family of humanity around the world.

These folks were serious about the international vibe. An eight-minute introductory video presentation is offered to all FHL visitors. I noticed a French FHL volunteer—a missionary sent to the FHL for her term of service—assisting a French-speaking couple with their research. ("As you can imagine, this is a very plum mission to get," an FHL staffer whispered to me. I remembered the stories an old high school friend—a Mormon—had told me about his disastrous mission to Ireland at age eighteen, where Catholics and Protestants managed to overcome their religious differences and unite just long enough to pelt him with beer bottles, and I suddenly understood what she meant.) A few feet away, a white American FHL volunteer was discussing the family history of a visiting Japanese family—in Japanese.

"How many languages does this video come in?" I asked.

"All of them," she replied. "Well, I take that back," she said. "Last week a group from Vietnam came in and it turned out we didn't have the audio in Vietnamese yet. But we're working on it."

Like most of her fellow staff members, this one was polite, helpful, and dressed in a style I thought of as Amish Lite. Nothing about their outfits screamed, "I'm devoutly religious!" yet everything seemed a bit more modest than the average American woman's ensemble. No head coverings were involved, but skirt lengths hovered around the ankles; shoes were resolutely flat-soled and sensible; collars were buttoned to the tippy top. My host in the video room had a short hairstyle that reminded me of those you see on little girls in Dorothea Lange photographs from the Depression—its style was almost avant-garde in its severity. Almost.

The look of the male staffers was less obviously Mormon; this was probably because the male uniform of white shirt + dark tie + brown slacks looks the same everywhere. These guys had really, really short hair, but other than that, they could have passed for Unitarians. (A Mormon friend of mine back in Denver later broke it down for me: when he went as a Typical Mormon Missionary for Halloween one year, he wore the shirt/tie/slacks combo but accessorized it with a bike helmet—the ultimate signifier of a young man pounding the street on a divine mission.) When I walked through the maze of cubicles in the Joseph Smith Memorial Office Building to interview Chief Genealogical Officer David Rencher, it occurred to me that this was exactly what the set of the TV show *The Office*—both the British and the American versions—looked like. Actually it seemed especially British: the determinedly nonglamorous aesthetic of the FHL staff evoked a beigeness that seemed very Philip Larkin.

David Rencher (strawberry-blond crew cut, freckles, notably stylish silver-rimmed glasses, standard-issue office attire) told me that the on-site FHL staff could address over thirty languages and up to ninety in the broader LDS network. Some FHL staffers speak up to nine languages. This is all an offshoot of the vast missionary effort of the LDS Church, of course, which touches every continent.

The consequences of the LDS's international evangelism are significant, both for the church itself, for the FHL, and for Salt Lake City. Rencher told me that the city's unparalleled language skills were a key factor in persuading the International Olympic Committee to award Salt Lake City the 2002 Winter Olympics. Did this mean Vatican City has an shot at the Olympics, too? I liked the possibility.

The NORAD of genealogy

As a result of recording genealogical data from so many foreign countries, the FHL now serves as a kind of "world backup" for this information. When the South Pacific Cook Islands suffered a major hurricane in 1997 that destroyed their national archives, for instance, the FHL was able to present them with a fresh copy made from their own photographed version. "Whenever we hear about a natural disaster somewhere in the world," one librarian told me, "we all look at each other and ask: 'Did we get there yet?'" The answer is often yes.

This is part of the deal offered by the FHL when it approaches archives: you give us access to your records; we give you a digital copy as well as the knowledge that another master copy will be preserved forever in our vault, just in case you ever need it.

And they're serious about the vault. Its official name is Granite Mountain.

"We needed a secure area to preserve and store our records,"

Rencher explained. "In the East, some companies use abandoned coal mines but we didn't have a facility here like that. This led to the creation in 1964 of the Granite Mountain Record Vault up Little Cottonwood Canyon. It was blasted out of a solid piece of granite. It won't collapse in an earthquake—it's solid rock, ideal storage. When we negotiate with archives, we can tell them we have this ideal storage."

Glamour and conspiracy tend to accrue to private, blasted-out mountainside caves—think of Dr. No's island hideout, or NORAD's Cheyenne Mountain Complex, the high-security cave built for the North American Aerospace Defense Command just two years after the FHL's Granite Mountain. From the way genealogists refer to it, I could tell this was true for Granite Mountain, as well.

"Most of the records are in the Mountain, you know," my BGS friend Birdie Holsclaw told me before I left for Salt Lake City. "You should call ahead to make sure they have the microfilm you want—they might have to get it from the Mountain."

"Can you visit the Mountain?" I wondered. Most genealogists I asked scoffed at this. "No one visits the Mountain," they said.

"We actually gave tours at first," Rencher said when I asked him about access. For a religion with so many colorful details—the golden plates, the special "garments" (underwear) worn by the faithful, the caffeine ban (which apparently applies only to hot beverages)—the genealogical aspects of the LDS Church were disappointingly conventional. Yes, there's a big underground bunker in a canyon filled with genealogical records—and they'd love to give you a tour, if only they were permitted.

"What we found was that taking people through it raised the temperature," Rencher said, "so we had to stop doing that. It's not a security issue, really; it's the temperature." The exact archival conditions of the place are so delicate that changes in temperature and humidity might negatively affect the microfilm. "Unless I have a business need," said Rencher, "*I* can't go out there. Even the chief genealogical officer can't go in just to see it."

"Have you ever been inside the Mountain?" I asked.

"I have seen it, but it was work-related."

"So . . . what does it look like?"

"It looks like a giant Quonset hut from World War Two," Rencher said. "It's painted a dull army green. They blasted tunnel-shaped holes and then lined them with corrugated steel and back-filled it with concrete. It looks like a giant bomb shelter filled floor to ceiling with microfilm cabinets." This sounded a little more like the *Raiders of the Lost Ark* vision I expected. Not that I'd be able to verify it, of course.

The Mountain was built as a permanent solution to the storage problems of the FHL, but Rencher now admits "there isn't enough space there for the next fifty years of storage." Although the FHL has swapped 150 of its 200 field cameras from film to digital, they're still going to run out of room in the next few decades. The FHL itself has 1.4 million rolls of film; a million more are stored in the Mountain, with new rolls arriving all the time.

The goal, of course, is to abandon film entirely and digitize the entire collection. Once that's completed, the FHL plans to make the whole data set available through the Internet. For free.

Again, with the demystification! Wouldn't it be in the FHL's best interest, I asked, if only from a market-share standpoint, to make its archives a little more . . . if not secretive, then exclusive?

"That's not our goal," Rencher said. "If other entities want to be in the record-preservation business, we'd like to share the data. We believe that at some point data won't be the issue. It's kind of like food. You go to your favorite restaurant because you love their chicken. But, in fact, pretty much everyone serves chicken. You can get chicken anywhere. You go to this particular restaurant because of the experience. Likewise, we think that in the genealogical commu-nity, people will buy into the experience.

"Everyone will have the data in the long term—the data will be secondary," Rencher said. So will the Mountain, which will be supplanted by the Cloud: cloud computing, that is. Rencher is banking on cloud computing, a structure in which massive numbers of computer users access massive amounts of data stored on massive numbers of individual servers. In effect, the FHL's data would be stored in various locations but accessible online from any computer. While Granite Mountain will be maintained as a film storage facility, at some point the film will no longer circulate; only the digital information it contains will.

With all the data available, the search environment will become the key factor in deciding which service genealogists use. "We spend a lot of time trying to create an experience that we think will engage the absolute novice, the beginner. We believe that if we can create that kind of experience, you will learn more about your family, become more connected with your family, and as you compile that data you will want to share it. When you share it, other people who tie into that line will connect with you. That network expands and grows."

And that's their goal at the FHL and the LDS Church as a whole: to keep adding to the world's family tree. So while it's true that the work of many non-LDS members is contributing to what is essentially a religious commandment of the LDS Church, it's likewise true that the LDS Church is contributing to the family history knowledge of millions of non-LDS members. From what I've heard and seen, both parties generally seem happy—even thrilled—with the arrangement. Genealogists talk about the FHL and the genealogical mission of the LDS Church with a sort of amazed gratitude. It reminded me of the two graduate students of Renaissance history I knew who'd been granted access to the Vatican Library. When a thousand years of scholarship was suddenly opened to them, they nearly wept with thanks. You've never seen two Jewish kids so thrilled to visit a Catholic church.

So it is with genealogists and the LDS Church. Apart from the Holocaust-victim controversy, you don't hear any criticism of the church's interest in genealogy from the greater genie community. They just sort of tiptoe around the place—virtually, if they're researching online—and hope that no one ever cuts off their access to the records.

Genealogists also give back to the FHL, a generous gesture typical of genealogy culture. While the FHL's two hundred camera operators are roaming the globe digitizing data, that information must be processed before it hits the virtual shelves of the library. Many records, such as census records, were handwritten and must first be transcribed, then indexed to make them searchable. Once indexed, each record is triple-checked for accuracy, a standard that is unique to the FHL (just ask a genealogist about the spelling mistakes they've seen on other census indexes; it's a problem).

This laborious editing process is helped along by volunteer indexers from around the world, who access the raw records online and then index them in small batches. Several Boulder Genealogical Society members I knew were involved in this effort, along with their other volunteer indexing work for the local historical society. An FHL employee told me she knew a genealogy-crazed Delta Airlines pilot who indexed LDS records during layovers as a way to relax.

Transforming physical records into digital data is one of the biggest challenges facing the FHL and every other would-be repository of information on the Web. One of the FHL's most significant digitization and indexing projects was the the Freedmen's Bank Records Project.

Founded by the U.S. Congress in 1865 to help a newly emancipated black population attain financial security, the Freedmen's Savings and Trust Company collected not only the financial deposits of its over 480,000 members, but a great deal of biographical information about them, too: family names and relationships, stories of family members who had disappeared or been sold into slavery elsewhere, and in some cases brief oral histories. Although the story of the Freedmen's Bank ended tragically when, as a result of mismanagement, fraud, and a national depression, it collapsed in 1874, causing economic ruin for most of its members, the bank's records have long been valued by historians seeking information about black families before and during Reconstruction. Without a usable index, however, those records were nearly impossible to access in an efficient manner.

"It was a huge undertaking," admitted Dale Labrum, who worked on the index for eight of the eleven years the project required. Plenty of genealogists make time in their already busy schedules to do indexing; for Labrum, time was on his side. Dale Labrum is an inmate in the medium-security unit of the Utah State Prison in Wasatch. In fact, he's the head clerk in one of the prison's four Family History Centers, which are run by LDS missionaries and staffed by volunteer inmates who compete for the chance to do the genealogical work. Sometimes they work on their own family histories but often they index the FHL records on behalf of the LDS Church, which funds the centers. Inmates are only allowed access to the records of those long dead, to avoid potential identity-theft issues.

"I'm getting to pay back society through this service work that I'm doing right here, that's what I like," explained inmate Steve Deeter. "I've done a lot of my own personal genealogy, and somebody had to do exactly the same thing I'm doing so I could get those records, so that's what I'm doing, too. It's a pay-it-forward thing." Just as David Rencher might say.

In the case of the Freedmen's Bank records, the work of the Utah State Prison inmates established an invaluable new historical resource for those studying the lives of slaves and their descendants. Notoriously difficult to locate in official records, because of their noncitizen status, the genealogical records of enslaved families must often be pieced together through other records, such as wills, probate records, and deeds of sale. The Freedmen's Bank index was released by the LDS Church in 2001 in honor of Black History Month and immediately made available to the public. By that point, the Utah State Prison inmates were already at work on new projects.

"In a lot of cases, they come out to prison, and they've done some pretty bad things and the family cuts them off," Family History Center coordinator Keith Jepsen said. "But as these men start to do family history work, these bridges start to get mended again." One of the most skilled genealogical researchers among the inmates, Dan Maroney, has been working on his family history for thirty years. When he finally found some information on his great-grandmother, the woman who'd abandoned his grandmother in 1897, he began to cry. "I piece together this mystery of her life, and as I record it into her files and have shared it with other family members, I've been able to show that maybe some of the trials and tribulations I'm going through now aren't nearly as tough," he said. "Prison's a piece of cake compared to what my grandmother went through."[5]

While no one would voluntarily go to prison, the idea of spending eight hours a day, seven days a week, doing genealogical research is a fantasy held by many genealogists I met during my travels. There's a parallel to be drawn here between medium-security prison units and retirement, though, I won't be the one to make it.

The Jackson Five . . . thousand

Thanks to the work of volunteer indexers, I'd spent some time at home using the FHL's online site, FamilySearch, just to get an idea of their holdings and to identify items that might be of interest to me. I'd brought along those notes, but when it finally came time to research, I was drawn to a collection of books on the main floor: Family Histories and Biographies.

While the FHL is known for its collection of official archives—data collected from national and local government agencies—it also holds thousands, perhaps millions, depending on how you enumerate them, of more intimate genealogical records. These are the home-made genealogies. Some are hand-painted, poster-size family trees dating back hundreds of years, such as a German family tree from the nineteenth century, depicted as a giant black oak tree with hundreds of hand-painted names sprouting from its many branches. One of the most incredible examples of genealogical homespun was the king-size family quilt displayed on the second floor, which the artist had illustrated with hand-sewn versions of old family photographs, each captioned with the name and pertinent genealogical information for each person depicted.

"Gifts of family genealogies, organized collections and other records that contain genealogical information are welcome" at the FHL, according to their Web site. "You can even write a history of your family and place a copy in the library." Thousands of people had done exactly that. I headed for the family-histories-and-biographies section and walked to the *J*s.

There they were: the Jackson family histories. These were ge-nealogical accounts written by various Jackson descendants, perhaps two hundred of them. Their titles ranged from the maddeningly general (*My Family*) to the specific (*History of the Jackson Family of Hempstead, Long Island, N.Y.*) and the research standards varied as well; some were heavily footnoted, while others provided no clue to the origin or veracity of the data they contained.

I flipped through a few of them—Jacksons from Kentucky, from South Carolina, from Texas. *Three Hundred Years American* and *The Jackson Grist Mill.* Each one of these books—some several hun-dred pages long, some with photographs, some with hand-drawn pedigree charts—was the work of a genealogist somewhere, piecing together scraps and memories and vital records of the family history. I was reminded of David Lambert of the New England Historical Genealogy Society, way back on the genealogy cruise. He knew these people, the dedicated genealogists who spend decades on family his-tory projects and then find that no one else in their family has any interest in carrying on the work. "We're everyone's attic," Lambert said, referring to NEHGS, "because we're interested in everyone."

Institutions such as NEHGS and local history museums had long served this function for genealogists and amateur historians, collecting information for the future when no one else in the present recognized its value. The Family History Library was simply a larger, global version of that. David Rencher demurred when I suggested the FHL was "the world's backup," but it seemed to have come true whether they were aiming for it or not. The family-history-and-biography section of the library currently occupied about a quarter of the main floor, but it would eventually take over the entire library, given enough time.

These books stood apart because they were qualitatively different from the rest of the FHL's holdings. While the rest of the library contained primary sources, raw data, these books represented analysis. Whether or not one should accept that analysis at face value was another thing. I thought of Elizabeth Shown Mills and her crusade for professional standards of citation in genealogy; how many of these books met her expectations: three primary sources of proof for every genealogical fact? Probably very few. But a hundred years hence, perhaps most of the newer additions would, thus saving future genealogists thousands of hours of fact-checking. A genie can dream.

Microfilm: not dead yet

I read the Jackson books until my brain began to grind into low gear: so many Jacksons, so few familiar place-names or distinguishing details. I decided to head upstairs to the beating heart of the FHL: the microfilm machines.

If there's one twentieth-century technological artifact I will happily watch fade away, it's microfilm. How many researchers have lost their sight and their sanity to the nearly illegible strips of film? I almost lost both on several occasions. Yet they were a necessary evil.

As a graduate student in the Bay Area during the height of the dot-com boom, I watched as one cultural practice after another became transformed by innovative tech designers: shopping, maps, phone books, music . . . and I waited in vain for someone to magically convert all the goddamned microfilm in the Berkeley library to beautifully bright, easily searchable ones and zeros. My fantasy of a binary future didn't come true before my dissertation research ended, and it's still not true. Microfilm still exists. I felt a pang of tender love in my heart when I remembered David Rencher's commitment to digitizing the filmed contents of the FHL. All this time I'd been waiting for some whizbang kid in Palo Alto to solve my microfilm nightmare, when I should have turned my eyes to Salt Lake City. These people—the Mormons—understood microfilm. And they knew the cure. They were working on it, but in the meantime we still had to suffer through.

Every item in the FHL has a corresponding call number. The call number for the first roll of microfilm I selected was 1293882. That's one million two hundred ninety-three thousand eight hundred and eighty-two. Not to be pedantic, but this meant there were over a million other rolls of microfilm in line before this one. Thanks to my conversation with David Rencher, I knew there were also a million more after it. That's a *lot* of microfilm. Maybe too much.

Naturally, there are also a lot of microfilm machines at the FHL. And the one place I've ever found researchers overjoyed to be sitting in front of them, bathed in that telltale gloom and the scratchy shadows of faded handwriting, was here at the FHL. As a rule, graduate students are grouchy. Genealogists are grateful. I was somewhere in between.

I threaded my roll of microfilm into its spool and began to crank the handle. I'd already looked through a book I'd found on the second floor, *The Sumter County, Alabama Index to Wills* compiled by Joseph Stegall, a name I greeted almost like a friend, for this was the same Joe Stegall who'd done so much other genealogical work on Sumter County and whose family name graced the defunct Stegall General Store in Emelle. Armed with some helpful information from old Joe, I now began to look for the will of my third-great-uncle Jacinth Jackson.

I found it. It had been recorded in Sumter County on November 8, 1869. "In the name of God Amen, I Jasin [sic] Jackson . . ." The misspelled name was no surprise; that kind of thing happens a lot in genealogical records, especially when the name is unusual. Although there were no outright bombshells in the will, and no mention of slaves, it did name thirteen descendants, many of whom I'd never heard of before—a genealogical reward in itself. Why? Because the ongoing reward in genealogy is the discovery of more names of relatives, thus providing new avenues of research.

What happens in the U.S. Census stays in the U.S. Census. But only for seventy years.

Genealogical research never ends. This much should be obvious by now. More research simply leads to more names, and more research. Rencher reminded me of yet another factor in the reverse-entropy process that is genealogical research: death cutoff dates.

Death cutoff dates are sort of like copyrights. Both are a form of protection for individuals, based on the inevitability of both death and the forward-pointing arrow of time. A common term for copyright is seventy-five years; the idea being that after seventy-five years of collecting royalties from, say, your hit song, you've profited enough. The ownership of that song now moves into the public domain, where anyone can play or record it for free. In genealogy, death cutoff dates protect the privacy of individuals by preventing the publication of detailed vital record information for seventy years. The individual records for each U.S. Census are therefore kept secret until seventy-two years after the count—the death cutoff date here based on the average life span as calculated earlier in the twentieth century.

Now, not everyone who was counted in the 1940 U.S. Census will be dead in 2012. But at the very least they'll be seventy-two years old. The thinking behind this, presumably, is that none of the census information gathered on a child will be damning or embarrassing . . . I guess? Given the lengthening life spans of Americans in the twentieth and presumably in the twenty-first century—not to mention the relatively older population of genealogists as a group— the Census Bureau might have to consider extending its cutoff dates. As a librarian at Wisconsin's La Crosse Public Library observed, "About a third of the people who came into the Archives Room to see the 1930 Wisconsin federal census . . . did so to find *themselves* on the census! 'Yup, there I am!' a searcher would tell me, pointing to his family on the microfilm image of the 1930 census. 'And there's our neighbor, Mr. Crudmucker. Boy, he was grumpy!' So much for the right to privacy." Genealogists would, of course, argue for shorter cutoff dates: privacy be damned, they want the information now.[6]

For places like the FHL, the practical consequence of cutoff dates is to ensure that the contents of no archive are ever fully compiled, because every ten years a new batch of information will be released. Cutoff dates apply to local records, as well, so all those little county courthouses visited by the LDS photographers must be revisited every decade, or as close to that as possible. It's exhausting just contemplating this Sisyphean job.

The release of a new batch of census records thrills the genealogy crowd, of course. While the aggregate demographic data from a census is analyzed and published as soon as possible after each collection, descendants must wait seventy years to discover any interesting details about their grandmother's household. Not that it's always interesting; often the census data merely confirm the names, addresses, and ages of people that you already knew. Sometimes, though, you might find a name that appears in one census and not another—depending on the age, it could be a baby who died in childhood, or a relative or neighbor who stayed with the family for a while and then moved on. All are valuable details in reconstructing the texture of your ancestors' lives, seven decades past.

Cow poop in Ukrainian cemeteries

Genealogical research never ends, but my time at the FHL was limited. Because any of the dastardly microfilms at the FHL could be mailed to my local Family History Center, I reasoned that I should spend my time in Salt Lake City doing things that could not be replicated elsewhere. I decided to seek out Kahlile Mehr.

I'd heard about Mehr from Ellen Shindelman Kowitt, the specialist in Jewish genealogy. She and I met for coffee before my trip to the FHL and discovered that we had similar genealogical backgrounds, just reversed: her mother was from a Christian family (my father was); her father was Jewish (my mother was). But both of us shared a similar regional Jewish ancestry, hailing from an area that was a center of the European Jewish population for hundreds of years before the twentieth century: the Ukraine.

"There are lots of assumptions made about Jewish genealogy," Kowitt said. "The first is: 'Everybody died.'" This is the belief that the rest of the family, those individuals who didn't leave Eastern Europe before or during the various anti-Semitic genocides of the twentieth century, perished. Thus, there can be no surviving relatives to look for in the records or anywhere else.

"The second is: 'The records were destroyed.'" You hear different versions of this one. Sometimes a conspiracy is involved: the ruling classes separated Jewish vital records and burned them as part of a larger program of Jewish extermination. Other times the "fact" of Jewish record loss is attributed to the usual bureaucratic mismanagement or natural disaster. Whatever the cause, the consequence of this assumption is that research is never begun, because "there are no records" to research.

As Kowitt rattled off these assumptions I thought about the conversations I'd had with my mother about our Ukrainian Jewish roots. I had a few records already, including a 1929 Palestinian passport issued to my grandfather Ephraim Hirsh Baum (1902–1948), as well as the copied pages of *The Birth-Book of the Sambor Jewish Registration District*. I wasn't quite sure how my mother had gotten ahold of it, but it definitely existed.

"My mom was thinking about visiting the Ukraine to see the cities her ancestors came from," I told Kowitt, "Sambor and Rovno [now known by their Russian names, Sambir and Rivne]. But when she started doing some research on the Internet about the area, she got pretty discouraged. Not only did it seem depressing—it's near Chernobyl—but it seems to be some kind of Eastern European hotbed of neo-Nazi activity. And, I guess this shouldn't have been a surprise, but there's basically no Jewish population there now. It's just . . . gone."

Kowitt nodded. I thought she was sympathizing—and she was—but she was also waiting for me to finish before informing me of Jewish Genealogy Assumption 3: "Everyone in current-day Russia/Poland/Ukraine is anti-Semitic. That's a big one."

Kowitt has led two genealogical tour groups to the Ukraine. "I was obsessed with my grandfather and his family," she said. "I learned Russian just so I could read the records—and so I could read the Shindelman name in them." After getting up to speed linguistically, she traveled to Lubar, Ukraine, in search of her ancestors. She hoped to find their graves.

"I heard the same thing about the anti-Semitism," Kowitt said. "People talk about how, after the Jews were gone, the locals used headstones from the Jewish cemeteries to pave the streets, or that they let cows in the Jewish graveyards, and they poop in there—so disrespectful!"

She'd heard all this, but she still wanted to go. "We went to the Jewish cemetery in Lubar. I brought along some family members: my dad, my brother, my cousin, but they're not genealogists," she said. "I was going to find a Shindelman grave in this cemetery. So I taught my cousin how to look for the Russian letter *S* on the gravestone and sent him off. All of a sudden this pack of kids shows up. I was nervous—Ukrainians! Anti-Semitic! Jewish cemetery—they're following us! I did the American thing: I tried to make nice; I gave them a bag of Tootsie Pops. Then, in perfect English, the tallest kid says, 'What are you looking for?'"

Kowitt smiled. "We had a long conversation in perfect English— he was in sixth grade. I told him what we were looking for and he said, 'Oh, we'll help you.' So I taught him, just like I taught my cousin. I showed them the *shin* [the Hebrew letter, written as *S* in English]—in Russian and English, and I explained that on a Jewish headstone it would read backward, from right to left. I told him just what I'd told my cousin: anytime you see one of these letters on a grave, come get me and we'll look at it together.

"These kids spent the whole afternoon helping us in the cemetery. So, you might want to believe these stories you hear about anti-Semitism and Ukrainians and yet these boys were curious about what we were doing, and they were willing to hang out with us all day in the Jewish cemetery. I never found the headstone, but I wanted to light a memorial candle in the Jewish tradition, something you usually do on the anniversary date of an ancestor's death and I wanted to say a couple prayers. These boys were respectful; they wanted to know what we were doing and they stayed with us while we did it.

"There's probably anti-Semitism in the Ukraine," Kowitt conceded, "but in this case a younger generation had an educational experience with us and I thought . . ." She paused for a moment to choose her words. "I thought it was a bridge. They don't know any Jews; all they know is dead Jews in the cemetery. But if American Jews come back like my family did that day, they'll never forget us.

"And they'll probably look at the cemetery differently," I said, "as a special place that has meaning for someone, somewhere—"

"—because they have descendants in America," Kowitt said, completing the thought. "Even though I didn't find a gravestone with my family name on it and there was no Jewish community left, just being there had great meaning for me. It's honoring your ancestors, in a way, by just being in the same physical space they were in."

So what about the first Jewish Genealogy Assumption: *Everybody died?* Kowitt had a story to debunk that one, too. Like many genealogists, Kowitt wanted to extend her research to include her husband's family. But, according to her mother-in-law, " 'Everybody died in the Holocaust.' And that was it: they didn't know names, places, anything. So one day—it happened to be International Holocaust Remembrance Day a few years ago—I got online and went to the Yad Vashem Holocaust Remembrance site and ran some names. I'd done this before, with the Shindelman name, but people are constantly adding to it so it's always a good idea to check again. I ran the family name Zekser and some new pages showed up. I'm looking at the information about these Holocaust victims, and it listed their parents' names, from Warsaw. So I tracked down the name of the person who submitted the record, a woman living in France. We compared photos: there was a resemblance. We compared naming patterns: there were similarities. This woman was my husband's second cousin, the granddaughter of the brother of my husband's grandfather. They'd had no knowledge that each other existed.

"The European descendants had no knowledge of this brother or the fact that he'd gone to America in 1913, long before the Holocaust. Her grandfather had left Warsaw and went to Paris, but he, his wife, and his daughter were all killed at Auschwitz. Yet the son—her father—survived a work labor camp. He had two children, and she was one of them.

"Everyone in my husband's family was shocked. It was true that they had family who died in the Holocaust, *but some of them survived.* Even I had accepted the story," Ellen said, shaking her head, "and there's still a lot of Americans who make this assumption . . . but if you don't look, you don't find out."

As for Jewish Genealogy Assumption 3(a): *They let the cows poop in the Jewish cemeteries!*, Kowitt laid that myth to rest, too. Sort of. Cows are allowed to walk through Jewish cemeteries in the Ukraine, Kowitt said, and they often poop there. But they walk—and poop— in the Christian cemeteries, too.[7]

Kowitt encouraged me to talk to Kahlile Mehr at the FHL if I got the chance. Mehr is the manager of the Slavic Collection Management and Cataloging Department, the FHL's resident expert on Russian and Eastern European genealogical records. I contacted him and gave him the name of the town I was most interested in, Rivne. When I met him in Salt Lake City, he handed me a stack of documents related to the Rivne genealogical archives. As it turned out, he'd traveled there in 2008 on a research trip. Ever since the wall came down in 1991, the LDS Church—specifically, Kahlile Mehr— had been working on gaining access to the genealogical archives of the former Soviet Union.

I flipped through the papers: a map of the region; an overview of the archival holdings; a typed list of specific archival records that might interest me; and a photograph of a pink two-story building with two fir trees growing in front. "What's this?" I asked, holding up the photo.

"That's the Rivne archive," Mehr said with a smile. "It's pink. Most of them aren't pink."

We started talking and I brought up one of the Three

Assumptions of Jewish Genealogy: *All the records were destroyed.* "Most people who are not well acquainted with records history don't know that there are two kinds of records," Mehr said. "There's the record that was kept locally and the one that was turned in to the government. In the case of Jews, it was usually the town council. In 1918, after the revolution, the Soviets created the first civil registration. None existed before 1918, so they went out to the churches and gathered their records—the originals went to the civil registrars' offices. There was only one census conducted in Russia: in 1897. The religious records were the only other records.

"There was no reason to destroy the records of Jews," Mehr said. "Most destruction, if it did occur, occurred as a result of war. Or maybe some rabbi took his records and buried them in the ground and nobody knows what happened to them. Generally speaking, the Jewish records ended up in the civil registrar offices. The idea that Jewish records were intentionally destroyed is a myth." Mehr's work over the past decade has revealed a pretty convincing argument to refute this myth: the Jewish records are there. Now the FHL just has to convince the Ukrainian government to let the digital cameras in.[8]

> Like all those possessing a library, Aurelian was aware that he was guilty of not knowing his in its entirety.
>
> —Jorge Luis Borges

There is something paradoxical about a library. Many of the answers we seek may be found inside . . . but where, exactly? You have to know how to look. And, as I've often experienced, sometimes it's only after a few hours of looking that you realize you're not quite sure what to look for. The genealogists I met usually divided their research by question: tracking down this great-aunt, or finding the birth certificate for this third-great-grandmother. The more specific the task, the better. Yet it's easy to get lost in the minutiae of such tasks and forget to step back and look at the bigger family picture. Instead of missing the forest for the trees, we miss the family tree for the leaves.

I left the FHL with a sense of gratitude and a feeling of humility: there was so much there waiting to be researched, and so much more I needed to learn about my family history before I would learn how to find the answers or even what I needed to know. On the genealogy cruise I'd heard one of the professional genealogists claim that she specialized in "complete genealogies," a term that struck me as an impossibility. I chalked up my reaction to my own inexperience, but over time I'd asked other, more experienced genealogists about it and they all scoffed. "What would that be?" one of my BGS friends asked. "A family tree going back to Adam and Eve?" There are no "complete genealogies." But if anyone ever manages to create one, no doubt the FHL will deserve much of the credit.

Unaccompanied minor

I have a soft spot for the Salt Lake City airport, known to travelers as SLC. It's nothing special to look at or travel through, just your typical midsize western metro hub, but I spent a lot of time and psychic energy there in my youth.

My parents split up when I was three, and eventually we all got sorted out this way: I lived with my mom in Northern California during the school year. From age seven to my sophomore year of high school, every summer and Christmas break I'd fly up to Montana to stay with my dad. Those flights were invariably routed through Salt Lake City: Reno-SLC-Helena, Reno-SLC-Butte, Reno-SLC-Missoula.

I was an "unaccompanied minor," one of those serious-looking kids you see sitting near the check-in counters at the concourse gates. I enjoyed my status: boarding the plane early; receiving lots of attention from the flight attendants; always getting a window seat; unlimited refills of Coke. No matter how many times the staff checked on me, it still felt much more free than traveling with a parent—something I rarely did, anyway. I made so many trips through the SLC airport that it became a favorite destination in itself. I knew where to find McDonald's. I could find the VIP lounge, where we unaccompanied minors passed our layovers reading books and eating peanuts; I could find my gate. I felt as if the SLC airport were my private getaway. I certainly knew it better than either of my parents did.

Walking through the A concourse the morning I arrived in Salt Lake City to visit the Family History Library, I tried to spot something I remembered from those days. The airport had been remodeled several times since I last traveled there as an unaccompanied minor. Yet as I neared the security gates (new, of course), I recognized a certain sloping approach to the main terminal. I knew that sunlit ramp. I'd walked it decades earlier. I was walking it again.

This time, for the first time, I walked out the doors of the SLC airport and stood in the sun. I'd never been outside the airport before. I used to travel through here to reach my family: Mom or Dad. This time I was coming to find family that had passed on long ago. They weren't here, in Salt Lake City, exactly, but records of their life were. And they'd probably been here way back when I was an unaccompanied minor, just passing through. As a metaphor for life, it had a certain symmetry.

Our time here on earth may feel permanent and essential, because it's all we know. But in fact we're just passing through. We're all unaccompanied minors, in that sense: we enter alone and we exit by ourselves. Finding the names of others whose own brief lives made ours possible—this process of genealogy—perhaps it's a balm, making the recognition of our solo journey a little easier to bear.

9

Ask Yourself Why You're Doing This . . . and Keep Asking

When my son was born in 2000, my husband and I both wanted him to have a family name," Pamela explained. I'd met Pamela at a local Daughters of the American Revolution meeting and invited her out for coffee so I could learn more about her participation in lineage societies—she belongs to twenty-six of them.

"I really wanted John," she said. "The name John is in both our families. But my husband wanted William. So I said, 'Okay, when he's born, if he has blond hair he'll be William; if he has dark hair he'll be John.'"

An adorable blond boy walked up to our table holding an encyclopedia of dogs. "Mom, I need to show this to you," he said. This was William.

"And William is a family name, too, I assume?"

Pamela nodded.

"He's named after my ancestor. William the Conqueror."

Lineage societies: as American as throwing off a tyrannical king

When I started my genealogical journey, I never expected to meet two descendants of the leader of the Norman Conquest in a mall outside Denver. Yet here I was and here they were: Pamela Dudley Winthrop Underhill and her son, William, blood relatives not only of William the Conqueror (1027–1087) but also King Henry II (1133–1189); King Henry III (1207–1272); King Edward I (1239–1307); and, more recently, two of the original governors of the Massachusetts Bay Colony, John Winthrop (1587/8–1649) and Thomas Dudley (1576–1673). Oh, and one other fellow you may have heard of: Charlemagne (742–814). When you start tracking ancestors who died before the first millennium, you know you've really met a serious lineage enthusiast.

My recent discovery of seventeenth-century Jackson colonial heritage forced me to confront the Daughters of the American Revolution question for myself: if I were indeed eligible, would I actually want to join? I'd had my doubts about heritage societies ever since that DAR scholarship application back in high school. The very idea of a club whose exclusivity was based on lineage seemed, well, un-American. Lots of people still see it this way.

One of the events DAR chapters commonly host is a reception for people who have just become U.S. citizens. This service is inspired by the DAR's mission of "patriotism" (they also promote "historic preservation and education"), but some new citizens wonder why they're being feted by a group that would, by definition, never admit them as members. The infamous 1939 Marian Anderson incident at DAR's Constitution Hall in Washington, D.C. (when Anderson was denied the opportunity to perform based on her race) remains a public-relations problem for the organization, which dedicates an entire section of its Web site to an apology and overview of the changes of DAR's policies since that time (Anderson later performed at Constitution Hall half a dozen times and in 1992 received the DAR's Centennial Medallion for her service to her country). Although the DAR Web site boasts that its members now include women of every race and religion, it's still seen by plenty of folks as a bastion of white privilege.

Lineage societies are a huge part of genealogy, though, as the existence of books such as *Burke's Peerage, The Almanach de Gotha,* and the ongoing popularity of various American social registers demonstrates. Discovering the seventeenth-century roots of the Jacksons provoked my curiosity. I mentioned it to my cousin Jannelle when I stayed with her in Alabama and she confirmed it: not only were we entitled to DAR membership; she had been a member since 1964. I was therefore entitled to join based on her research—I simply had to prove my relationship to her.

I began asking folks in the genealogical community about their opinions of the DAR and other lineage societies. Most of the genealogists I spoke with expressed either indifference to the groups (very few had ever tried to join one) and a few people were outright hostile to the concept. Among the genealogists who had joined the societies, they'd often done so solely because of the access they gained to the extensive genealogical archives, archives based on generations of membership applications like Jannelle's, listing hundreds of thousands of family trees going back to revolutionary times. I found one BGS member, however, who was eager to join. When I told her I was eligible, she encouraged me to attend a meeting of our local chapter with her. That's where I met Pamela Dudley Winthrop Underhill.

Charlemagne at the mall and patriots at the country club

"Ask yourself why you're doing this," Pat Roberts had said. She wasn't the only one. Genealogy skeptics constantly speculate about the reasons why anyone would want to spend her time looking up the names and marriage certificates of dead relatives.

Genealogists are often accused of narcissism. Isn't researching one's family simply a socially acceptable way of thinking about oneself? Perhaps, though as I'd seen and felt for myself, the geometric progression of ancestry explodes the notion of a "self" pretty fast. Just three generations back and you're looking at sixteen individuals who lived a century before you, in a very different world. One more generation and you've got enough ancestors to fill a classroom. Who are these people? They have something to do with you, sure, but they're not really you, are they?

The other major critique lobbed at genealogy is the suspicion that the whole enterprise is simply an exercise in status seeking, "the oldest form of social climbing in the world," as one journalist put it. For some, this may be true. The popularity of lineage societies such as DAR, the Mayflower Society, and the Order of Founders and Patriots of America (and hundreds of other, even more hairsplitting groups: Daughters of Indian Wars, for example) suggests that almost as soon as the American colonists abolished hereditary titles of European royalty, they got to work inventing some new ones for Americans. Exactly what kinds of privileges or status accrue to, say, a Colonial Dame is debatable, but surely it means something to the Dame in question.[1]

Genealogists tend to have a sense of humor about the criticism, but most of them would probably argue that the genealogical impulse is the opposite of narcissism: it's an effort to connect with others—other people, other eras, and other histories. In 1820, the Pilgrim Society, an early lineage society made up of descendants of the original Pilgrims, asked the American statesman Daniel Webster to speak on the bicentennial anniversary of the landing of the *Mayflower*. The arguments Webster made for the virtues of genealogy have remained the same ever since.

"It is a noble faculty of our nature," Webster said, "which

enables us to connect our thoughts, our sympathies, and our happiness with what is distant in place or time; and, looking before and after, to hold communion at once with our ancestors and our posterity." This notion, that actively seeking to connect with one's long-gone ancestors is actually a "noble" pursuit, resonates with many genealogists. Thinking back to my own experience in the graveyards of Alabama, I could relate to it, too. It's something like the feeling I get when staring up at the stars on a clear night: that humbling sense that I'm just a tiny part of a much bigger system. Such humility does feel noble, in a way: it's a recognition of how small a part each individual plays in the bigger story of life and the universe.

Webster argued that "there is also a moral and philosophical respect for our ancestors, which elevates the character and improves the heart . . . and we would leave here, also, for the generations which are rising up rapidly to fill our places, some proof that we have endeavored to transmit the great inheritance unimpaired; that . . . in our regard for whatever advances human knowledge or improves human happiness, we are not altogether unworthy of our origin."[2] This argument, focused on a respect for tradition, resonates with many who study history, genealogists included. Santayana's idea that "those who cannot remember the past are doomed to repeat it" still holds a lot of traction.

I've seen it in action in genealogy gatherings, as the participants shake their heads in pity and disgust at the level of historical ignorance displayed by their non-historical-minded contemporaries. (*They want to put a Starbucks where?! Surely they realize that's the site of the town's first granary?!*) Genealogy is a popular pastime around the world, but in the United States the tension between the past and the present/future (these two seem to join forces in the competition) is particularly strong. It's very American to pooh-pooh the past: Nathaniel Hawthorne was horrified by what he perceived as the "deadweight" of English history after he visited the British Museum in 1856. "I don't see how future generations are to stagger onward," he wrote, "with all the additions that will continually be made to it."[3] Americans regard their country as "young" but, as any genealogist knows, each year that classification grows weaker. One day, if all goes well, America will be old (it's better than the alternative, as they say). When America is old, perhaps genealogists will finally get some respect.

This probably explains some of the appeal of lineage societies: if you're into history and you're into respect for the past, the Sons and Daughters of the Plantagenet (for example) offers safe haven among others who understand. It's never been complicated for Pamela Dudley Winthrop Underhill: as soon as she joined her first lineage society, she felt as if she'd found family. In fact, she had.

"My mom calls me a 'joiner,'" Pamela said with a laugh. With her long blond hair and dazzling smile, Pamela is every inch the gorgeous, grown-up California girl and it's easy to imagine her as one of those intimidatingly pretty sorority sisters you saw in college.

Pamela's mother does not belong to a single lineage society and has no formal interest in genealogy. Although her mother's family, the Dudleys, still own a farm in Exeter, New Hampshire, that was an original land grant from King George III, Pamela's mother lives in Hawaii. "She's not into DAR," Pamela says, "because of the Constitution Hall incident. Sometimes I'll bring something up about DAR and she'll say, 'Are you doing things to help the community? Because that's all I want to hear about.' She's not interested in family history per se, because . . ." Pamela shrugs. "She grew up in it."

The more I talked to Pamela, the more I began to understand what she meant by "growing up in it." Pamela and many of her relatives, for instance, attended Harvard. While there, they would have passed through the Thomas Dudley Gate every day on their way to Harvard Square and walked by the Dudley House and the Winthrop House on campus. When checking out books at Widener Library, they would have passed underneath the 1636 charter for Harvard College, signed by Thomas Dudley, who insisted that the school not be named after him, but instead after his friend John Harvard, who had recently died and donated his library to the school. Driving up to New Hampshire to visit the family homestead in Exeter, they would have passed the town of Winthrop, just outside Boston, as well as Phillips Exeter Academy, founded by another ancestor in the Gilman branch of the family (one of the Gilmans was a signer of the Constitution). Did I forget to mention that the Underhills—Pamela's father's family—came over to Massachusetts on the same ship in 1630 as the Dudleys and the Winthrops? Pamela's mother didn't merely "grow up" in the family history: she was soaking in it.

Pamela, who was born and raised in Los Angeles, is one of the few in her auspiciously extended family to embrace their genealogy. For Pamela, it all began in the late 1990s when she inherited four boxes of papers from her grandmother Louise May Carlisle, a woman famous (in her own family, at least) for two unverifiable achievements: once beating out Robert Frost as "Person of the Year" and patriotically renaming German toast "French toast" during World War I. It was among the redoubtable Louise May Carlisle's papers that Pamela discovered letters from her great-grandmother Ariana S. Dudley, a member of the Colonial Dames of America and a charter member of the DAR. Although Ariana Dudley had no children of her own, her letters expressed the hope that some of her family's descendants would continue in the tradition. Very few had.

"I was overtaken," Pamela told me. "I decided I would join. My mom and her sisters didn't like DAR because of the Marian Anderson incident—we've always been left-wing," she explained, "like the Kennedys. In our family it was always, 'To whom much is given, much is expected,' that kind of thing. We've always fought for civil rights." Pamela shared the family politics, but born in California in the late 1960s, "I only saw the philanthropic side of DAR," she said: "raising money for schools, helping the needy, that kind of thing.

"I love history. I wanted to find out more about other people's history—that's why I joined," she said. "I love meeting other smart, interesting women. I felt a bond with the other members—many of us have the same ancestors. It was just a nice bond and I got hooked."

Although Pamela is the most genealogically minded member of her family, the Dudleys and Underhills do the sorts of things that make genealogists happy—and envious. They host family reunions every other year at the Exeter farm, for example. Although she lives in Colorado, Pamela sleeps on what's known in the family as "the George Washington bed," because Washington (another cousin) once slept in it during a tour of the colonies in his prepresidential days.

All this reminded me of what the actress Tilda Swinton said about "old families": that they're regarded as old simply because, unlike everyone else, "they wrote everything down." The truth is, if your family achieves a certain level of prominence, others will take over the genealogical legwork for you. That's one definition of celebrity: when other people are interested in whether they're related to *you* instead of the other way around.

Take the William the Conqueror claim, for example, or Charlemagne. Don't imagine that Pamela Dudley Winthrop Underhill spent the last decade combing through a thousand years of archives to connect herself to these illustrious ancestors. When it comes to royal heritage, the bulk of the work has already been done (by *Burke's Peerage,* among others). All you need to do is prove your relationship to a "gateway" ancestor. In Pamela's case, it was Thomas Dudley: his ancestral line is the one connected to Charlemagne—at least according to the Charlemagne Society.

Amazing, some will say. Absurd, say others. They're both right. Tracing one's heritage back a thousand years requires a certain level of tolerance for hazy "facts" and irregular record keeping. Even if one's ancestors were of royal blood—perhaps especially if so—the accuracy of paternity is questionable (in the DNA testing world, infidelity is referred to as a "non-paternity event," and it occurs on average 5 percent of the time, per generation—with much larger percentages possible).[4] Regardless, the mathematical laws governing genealogy predict that whether or not they know or care about their genealogy, 70 percent of living humans with French, German, Benelux, northern Italian, Swiss, or English ancestors probably carry some trace of Charlemagne's DNA in their bodies. So maybe the idea of sharing a latte with a descendant of the King of the Franks isn't so bizarre, after all. Pamela Dudley Winthrop Underhill and I are probably cousins. In the broadest sense.

I'd met Pamela at the local DAR chapter's annual summer luncheon, and although it was held at a country club, it was hardly the white-glove-and-tea-cake affair I'd suspected. For starters, the chapter president was attired in what appeared to be Native American costume; it turned out that although she had the requisite revolutionary patriot lineage (defined as "an ancestor who aided in achieving American independence"), she was most interested in her indigenous American heritage—thus the braids, the moccasins, and the beaded jewelry.

The DAR's definition of revolutionary patriotism is broad. To join, you must prove a direct connection to someone who provided assistance to the revolutionary cause between the 1775 Battle of Lexington and the 1783 withdrawal of British troops from New York. In addition to the expected patriotic actions—military service, action in the Boston Tea Party, and signing the Declaration of Independence—many other acceptable forms of assistance are valid, including medical service, supplying cattle for Galvez's forces after 1776, and lending money to the Colonies during the war. The DAR ladies were friendly and, indeed, quite patriotic: American flags fluttered from every table's centerpiece.

Here's what I learned from attending the DAR luncheon: if you're looking for a way to jump-start your genealogical quest— whether you're a novice or a veteran who's simply hit a brick wall— and you think you might possibly qualify, run to your local DAR chapter and tell them you want to join. If my experience was representative, you will have lucked into a handheld tour of your own genealogical history.

Mollie volunteered to be my DAR guide. She e-mailed me the day after the luncheon: "I am going to try to help you find a patriot," she announced, and then asked me for the general outline of my history. I told her I knew I had ancestors in colonial Virginia during the late eighteenth century but no idea whether they'd served in any kind of revolutionary capacity, but I gave her some names. That was enough to get Mollie started. A week later she e-mailed me a list of DAR-approved revolutionary patriot Jacksons from Brunswick County, Virginia.

"Are any of these your ancestors?" Mollie asked.

Yes. Randle Jackson (1763–1839). According to the DAR's proprietary archive, Randle "served as a soldier and received bounty land in Georgia—Green County, the part reserved for Revolutionary soldiers." This matched with the information I'd discovered back in the Sumterville Methodist Cemetery in Alabama, where I'd found both his gravestone and that belonging to his wife, Elizabeth:

RANDLE JACKSON
BORN IN BRUNSWICK CO., VIRGINIA
OCT 17, 1763
AND DEPARTED THIS LIFE MAY 17, 1839 AGED 75 YEARS
AND 9 MONTHS

ELIZABETH WIFE OF RANDLE
B. SOUTH CAROLINA
MOVED TO GEORGIA AT AN EARLY AGE AND REMOVED TO
ALABAMA IN 1818. SHE DIED JUNE 1854. 78 YEARS OLD

All the pieces of the genealogical puzzle suddenly fit together with an almost audible *click*.

It was then that I felt something change. A year earlier, I'd been someone interested in her family history, thrilled simply to see a list of names on a pedigree chart. Now, after months of stumbling through interviews, archives, and graveyards, a small part of my family's past presented itself in a small but comprehensible image, like a slide snapping into focus on the carousel.

I felt the accomplishment of contributing something of my own to the family history; Judy Bennett had provided Randle's name and Mollie provided the link to his military service, but I brought my firsthand visit to his grave to the equation, and the inscription on Elizabeth Jackson's tombstone added the final clue to the puzzle. "We struck gold!" Mollie said. Yes, together we had.

A more perfect union?

I'd begun my genealogical journey at the Boulder Public Library. That was over a year, several thousand frequent-flier miles, many credit-card transactions, multiple cemeteries, dozens of genealogy meetings, and many files of documents earlier. Back then, I had questions about my family history. Now I had some answers.

Yes, my grandfather Jabe Cook Jackson did, in fact, claim to have performed—or at least witnessed—a miracle, saving his father's life.

Yes, I now knew all about Bullwhip Jackson. And bats.

No, it didn't seem likely we were related to William Faulkner.

Yes, my father and his entire family had, in fact, lived for a brief time in a circus tent.

Why was the house in Kingsley named Windswept? Because of the sand dunes in the back of the property, blown there by the wind off Lake Michigan. Grandpa Jackson eventually planted trees back there to hold things down a bit. Not quite as romantic as Tara, but I appreciated the logic.

Yes, Grace Jackson had seen ghosts—many times. Lots of my ancestors had, in fact. The tiny ghost train was still haunting me a little bit.

And what about that little black boy who supposedly grew up alongside Grandpa Jackson back in Emelle? What of him? That one was still a mystery. My aunt Mary said she'd heard the story and was sure the boy's name was Arthur. But according to my father, "His name was Thomas, for sure," Jannelle thought she'd heard something about him . . . hadn't Jabe saved that boy from drowning once? No one knew. This was one family mystery that still hadn't been solved.

Judy Bennett provided me with brand-new information, however, about another offshoot of the Jackson family that was new to me—but familiar to her, because her husband, Kent, descended from Mark Jackson.

"As I looked back through your line," Judy wrote me in an e-mail, "I saw that Randle Jackson went to Alabama. All of Kent's ancestors went to Georgia and had huge plantations there. One of them, Albertus Jackson, son of Jethro Jackson, eventually moved to Texas."

Judy went into all this detail about Kent's ancestors to make this point: Albertus Jackson moved from Georgia to Texas around 1860 and brought several slaves with him. As recently as the 1970s, the descendants of these people—the Jacksons and their slaves—remained in the vicinity of Tyler, Texas, where their names reflected that heritage. Many of the African-American descendants were named Jethro or Albertus, apparently after the Jackson patriarchs.

Judy connected me with Kent's cousin who'd grown up near Tyler. She wrote me an e-mail describing the relationship between the families.

"When I was a child being reared on the farm it was apparent that the African-Americans favored working for daddy [Earl Ansley Jackson] more than other farmers in the area when he needed help gathering the crops," she wrote. "My mother used to cook lunch for them as well as for our family. There was never any arguments or disagreements between them and my daddy." And, just in case I was wondering, "There were never mixed marriages or anything like that between them."

Questions about race—about whether my white Jackson family was connected to any of the African-American Jackson families out there—had been among the first to set me on this genealogical path. I'd discovered so much about my family history but I still hadn't found any answers to this question—just more interesting nuggets of information, like the story of the Jethros and Albertuses in Texas.

I'd done DNA testing, so theoretically I had a surefire proof of paternity on hand . . . if only there were a way to casually compare my Y-DNA (i.e., male Jackson line) signature with a male Jackson who happened to be black. Funny how rarely those opportunities arise. It just felt weird to contact, say, a random African-American genealogy enthusiast by the name of Jackson and ask him to compare genetic samples.

I'd first met Megan Smolenyak Smolenyak on the genealogy cruise. We'd kept in touch over the following months; to be more accurate, she had generously responded to all of my e-mail queries despite her incredibly busy schedule, not to mention the yawning chasm of experience that existed between her professional-level genealogy work and my own. She had all kinds of experience, but I knew that lately she'd been working on the family tree of Michelle Robinson Obama. She was familiar with the special challenges in African-American genealogy, so I asked her for advice.

"Dear Megan," I wrote. "I know my Y-haplogroup (I1a) for the Jackson surname. I also know there are lots of African-American Jacksons in this country. My ancestors owned slaves. You can see where this is headed: is there any efficient way to find out if any of the African-American Jacksons out there are related to me (presumably through one of my slaveholding ancestors)? It's not pretty, but as a historian of this stuff I know it happened all the time. If you have any thoughts on this, I'd greatly appreciate it."

Smolenyak had been asked about this kind of thing before. She suggested I "work the property deeds" of Sumter County for my ancestor Jacinth Jackson (son of Randle), one of the biggest slave owners in Sumter County. She recommended I search the probate records for Jacinth's sons, who died before their father during the Civil War. She looked at the 1870 U.S. Census for Sumter County and found a "mulatto" man named Chas Jackson who'd been born in Georgia in 1818—the year that Randle and Elizabeth Jackson moved from Georgia to Alabama. And she found one other thing.

She'd glanced at the mid-nineteenth-century censuses for Sumter County, Alabama, and discovered at least one very interesting detail: a listing reading:

NAME: JACINTH JACKSON   RACE: COLORED

As Megan put it, "This, I believe, falls under the category of 'things that make you go hmmm . . .'" Like the Jethros and Albertuses, this Jacinth Jackson was . . . what? A friendly former slave of my great-great-great-uncle Jacinth? A descendant of his?

While in Livingston, Alabama, I'd picked up a book of slave narratives edited by two historians at the University of Western Alabama. Culled from the incredible Works Project Administration Slave Narrative Project of 1937–1938, the book contained transcripts of interviews with local African-Americans born in the time of slavery. The questions were usually asked by white interviewers and the answers transcribed in dialect, which often grates against contemporary sensibilities. One of the women interviewed was Martha Jackson, born in 1850. Eighty-seven years old at the time of her interview, Jackson told stories of working for "Marsa" and for "Miss

Betty," who tried to get her to provide information on an escaped slave.

"I never said nothin'," Martha Jackson said, "and he ain't never showed hisse'f in daylight till he peered up atter de S'rrender."[5]

Martha Jackson's story of protecting a fellow slave was compelling in its own right, but it caught my attention for another reason: her surname (Jackson) and the name of "Miss Betty." Given the fact that my great-great-great-great-grandmother Elizabeth Jackson died in 1854 (when Martha was only four years old), it seemed impossible that she and "Miss Betty" could be the same person—Martha Jackson's mistress. But perhaps there was another Jackson ancestor, one I hadn't found yet, who would fit into this puzzle? I added it to the growing list of "things that make you go hmm . . ."

Three of every ten African-American men who test their DNA with the genetic testing company African Ancestry find they have European male chromosomes. According to sociologist E. Franklin Frazier, most of the 600,000 "mulattoes" listed on the 1860 Census were the children of white men and enslaved black women. And many slaves were given the surnames of their owners (though many, but not all, changed their surnames after Emancipation).[6]

I'd have to trace this "colored" Jacinth's line forward to the present and then I'd face the same problem I faced in the other situations . . . how to suggest a DNA comparison? I wanted to find out if any of the African-American Jacksons who lived among my ancestors were related to me, but did they want to know that history?

This quest began during a particularly interesting time in American race relations. The campaign and election of Barack Obama brought issues of race into everyday conversations all around me. I thought about candidate Obama's speech on race in America, "A More Perfect Union," that he'd delivered in March 2008.

"I am married to a black American who carries within her the blood of slaves and slave owners," Obama said, referring to his wife,

Michelle, "an inheritance we pass on to our two precious daughters. I have brothers, sisters, nieces, nephews, uncles and cousins, of every race and every hue, scattered across three continents, and for as long as I live, I will never forget that in no other country on Earth is my story even possible."[7]

Reaction to Obama's speech was overwhelmingly positive, a national sigh of relief as if the elephant in the room had finally been acknowledged publicly. "We want for there to be [racial] healing and reconciliation," said the Reverend Joel Hunter, pastor of a mainly white evangelical church in Florida who loved the speech, "but unless it's raised in a very public manner, it's tough for us in our regular conversation to raise it." Janet Murguia, the president of the National Council of La Raza, expressed hope that the speech would help all Americans "talk more openly and honestly about the tensions, both overt and as an undercurrent, that exist around race and racial politics."[8]

I hope we can talk more openly and honestly about it, too. As more Americans investigate their family histories, whether through DNA testing or traditional genealogical techniques, more of us will confront this issue: Who are we and how are we related to each other? Because we are all related to each other.

Time: *kairos* and *chronos*

"Ask yourself why you're doing this." For many, the issue of identity—are you who you say you are?—is the motive.

Another one is time. The rituals of time spurred my own quest: my wedding, the trimesters of my pregnancy, the birth of my son. Aging is a powerful genealogical incentive. The further from our birth we get, the closer to our past we want to be. As anyone over the age of thirty knows, Einstein was right: time really is relative. It speeds up as we get older (though it seems to slow down in airport security no matter what your age).

The ancient Greeks knew everything before we did; even, apparently, the theory of relativity. The Greeks had two words for time: *kairos* and *chronos,* each with a distinct meaning.

Kairos referred to time in the moment—it's often used synonymously with "opportunity." *Kairos* is now. *Chronos,* in contrast, meant time in the longest sense: eternal, ongoing time. Though it's a word that's disappeared from common usage, most of us in the twenty-first century are more familiar with *kairos,* living from moment to moment, busy and busier. Our ancestors, though, exist in *chronos.* In fact, we all exist there, too, but we rarely recognize it. Yet it feels comforting when we alight in a *chronos* moment, whether through meditation, prayer, or some other form of deep, still contemplation.

The pursuit of our past—of our ancestors' pasts—is a small attempt to bring us closer to *chronos.* Engagement with the smallest details of our ancestors' lives—their names, their addresses, their faded wedding photographs, their DNA—can pull us out of *kairos* and back into the eternal sense of time, the one we'll all return to eventually.

A funny thing happened as I neared the completion of writing this book. Several years earlier I'd published an article and the editor asked me to write a brief bio, including something about my future writing projects. I remember thinking what I always do when I'm faced with such a query. *Great—now I have to invent something interesting.* This was well before I'd gotten interested in my family history, yet as I read the bio years later I was struck by what I had written: "Buzzy Jackson is currently working on a project designed to inspire extremely long-term thinking."

I'd gotten back to colonial Virginia, but I still had a long way to go.

Acknowledgments

No family tree can be completed alone and neither can a book. So many generous people helped make *Shaking the Family Tree* possible, and it's a pleasure to credit some of them here.

First I want to thank my family. Everyone was so enthusiastic, helpful, and patient with me as I worked on this project. Many of my aunts, uncles, and cousins provided me with facts and anecdotes that, although they may not all have made it into the final version of the manuscript, nevertheless influenced my understanding of our family history. Thank you all for your good humor and your trust.

Also providing support and, crucially, childcare that enabled me to enjoy genealogy cruises and southern road trips were Jackson's grandparents, Kathryn Kirshner, Ruth Jackson Hall, Lewis Kirshner, Dawn Skorczewski, and Jon A. Jackson, as well as our friends Tania Schoennagel and Steve Leovy and the wonderful staff of Sunflower Preschool. Thank you all.

I was overwhelmed by the kindness of the genealogical community. In particular, I must thank the members of the Boulder Genealogical Society for their willingness to share their wisdom and their fellowship with me. Patricia "Pat" Jordan Roberts helped me get started on my journey and provided encouragement all the way through. I also benefitted from the advice and good humor of Donlyn Arbuthnot, Dina Carson, Birdie Holsclaw, Shirley Huntbach, Mona Lambrecht, Mary Ann Looney, and Cari Taplin.

The Arapahoe Chapter of the National Society of the Daughters of the American Revolution was so welcoming. Thanks to Valerie Turner and Mollie Sue Morton for their help in researching my revolutionary patriot credentials. I also must express my gratitude to the lovely Pamela Dudley Winthrop Underhill, who responded to my unending list of questions with grace and wit.

I benefitted from the work and assistance of many genealogy professionals during the research phase of this book. Many thanks to Megan Smolenyak Smolenyak, Elizabeth Shown Mills, John Grenham, John Titford, Tony Burroughs, Cyndi Howell, Dick Eastman, and Bob Velke.

The staff and administration of the Family History Library in Salt Lake City could not have been more helpful during my visit. I thank David Rencher, Kahlile Mehr, Cody Craynor, Laurie Hillier, and the staff of the Louisville, Colorado, Family History Center for their insight and assistance, and for their invaluable genealogical work.

Other members of the genealogy community helped me immesurably. I thank Ellen Shindelman Kowitt for insights into Jewish genealogy. Thanks to Christin Loehr for making my trip to the UWA Julia Tutwiler Library one of the most productive days of research I've ever experienced.

I benefitted from the generosity of many friends and family members during my travels. My mother, Ruth Jackson Hall, and my son Jackson were wonderful companions during our trip to Michigan. Thank you to the Baum families of Detroit, my aunts and uncles Barry, Pat, Martin, and Bernie, and my cousins Michael, Bunny, Lewis, Isaac, Daniel, David, Jeanine, Adam, and Mark. I send my love to my remarkable great aunt Selma, who entertained everyone with her wit and charm while we visited. I wish she could have seen this book published.

My aunt Mary Brewer was incredibly patient with me during our conversations in Kingsley. Thanks, Aunt Mary and Cousin

Candiss Brewer for your assistance with this book, and thanks, too, to my dear uncle Jabe Jackson. My aunts Nancy Schwarz and Claudia Apfel were especially helpful as I began this project—thank you both for your enthusiasm and your help in getting all the details of our family tree in order. My gratitude also goes out to the Veeder family and to Pat and Vesper Paton for their friendship and hospitality over many decades.

I offer a special debt of gratitude to my extraordinary cousin Mooner, who helped plan and execute a truly epic trip to our "home place." I love you. I thank Carol and Howard Kirshner for introducing Mooner and me to the South and its cuisine. Allan Gurganus, thank you for your friendship and your matchless insights into southern culture.

My cousins Tim Schwarz, his wife Julie, and their children Ava, Caz, and Bennett are amazing. Thank you for inviting me into your lives. I thank the remarkable Dr. Rebecca Buckley, M.D., Distinguished Professor of Pediatrics at Duke University Medical Center, both for taking the time to speak with me about Caz's case and for saving his life.

Two other scientists provided help as I learned my way around the double helix. Thank you to Jennifer Knight, Ph.D., of the Department of Molecular, Cellular, and Developmental Biology at CU Boulder, who allowed me to audit her course on Human Genetics, and to Ken van der Laan, Ph.D., for correcting my errors both scientific and syntactical.

I can never adequately express my gratitude to Jannelle and George Gent. They graciously invited us into their home and provided us with details and stories of Jackson history that we would never have found anywhere else. Mooner and I also enjoyed the welcoming hospitality of our cousins Jackie Gent Drennan, Janet and Ted Parker, and Gent and Carl Davis Parker. Thank you for your kindness and especially for the amazing barbecued steak.

As should be clear by now, Judy Bennett's help in filling out my Jackson family tree was indispensable. Judy, thank you for your enthusiasm, your kindness, and your friendship. You are a gem. And thank you to Joyce Wick for your insight into the Texas branch of our Jackson family tree.

Sara Doolittle provided both her ongoing friendship and the use of her sweet mountain cabin to me, both of which made the completion of this book much more pleasurable. I'm grateful for the ongoing support of Patty Limerick and all my colleagues at The Center of the American West at CU Boulder.

And as always, my writing was inspired by the sound of music: Bill Evans, Keith Jarrett, Torlief Thedeen, Anner Bylsma, Bon Iver, Sigur Ros, Iron and Wine, and Tom Waits.

It is my great fortune to have a dear friend for a literary agent. Thank you, Gary Morris, for your wit and your willingness to answer the phone. And thanks to the rest of the charming and helpful team at the David Black Literary Agency.

I was also lucky to work with a wonderful editor at Touchstone/Fireside, Michelle Howry and her assistant, Alexandra Preziosi. Michelle, thank you for the energy and insight you've brought to this project from our first conversation on. I couldn't ask for a better partner in this endeavor.

Finally, I thank my parents, Ruth Jackson Hall and Jon A. Jackson, for providing, well, everything, and my brothers, Keith Hall and Devin Jackson, for their support. The Mescherys—Tom, Joanne, Janai, Megan, and Matthew—have always shown me that family is defined by love, not DNA. And I thank my dear husband, Ben Kirshner, and my son, Jackson, for their support during the research and writing of this book. You were my inspiration.

Notes

1. Ask Yourself Why You're Doing This

1. U.S. Census Bureau, Year 2000 Census data, www.census.gov/genealogy/www/freqnames2k.html.
2. Oscar Wilde, *The Importance of Being Earnest* (1895).
3. John Tierney, "Is There Anything Good About Men? And Other Tricky Questions," *New York Times* (August 20, 2007). Richard Dawkins, *The Ancestor's Tale: A Pilgrimage to the Dawn of Evolution* (Boston: Houghton Mifflin, 2005).
4. "Actress Swinton Moves from Art House to Hollywood," *All Things Considered,* National Public Radio (January 17, 2008).

2. They See Dead People But I Stick to the Living

1. Amos Oz, *A Tale of Love and Darkness* (Orlando, Fla.: Harcourt, 2004), p. 88.
2. Adam Davidson, "Nepotism: A Beginner's Guide," *This American Life,* Episode 171: "Election" (November 1, 2000), www.thisamericanlife.org.

3. Interview Your Relatives and Go to Your High School Reunion

1. Eilis O'Hanlon, "No One Will 'Find' Themselves in Dusty Old Birth Records," *The Independent* (Dublin), September 21, 2008.

4. *CSI: Lido Deck:* The Genealogy Cruise, Part I

1. Sharon Carmack, author of the forthcoming *A Genealogist's Guide to Discovering Your Ethnic Ancestors* (and a contributor to *Family Tree* magazine), debunks this legend: "No evidence whatsoever exists to suggest this ever occurred, and I have challenged countless people who insist their ancestor's name was changed on Ellis Island to provide me with proof. So far, no one has been able to . . . Inspectors compared the names the immigrants told them against what was recorded on the passenger lists. These lists were created at the ports of departure. There was no reason to record or change anyone's surname once they arrived. More likely, immigrants themselves changed their names after they settled in America to avoid prejudice and to blend more easily into American society." From David Fryxell, "Coming to America," www.genealogy.com/68_fryxell.html.

2. Megan Smolenyak Smolenyak, in Sam Roberts, "Story of the First Through Ellis Island Is Rewritten," *New York Times* (September 14, 2006), p. 1.

3. Megan Smolenyak Smolenyak, Interview with the Author, October 26, 2008.

4. Megan Smolenyak Smolenyak and Ann Turner, *Trace Your Roots with DNA* (New York: Rodale Books, 2004).

5. Hillary Mayell, "Genghis Khan a Prolific Lover, DNA Data Implies" *National Geographic News* (February 14, 2003); Hillary Mayell, "Global Gene Project to Trace Humanity's Migrations," *National Geographic News* (April 13, 2005); Spencer Wells, *The*

Journey of Man: A Genetic Odyssey (Princeton, N.J.: Princeton University Press, 2002).

6. There are hundreds of Web sites devoted to various genealogies of the Ui Neill/O'Neill name. One featuring the Egyptian connection is "Ancient Ireland and Our O'Neill Ancestors" by Jill O'Neall Ching. Ching admits that the story may be mostly mythological in nature; web.archive.org/web/20040214163141/; www.maui.net/~mauifun/oneall3.htm.

6. Information Wants to Be Free

1. There are many good resources for information on DNA and genetics, and new discoveries and interpretations are made all the time. Here are a few sources I used: Rob DeSalle and Michael Yudell, *Welcome to the Genome: A User's Guide to the Genetic Past, Present, and Future* (Hoboken, N.J.: Wiley-Liss, 2005), pp. 8–19; Megan Smolenyak Smolenyak and Ann Turner, *Trace Your Roots with DNA* (New York: Rodale, 2004); the International HapMap Consortium, "A Haplotype Map of the Human Genome," *Nature* (October 27, 2005), pp. 1299–1320, dx.doi.org/10.1038/nature04226; Luca Cavalli-Sforza and Marcus W. Feldman, "The Application of Molecular Genetic Approaches to the Study of Human Evolution," *Nature Genetics* 33 (2003), pp. 266–275; Christine Rose and Kay Germain Ingalls, *The Complete Idiot's Guide to Genealogy*, 2nd edition (Indianapolis: Alpha Books: 2005), pp. 291–301.

2. On mitochondrial Eve and Y-Chromosomal Adam, see Spencer Wells, *The Journey of Man: A Genetic Odyssey,* (Princeton, N.J.: Princeton University Press, 2002), pp. 14–60.

3. Richard Dawkins, *The Ancestor's Tale;* Spencer Wells, *The Journey of Man;* literature from FamilyTree DNA, the Genographic Project, and SMGF. Also, Rob DeSalle and Michael Yudell, *Welcome to the Genome.*

4. The Genographic Project, "Field Research," genographic.na
   tionalgeographic.com/genographic/lan/en/about.html.
5. On James Watson, see Charlotte Hunt-Grubbe, "The Elementary
   DNA of Dr. Watson," *Times* (UK) online (October 14, 2007),
   entertainment.timesonline.co.uk/tol/arts_and_entertainment/
   books/article2630748.ece; Tom Abate, "Nobel Winner's Theories Raise Uproar in Berkeley," *San Francisco Chronicle* (November
   13, 2000), www.sfgate.com/cgi-bin/article.cgi?file=/chronicle/
   archive/2000/11/13/MN111208.DTL; Jonathan Leake, "DNA
   Pioneer James Watson Is Blacker Than He Thought," *Times*
   (UK) online (December 9, 2007), www.timesonline.co.uk/tol/
   news/uk/science/article3022190.ece.
6. Erin Aubry Kaplan, "Black Like I Thought I Was," *LA Weekly*
   (October 7, 2003), www.alternet.org/story/16917/?page=2.
7. On racial identification, see Jonathan Peter Spiro, *Defending
   the Master Race: Conservation, Eugenics, and the Legacy of Madison
   Grant* (Burlington, Vt.: University of Vermont Press, 2009);
   Beverly Daniel Tatum, *Why Are All the Black Kids Sitting Together in the Cafeteria?: and Other Conversations About Race* (New
   York: Basic Books, 2003).
8. On the Virginia Racial Integrity Act and the Pocahontas Exception, see Kevin Noble Maillard, "The Pocahontas Exception: American Indians and Exceptionalism in Virginia's Racial
   Integrity Act of 1924" (March 23, 2006), Bepress Legal Series,
   Working Paper 1187, law.bepress.com/expresso/eps/1187. On
   changing classification of ethnic American groups, see David
   Roediger, *The Wages of Whiteness: Race and the Making of the
   American Working Class* (New York: Verso, 1991).
9. The Genographic Project, "Genetic History: Jackson Family."
10. Michael D. Lemonick et al., "The World in 3300 B.C.," *Time*
    (October 26, 1992), www.time.com/time/magazine/article/
    0,9171,976877,00.html.
11. Richard Willing, "DNA Rewrites History for African-

Americans," *USA Today* (February 1, 2006), www.usatoday.com/
tech/science/genetics/2006-02-01-dna-african-americans_x.
htm; Godfrey Mwakikagile, *Relations Between Africans and
African-Americans: Misconceptions, Myths and Realities* (Dares Sa-
laam, Tanzania: New Africa Press, 2007), pp. 267–268.

7. Get Back to Where You Once Belonged

1. Brunswick County, Virginia, *Will Book 2*, p. 127; cited in Evelyn Duke Brandenberger and Clara Jackson Martin, "The Jacksons of Lower Virginia," *The Virginia Genealogist* 33:1 (January/
   March 1989), p. 35.
2. Brunswick County, Virginia, *Will Book 3*, p. 575; cited in Brandenberger and Martin.
3. Nellie Morris Jenkins, *Pioneer Families of Sumter County, Alabama* (Tuscaloosa, Ala.: Willo Publishing Company, 1961), pp.
   128–129.

8. The Mountain and the Cloud

1. David Rencher, Interview with the Author, September 9, 2009.
2. Bernard I. Kouchel, "The Issue of the Mormon Baptism of
   Jewish Holocaust Victims and Other Jewish Dead" (2009), accessed at www.jewishgen.org/InfoFiles/ldsagree.html.
3. Will of John Jackson, written 22 February 1739/40 and proved
   1 January 1746/47; Brunswick County, Virginia, *Deed Book 3*,
   p. 575; in Evelyn Duke Brandenberger and Clara Jackson Martin, "The Jacksons of Lower Virginia," *The Virginia Genealogist*
   33:1 (January/March 1989) p. 35.
4. Will of Thomas Jackson, written 15 August 1751 and recorded
   24 September 1751; Brunswick County, Virginia, *Deed Book 3*,
   p. 28; in Brandenberger and Martin, p. 37.
5. Ben Winslow, "Inmates Use LDS Family History Centers to

Find Their Pasts and Help Others," *Deseret News* (March 20, 2009).

6. William Petersen, "Seventy-two Years Later, People Can Finally Come to Their Census" (January 2003); La Crosse Public Library, www.lacrosselibrary.org/archives/census.htm.

7. Ellen Shindelman Kowitt, Interview with the Author, September 4, 2009.

8. Kahlile Mehr, Interview with the Author, September 10, 2009.

9. Ask Yourself Why You're Doing This . . . and Keep Asking

1. John Seabrook, A Reporter at Large, "The Tree of Me," *The New Yorker* (March 26, 2001), p. 58.

2. Daniel Webster, "First Settlement of New England: A Discourse Delivered at Plymouth, on the 22nd of December, 1820"; in Daniel Webster and Edwin Percy Whipple, *The Great Speeches and Orations of Daniel Webster, with an Essay on Daniel Webster as a Master of English Style* (Boston: Little, Brown: 1886), accessed at the Internet Archive, www.archive.org/details/greatspeechesorat00webs.

3. Nathaniel Hawthorne, quoted in Jeanette Greenfield, *The Return of Cultural Treasures* (New York: Cambridge University Press, 1989), p. 310.

4. Family Tree DNA, "Test Results: Y-DNA," www.familytreedna.com/faq/answers/9.aspx#567; Steve Olson, "Who's Your Daddy?," *The Atlantic* (July/August 2007), www.theatlantic.com/doc/200707/paternity.

5. Martha Jackson, "Heaps of Dem Yaller Gals Got Sont Norf"; in Alan Brown and David Taylor, editors, *Gabr'l Blow Sof': Sumter County, Alabama Slave Narratives* (Livingston Press: Livingston, Alabama 1997), p. 75. Note: Despite the obvious problems with the interviews—possible lack of candor due to racial tension, age of the interviewees, skill of the interviewer, etc.—the

WPA slave narratives are recognized today as an invaluable historical resource.

6. Rick Kittles, "Whites in the First Family," African Ancestry Blog (October 19, 2009); E. Franklin Frazier quoted in same; blog.africanancestry.com/2009/10/whites-in-the-first-family/.

7. Barack Obama, "A More Perfect Union" (March 18, 2008), my.barackobama.com/page/content/hisownwords/.

8. Hunter and Murguia quoted in Larry Rohter and Michael Luo, "Groups Respond to Obama's Call for National Discussion About Race," *New York Times* (March 20, 2008), www.nytimes.com/2008/03/20/us/politics/20race.html?scp=1&sq=obama+race+speech+2008&st=nyt.

About the Author

Sarah Rachel Jackson was born six weeks late in Traverse City, Michigan, where she stayed for ten days, just long enough to earn the lifelong nickname "Buzzy" from her Jewish grandmother, Mary Mindl Yaffe Baum. (Actually, Mary called her granddaughter *buzik*, which means a burr—a tiny seedlike thing that clings to you. Since she meant it affectionately, think of it as the cute Jewish version of Velcro.) Inspired by both the difficulty of pronunciation and by the memory of a cool girl named Buzzy she'd known in high school, Ruth modified her daughter's nickname and began calling her Buzzy. It stuck.[*]

On the eleventh day she moved to Montana.

Since then, Buzzy has lived in five states and three countries. She earned a Ph.D. in United States history from UC Berkeley, where she wrote her first book, *A Bad Woman Feeling Good: Blues and the Women Who Sing Them* (W.W. Norton: 2005). Buzzy is the recipient of numerous writing and teaching awards, including those from UC Berkeley, PEN-West and the American Library Association. She is currently a research affiliate at The Center of the American West at CU Boulder.

To contact Buzzy and find out more about her current projects visit www.buzzyjackson.com.

---

[*] Note re *buzik*. According to family lore, *buzik* was either a Russian or Yiddish word (both were languages of my baba's childhood). Like many family stories, however, it's difficult to verify this one. No Russian, Yiddish, or Ukrainian speaker I spoke with was familiar with *buzik*. So please, if there are any linguists out there specializing in the Jewish shtetls of Galicia (and the city of Rovno in particular), let me know if you have any leads. There's a very small reward in it for you.